'An excellent introduction to one of the most fascinating periods of the European Middle Ages.' – **Bjorn Weiler**, *Aberystwyth University, UK*

Between 1095 and 1229, Western Europe confronted a series of alternative cultural possibilities that fundamentally transformed its social structures, its intellectual life, and its very identity. It was a period of difficult decisions and anxiety rather than a triumphant 'renaissance'.

In this fresh reassessment of the twelfth century, John D. Cotts:

* shows how new social, economic, and religious options challenged Europeans to re-imagine their place in the world;
* provides an overview of political life and detailed examples of the original thought and religious enthusiasm of the time
* presents the Crusades as the century's defining movement.

Ideal for students and scholars alike, this is an essential overview of a pivotal era in medieval history that arguably paved the way for a united Europe.

John D. Cotts is Associate Professor of History at Whitman College, USA.

European History in Perspective

General Editor: Jeremy Black

Benjamin Arnold *Medieval Germany*
Ronald Asch *The Thirty Years' War*
Nigel Aston *The French Revolution, 1789–1804*
Nicholas Atkin *The Fifth French Republic*
Christopher Bartlett *Peace, War and the European Powers, 1814–1914*
Robert Bireley *The Refashioning of Catholicism, 1450–1700*
Donna Bohanan *Crown and Nobility in Early Modern France*
Arden Bucholz *Moltke and the German Wars, 1864–1871*
Patricia Clavin *The Great Depression, 1929–1939*
John D. Cotts *Europe's Long Twelfth Century*
Paula Sutter Fichtner *The Habsburg Monarchy, 1490–1848*
Mark R. Forster *Catholic Germany from the Reformation to the Enlightenment*
Mark Galeotti *Gorbachev and His Revolution*
David Gates *Warfare in the Nineteenth Century*
Alexander Grab *Napoleon and the Transformation of Europe*
Nicholas Henshall *The Zenith of European Monarchy and Its Elites*
Martin P. Johnson *The Dreyfus Affair*
Tim Kirk *Nazi Germany*
Ronald Kowalski *European Communism*
Paul Douglas Lockhart *Sweden in the Seventeenth Century*
Kevin McDermott *Stalin*
Graeme Murdock *Beyond Calvin*
Peter Musgrave *The Early Modern European Economy*
J. L. Price *The Dutch Republic in the Seventeenth Century*
A. W. Purdue *The Second World War (2nd edn)*
Christopher Read *The Making and Breaking of the Soviet System*
Christopher Read *War and Revolution in Russia, 1914–22*
Francisco J. Romero-Salvado *Twentieth-Century Spain*
Matthew S. Seligmann and Roderick R. McLean
Germany from Reich to Republic, 1871–1918
David A. Shafer *The Paris Commune*
Graeme Small *Late Medieval France*
David Sturdy *Louis XIV*
David J. Sturdy *Richelieu and Mazarin*
Hunt Tooley *The Western Front*
Peter Waldron *The End of Imperial Russia, 1855–1917*
Peter Waldron *Governing Tsarist Russia*
Peter G. Wallace *The Long European Reformation (2nd edn)*
James D. White *Lenin*
Patrick Williams *Philip II*
Peter H. Wilson *From Reich to Revolution*

European History in Perspective
Series Standing Order
ISBN 978–0333–71694–6 hardcover
ISBN 978–0333–69336–0 paperback
(*outside North America only*)

You can receive future titles in this series as they are published by placing a standing order. Please contact your bookseller or, in the case of difficulty, write to us at the address below with your name and address, the title of the series and the ISBN quoted above.

Customer Services Department, Palgrave Ltd
Houndmills, Basingstoke, Hampshire RG21 6XS, England

Europe's Long Twelfth Century

Order, Anxiety, and Adaptation, 1095–1229

JOHN D. COTTS

palgrave
macmillan

First published 2013 by
PALGRAVE MACMILLAN

Palgrave Macmillan in the UK is an imprint of Macmillan Publishers Limited, registered in England, company number 785998, of Houndmills, Basingstoke, Hampshire RG21 6XS.

Palgrave Macmillan in the US is a division of St Martin's Press LLC, 175 Fifth Avenue, New York, NY 10010.

Palgrave Macmillan is the global academic imprint of the above companies and has companies and representatives throughout the world.

Palgrave® and Macmillan® are registered trademarks in the United States, the United Kingdom, Europe and other countries.

ISBN 978–0–230–23784–1 hardback
ISBN 978–0–230–23785–8 paperback

This book is printed on paper suitable for recycling and made from fully managed and sustained forest sources. Logging, pulping and manufacturing processes are expected to conform to the environmental regulations of the country of origin.

A catalogue record for this book is available from the British Library.

A catalog record for this book is available from the Library of Congress.

10 9 8 7 6 5 4 3 2 1
22 21 20 19 18 17 16 15 14 13

Printed in Great Britain by MPG Group, Bodmin & King's Lynn

For Afton

Contents

vii

Preface

Given its broad scope, this book must have modest goals. It was conceived as an attempt to fit, between two relatively inexpensive covers, a general survey of the twelfth century that could articulate what this period has meant and continues to mean to medievalists. It seeks, that is, to provide a basic introduction to the politics, society, and culture of Western Europe between 1095 and 1229 while also introducing the academic study of the period as a subject of considerable interest in its own right. As a result, I have annotated the work more thoroughly than is usual in such a survey. In cases where a particular point is common knowledge to medievalists, or has been discussed in several secondary sources, I have cited the one I thought would be most accessible and interesting to readers approaching the period for the first time. When presenting primary sources, I have tried to discuss things that work well when assigned as readings in introductory courses, and that are available in good English translations. Many of the texts cited are available online or in popular sourcebooks, so that readers may proceed to their own explorations as easily as possible. Several other aspects of this book have been shaped by the undergraduate classroom. Since many of the sections started out as lectures, they focus on material and examples that serve to illustrate key points rather than to provide comprehensive coverage (which would, at any rate, be impossible in a book of fewer than 90,000 words). The chapters and their subsections do not follow a single template, but vary based on the kinds of questions and problems that particular subjects inspire from engaged and motivated students. Although I am deeply indebted to many friends and colleagues for opportunities to discuss the twelfth century over the past 15 or so years, I would especially like to acknowledge my students in History 155B at the University of California, Berkeley, in History 233 at Grinnell College, and in History 181 at Whitman College, for pressing me to think about and articulate the importance of medieval studies in the twenty-first century.

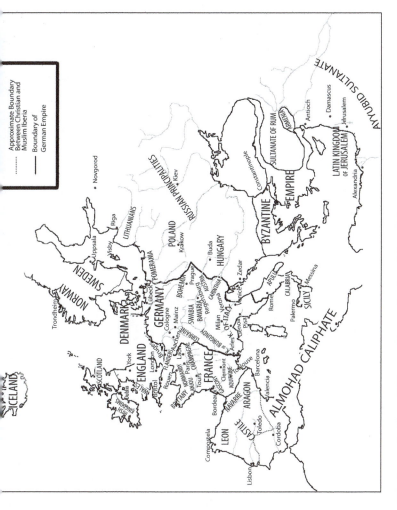

Map 1 The political organization of Western Europe in the mid-twelfth century

Introduction: Approaches to the Twelfth Century and Its 'Renaissance'

'You are divided in your attentions', wrote the nun Hildegard of Bingen to Pope Eugenius III, probably in the early 1150s. 'On the one hand your soul is renewed in the mystic flower that is the companion of virginity; on the other, you are the branch of the Church'. The pope, the leader of Latin Christendom, found himself caught between his love of contemplation, the 'mystic flower', and his role as defender of the Church in a turbulent political climate. The citizens of Rome had revolted against him, and he always had to beware the encroachments of the king of Germany on Italy. 'Choose for yourself the better part', Hildegard urged, quoting the Gospel of Luke.[1] Eugenius, she argued, had to make the difficult choice to forego contemplation and intervene in the messy world of politics for the good of the faithful. Anxiety over difficult choices emerges from a rich variety of other texts from the long twelfth century. In the late 1180s, the cleric Peter of Blois told an educated young man in search of a job that 'you are conflicted, and your heart is pulled in opposite directions. Seized by a wavering fluctuation, you hesitate as to whether you will turn to the knowledge of the laws or the pursuit of the sacred page'. This job-seeker could either pursue theology, the study of which had made great strides in the previous generation, or he could become a legal expert for the king of England. Perhaps bruised by his own experience in royal and ecclesiastical courts, Peter of Blois urged him to 'let the knowledge of truth devour the knowledge of avarice'.[2] Monks and bishops were constantly writing to young men and women about the various monasteries they could enter, while members of different religious orders continually argued about how to live the best possible life in the world.

1

The writers of these letters confronted tough decisions amidst irreconcilable tensions, and similar problems appear throughout our written sources for the period. The theologian Hugh of St Victor thought the human condition itself was poised between heaven and earth, 'as if ordered in a kind of middle place', on the verge of wildly contradictory possibilities.[3] The language of possibility and competing options similarly informs the titles of two of the twelfth century's most significant works of theology and law, respectively: Peter Abelard's *Yes and No* and Gratian's *Harmony of Discordant Canons*. Even a quintessential contemporary hero like Lancelot distinguished himself through indecision when he allowed himself to take two tentative steps before pursuing his true love (adulterously) with absolute devotion.[4] In political life, the people in power—be they popes, bishops, emperors, kings, dukes, or lords of one-room castles—negotiated between the universal and the local, between customary law and written law codes, while, on what we now would call the periphery of Europe (in culturally central areas like Spain, Sicily, and the Near East), warriors and lawgivers negotiated the boundaries of Christendom and encountered foreign civilizations. Basking in the triumph of the First Crusade, a French historian in Palestine observed a cross-cultural blending of habits, clothing, and families, and rejoiced that 'we who were Occidentals now have been made Orientals', calling this a 'great miracle'.[5]

Intellectuals also confronted new options. Since the late tenth century, new schools had been forming around charismatic masters in European towns, providing educational alternatives to the traditional monastic schools. During the long twelfth century, these cathedral schools would coalesce into the first universities, and young scholars went back and forth between them, often agonizing over their choices and just as often failing to achieve the success or wealth they thought possible. Their courses of study sometimes integrated Arabic writings and translations of Greek philosophical texts, many of which had been produced in Spain and other areas that had been under Muslim political control during the early Middle Ages. Shortly after the Englishman Adelard of Bath crossed the Pyrenees to find astronomical texts in Spain, monks at the French monastery of Cluny translated the Qur'an from Arabic into Latin.

Religious life reflected shifts in European demographics. In 1100, most of the spiritual energy of the Latin West radiated from traditional Benedictine monasteries, but by the 1220s members of the new Franciscan and Dominican orders of Friars ministered to the poor in cities, whose populations had grown substantially over the course of the century and which played an increasingly prominent cultural role. Religious dissidents also entered the historical record in greater numbers, and ecclesiastical and secular authorities wrote statutes and manuals about how to identify and persecute heretics on an unprecedented scale. Jewish communities similarly found themselves suffering more frequent persecutions after 1095.

In all these ways, Europeans made choices in response to shifting political, cultural, spiritual, and economic realities, and often worried about them. Presumably, there are anxious human beings in any given century, and anxiety has been suggested as a lens with which to approach the late Roman Empire, the Renaissance, and the seventeenth century.[6] The argument implicit in this book's subtitle is not that anxiety over difficult choices was any more pervasive in the twelfth century than in any other century. Rather, the claim here is that it provides a uniquely valuable approach for a historian who wants to explain the cultural energy that fills the manuscripts, histories, laws, and cathedrals that appeared between the years 1095–1229.

This approach is offered in part as a corrective to earlier historiography, which has too often seen the period as one of unproblematic and steady development. The seismic shift in source materials and their nature (manifest in new literary languages and genres), the diversity of religious orders, and the new institutions of learning cry for explanation, and historians have brought no shortage of imagination to the task of explaining them. According to the titles of books produced in the last hundred years, the twelfth century played a major role in a renaissance, a reformation, a period of 'renewal', the 'Discovery of the Individual', a 'revolution', and even the 'Making of Europe'.[7] All of these terms, of course, were originally applied by historians to other periods, and thus they often carry anachronistic expectations. The following chapters will synthesize the contributions of these studies, correct them when recent research has given cause, and evoke the anxious, halting series of cultural negotiations that Europeans confronted; the goal is not only to provide undergraduates and general readers with a survey of the key events and cultural currents of the period, but also to give them a sense of what is at stake in twelfth-century studies. More advanced students, it is hoped, will find a synthesis of historiographical approaches and insights, while advanced scholars may encounter new ways of considering familiar material.

When Charles Homer Haskins published *The Renaissance of the Twelfth Century* in 1927, he simply told a larger academic audience what medievalists had been arguing for as many as 90 years: that the twelfth century witnessed a cultural flowering marked by increased intellectual productivity, advances in speculative thought and science, and a greater use of and appreciation for the classical tradition. Already in 1839 a French historian had argued that developments in learning and piety deserved to be called 'a real renaissance'.[8] A few papers and chapters applied the term to the twelfth century in the early twentieth century, but Haskins took on the role of polemicist and relished it, beginning his great book by acknowledging the challenge before him: 'The title of this book will appear to many to contain a flagrant contradiction. A renaissance in the twelfth century! Do not the Middle Ages, that epoch of ignorance, stagnation, and gloom, stand in the sharpest contradiction to the light and progress and freedom of the Italian Renaissance which followed?'[9]

The popular view of the Middle Ages as an unsanitary morass of ignorance and intolerance owed much of its currency, rightly or wrongly, to the nineteenth-century Swiss historian Jakob Burckhardt, whose *Civilization of the Renaissance in Italy* (1860) created the modern notion of the early modern 'Renaissance' and confirmed that the preceding medieval era labored under a veil of 'faith, illusion and childish presupposition'.[10] Burckhardt, whose own work was more subtle and nuanced than is often recognized, saw in fourteenth- and fifteenth-century Italy a new artistic sensibility aided by an appreciation for classical antiquity, a revitalized and vaguely modern political order, a previously absent sense of individual human dignity, and the triumph of 'humanism' over religiosity. When merged with modernist (and often anti-Catholic) assumptions about progress, Burckhardt's Renaissance became a powerful indictment of the European Middle Ages. With Haskins's work, the twelfth century emerged as a powerful foil to the prevailing negative views of medieval civilization.

Haskins wove three distinct but related elements into his thesis. First, and most important, he argued that the genius of twelfth-century thinkers and writers found its highest expression in Latinity, which in turn depended on a revival of classical learning. Second, he called attention to the reception of Greco-Arabic science and philosophy as a catalyst to greater understanding and curiosity in the Latin West. Finally, he placed this cultural movement in the institutional setting of the urban cathedral schools, from which would spring the great European universities, especially that of Paris. The first two planks of this program insisted on the importance of classical literacy as a barometer of cultural progress, while the third tied his Renaissance to the economic and demographic transformations that Western Europe experienced after the year 1000. Haskins took Burckhardt on his own terms insofar as both agreed on the significance of antiquity to their movements; he agreed in principle with Burckhardt as to the contours of a 'renaissance', but relocated it in time to the twelfth century and in space to northern France.

Haskins's Renaissance was accepted, often with qualifications, by most medievalists, and it became a staple of European history textbooks. In the late 1940s and early 1950s, the journal of the Medieval Academy of America, *Speculum* (itself founded by Haskins), published a series of articles on the idea, and few scholars wanted to reject the phenomenon out of hand.[11] Most of the qualifications came from scholars concerned to distinguish the nature of what happened in the twelfth century from the 'real' Renaissance that occurred in Italy three centuries later. In addition, by the middle of the twentieth century, other medieval 'renaissances' proliferated in standard histories of the Middle Ages. One can read about of a Northumbrian, a Carolingian, an Alfredian, and an Ottonian Renaissance, among others, throughout the scholarly literature. This almost embarrassing glut of renaissances clearly required that the term be clarified.

In this vein Erwin Panofsky offered an unusually detailed and complex objection to Haskins in his classic *Renaissances and Renascences in Western Art*, which saw the Italian Renaissance's medieval precursors as being essentially medieval in character and classical only in form. When medieval artists used classical models, he argued, they made no effort to understand their original aesthetic sensibility. Although Panofsky's study focused on the visual arts, his claims applied by extension to literature and philosophy. The classical tradition provided medieval authors with decorations for a fundamentally Christian superstructure, and they did not lionize their Greek and Roman influences. In his most famous formulation, Panofsky wrote that 'the Middle Ages had left antiquity unburied and alternately galvanized and exorcised its corpse. The Renaissance stood weeping at its grave and tried to resurrect its soul'.[12]

The objections of Panofsky and others were enough to make untenable any idea of the twelfth century as a cultural flowering based on Greco-Roman traditions, but until rather recently historians were comfortable working within Haskins's paradigm, and eager to expand it. R. W. Southern and Colin Morris, for example, worked on the conjoined problems of humanism and attitudes toward the value of the individual, both of which were considered since at least Burckhardt as hallmarks of Italian Renaissance civilization. For Southern, the twelfth century was the crucial stage in the formation of an identifiable

European civilization consequent to revolutionary changes in social organization, economy, culture, and ideas. 'The results of all this', he claimed in his essential *The Making of the Middle Ages*, 'are still with us'.[13] Southern's twelfth century, developed in a series of books and articles over a 60-year career, was optimistic, ambitious, dynamic, and characterized by what he called 'medieval humanism'. By using this term, Southern boldly encroached on the territory of scholars of the 'true' Renaissance just as Haskins had done before him. Humanism carries with it connotations of the dignity of humankind, a love of Classical learning, and a secular outlook completely alien to the Dark Ages against which the Burckhardtian Renaissance positioned itself. In a 1970 article, he summarized the importance of this humanism in a passage that bears quotation at length:

> There was thus in the twelfth and thirteenth centuries a continuous and uninterrupted reassertion of the claims of human dignity. The intellectual enquiries of the period made God, man, and nature intelligible and coherent; the area of the natural world was enlarged at the expense of the supernatural, and the pressure of the unknown which had weighed heavily on many parts of life was lightened.[14]

Southern's work often veers toward the romantic, but he managed, more effectively than Haskins, perhaps, to locate an enthralling intellectual dynamism within a much larger vision of society.

Morris similarly brought the debate over medieval humanism to Burckhardt's own territory in his provocatively titled *The Discovery of the Individual, 1050–1200*.[15] The notion that medieval Europeans had granted individuals no special dignity captured the popular imagination as powerfully as any plank of Burckhardt's original argument, and Morris's re-framing of the problem inspired vigorous debate. These claims were commonly, but not universally, accepted in Anglophone scholarship when Caroline Walker Bynum argued that the question of individuality was misplaced; the twelfth century, she argued, instead discovered that individual piety and intellectual life were experienced most fruitfully within clearly defined groups. 'If the religious writing, the religious practice, and the religious orders of the twelfth century are characterized by a new concern for the "inner man", it is *because* of a new concern for the group, for types and examples, for the "outer man"'.[16] In a sense, the present study follows Bynum's lead and focuses on the way individual Europeans were assailed by options, by new means of self-realization. The 'new institutional structures' that Bynum claimed informed the individual experience of western Europeans here become a series of spiritually and professionally fraught choices.

The notion of a twelfth-century Renaissance is itself rich enough to inspire many other critiques, and those critiques have come from many angles. It is possible to identify a few main trends in criticism, beyond the basic problem of defining the nature and time-frame of any cultural flowering. The first line of critique centers on geography, and especially the Franco-centric focus of much of the scholarship. A side debate even developed on the place of England in the twelfth-century Renaissance (Southern felt it played a small role), and Germany and sometimes even Italy seemed to be effectively marginalized (and at any rate German and Italian scholars in the twentieth century depended less than their French and English counterparts on Haskins's framework).[17] C. Stephen Jaeger has been particularly adamant that Haskins, Southern, and others systematically ignored the eleventh-century German origins of twelfth-century cultural achievements. In addition, Haskins focused almost exclusively on intellectual production in Latin in a period that saw the emergence of increasingly rich vernacular traditions. Many subsequent scholars were content to incorporate developments in Old French, Middle High German, and other vernaculars into a vision of a renaissance; in doing so, however, they slightly shifted the foundations of Haskins's argument.[18] Recent work on the problem of language, however, has sought a more sophisticated approach to the relationship between Latin and vernacular writings, one that sees a dynamic interconnectedness between what have too often been regarded as parallel cultural spheres. The 'vernacularization' of a written word in which Latin had been predominant gave thinkers and writers the opportunity to re-cast the role of writing and its social and political implications in fundamental ways.[19]

Haskins and his immediate followers, perhaps predictably, had little to say about the place of gender in the twelfth-century renaissance. It was only in the 1970s that gender began to be taken seriously as a category of historical analysis. Since then, scholars have paid greater attention to female authors, such as Hildegard of Bingen, Heloise, Herrad of Hohenberg, and Marie de France, who together warranted a total of only five mentions in *The Renaissance of the Twelfth Century* (none for either Hildegard or Marie). Thus, the canon of representative texts has expanded because of greater attention to women's intellectual production, and all four of those writers, along with several others, participated in the major trends of the renaissance noted above. As Chapters 3 and 4, below, will demonstrate, gender also played an important symbolic role in twelfth-century culture. Monks referred to Jesus as a mother, and venerated the Virgin Mary, who was generally celebrated for not partaking of the characteristic weaknesses of her sex. Authorities often did not know what to make of the female saints who became increasingly common over the course of the century. Moreover, as the Church elevated the status of the male, Latin-literate, celibate clergy, women were further marginalized and emphatically excluded from positions of authority. Religious women often turned to mystical experience and vernacular writing to circumvent these power structures. In the secular world, a few women achieved positions of prominence, most famously the English queens Matilda and Eleanor of Aquitaine, the latter of whom had great power in the prevailing feudal order. But these and other examples were the exceptions that proved the rule, for even they were largely defined as wives or mothers. Certainly the marginalization of women by contemporaries, and until recently by historians, militates sharply against a romanticized notion of inexorable intellectual ferment.

One could also attack the positive assessments of twelfth-century culture by Haskins, Southern, and others as excessively romantic and dismissive of decidedly chilling developments. The twelfth century, after all, witnessed the height of the Crusading movement, an intensification of attacks on Jewish communities, persecution of religious minorities, and an increase in urban poverty. In the 1930s, the German historian Carl Erdmann suggested that the Crusades were an extreme example of idealism degraded into fanaticism. More recently, R. I. Moore dated the 'formation of a persecuting society' to this period, and argued that secular and ecclesiastical authorities began to identify dangerous 'others', such as Jews, lepers, and homosexuals, and mark them for discrimination.[20] Even more controversially, John Boswell argued in 1980 that, over the course of the twelfth century, what had been a comparatively tolerant period in European history for gay people gave way to hostility and persecution.[21]

Moreover, as Jaeger has persuasively argued, the twelfth-century renaissance fails the test of self-definition: few contemporary writers betray much sense of participating in a revival of antiquity or general cultural flowering. This contrasts sharply with later Italians like Petrarch, who convinced himself he lived in a golden age. After making the case that the twelfth century built on more important developments in the cathedral schools of eleventh-century Germany and surveying the pessimistic worldview of a series of writers and thinking, Jaeger zestfully concluded that the idea of a renaissance had outlasted its usefulness as a guide to understanding twelfth-century culture: 'It is time to scrap it. It is now more trouble than it is worth; it obscures more than it illuminates'.[22] This brief book has a wider scope than most of the studies noted above, but it too rejects the notion of 'renaissance' as deficient in explanatory power and profuse with intellectual baggage. Its inherent teleology and its claims to prefigure modernity rob the period of its contingency, or, to borrow a term once applied to the later Italian renaissance, its 'drama'.[23] Freed from its responsibility for prefiguring Petrarch and Leonardo, for discovering individuality, and for giving rise to other harbingers of the 'modern', the twelfth century can be explored as a locus of contradiction and possibility in several distinct scholarly areas.

The 'The Renaissance of the Twelfth Century' always referred to more than just Latin writing and even high intellectual attainment. Scholars like Southern and Morris focused on a kind of spiritual mood characterized by individuality and great emotional energy. The religious writings of the twelfth century have in this regard long enthralled casual readers as well as scholars. Two of the Middle Ages' most popular saints, Bernard of Clairvaux and Francis of Assisi, lived during this period, and new religious orders spread throughout Western Europe as laypeople participated more actively in religious life. Twentieth-century scholars identified a 'spiritual awakening' that stretched from the so-called Gregorian Reform of the mid-eleventh century to the Fourth Lateran Council of 1215, characterized by a new diversity of forms of the religious life, greater emotionalism in spiritual writing, and an emphasis on the human, suffering figure of Jesus Christ (in contrast to the more distant, stoic Jesus of earlier iconography). This energy was channeled into a series of new religious orders, most notably the Cistercians and, at the beginning of the thirteenth century, the Franciscans, and sometimes the institutional Church was a step behind these developments. As noted above, the spiritual dynamism of the period often manifested itself in heterodox ways, which required a concerted ecclesiastical response. Women, religious minorities, and heterodox thinkers came under increasing pressure as the Latin Church increasingly defined itself by systemizing its doctrine and insisting on the fundamentally distinct identity of its male clergy. The causes of these phenomena have not been precisely pinpointed, but the institutional and devotional developments of the period continue to form an important and distinct branch of twelfth-century studies.

Although the term 'Renaissance' implies a focus on forms of cultural expression like art and literature, for scholars of the twelfth century it came to encompass developments in other areas. Political historians, especially English and French ones, have long considered the twelfth century to be pivotal in the formation of the modern political order. The feudal monarchies of the period, especially those of England, France, and perhaps northern Iberia, contained the germ of what would sprout into modern-style nation states. In the late nineteenth century, the English historian William Stubbs claimed that to this period belonged the 'the beginning of the process which is completed in national self government'.[24] The political history of twelfth-century England has been seen by many to culminate in the issuing of Magna Carta in 1215, which in turn (supposedly) led to modern notions of law and rights. Recent approaches to this political narrative are decidedly less triumphalist, but the twelfth century still bears some weight when considering modern origins. Other national narratives depend on this period. While imprisoned by the Nazis during the Second World War, Robert Fawtier contemplated the Capetian dynasty of high medieval France and found that 'the original structure of France seemed to me so strongly built that it could not be completely destroyed'.[25] Germany, on the other hand, despite a few powerful rulers, fragmented into a universe of small states after the twelfth century, and thus its twelfth-century history often appears as a cautionary tale. This, however, has not prevented scholars from reasonably finding 'the beginnings of a national consciousness' then.[26] In all these cases, we can find origins if we wish to, but nothing in the political map of 1229 implied what the shape of Europe in 1648, 1815, or 1945 would be. Recent studies of government have focused less on the problem of the origins of modern political entities and more on cultures of power around rulers. During the twelfth century, royal and princely courts became not only centers of administration, but also arbiters of social values.[27] In addition, rulers depended more and more heavily on the written word to exercise power, and this occasioned a sea change in attitudes about memory and the function of government itself. As a result, a new class of literate bureaucrats entered European society. Scholarship relevant to the problem of state origins, then, has moved beyond stories of national beginnings to broader questions about how new kinds of government and administration transformed culture.[28] Thomas N. Bisson, for example, has recently suggested a new vision of power dynamics during the century in a book provocatively titled *The Crisis of the Twelfth Century*.[29]

As the grand political narratives of European history have been challenged in the post-colonial period, scholars have re-evaluated the place of medieval Europe in the wider world. Ambitious syntheses

by Archibald Lewis and Jerry H. Bentley, for example, have placed
Europe within a larger complex of political and cultural interaction
encompassing Africa and Asia.[30] Bentley, in particular, has argued that
'during the twelfth and thirteenth centuries, the Eastern Hemisphere
became more tightly integrated than at any period of history before
modern times'.[31] At the center of much of the work on Christian
Europe's encounters with different cultures has been the Crusades to
the Near East, which began just as the twelfth century dawned, caught
the imagination of rulers, writers, and peasants alike, and will never
be far from the main topic at hand in any of the chapters of this book.
Since September 11, 2001, cultural interest in the Crusades has been
at its most intense in recent memory in both the English- and Arabic-
speaking world. The Crusades do, in fact, offer something of a unified
theory for considering the twelfth century, since they bring together
so many of its central concerns. Conceived of by the papacy but executed by kings and assorted lesser nobles (depending on the crusade
in question), they demonstrated both the ambitions and limitations
of the medieval Church; they gave expression to the powerful but
volatile spirituality that one finds in most corners of twelfth-century
culture; they show how the conceptual and geographical limits of
Christendom were negotiated; and they provide a singularly useful
example of the conflict between peoples, cultures, and religions that
played itself out in most parts of Europe, with varying results. In the
mid-twentieth century, some historians (including a few who were
clearly influenced by the experience of modern Israel) were inclined
to see the Crusades as an early colonial misadventure on the part of
ambitious Europeans, a view which has been re-articulated by political commentators in the aftermath of US intervention in Iraq and
Afghanistan after 2001.[32] Most historians sensibly recoil from draw-
ing any clear parallels between the Crusades and modern conflicts,
but it is worth exploring why the medieval expeditions resonated so
clearly in the discourse of both the twelfth and twenty-first centuries.
The rhetoric of crusading profoundly shaped Europeans' conception of the world they inhabited, as well as what it meant to be a
knight. And although the idea that the expeditions to the Holy Land
were motivated by commercial ambitions has largely been discredited,
they did intertwine with an expansion of long-distance trade in the
Mediterranean and beyond.

The exciting and diverse recent scholarship on the long twelfth
century simply reflects the complexities of its culture, and it has necessarily rejected straightforward claims about its place in the origins
of modern Europe. Institutions insisted on an ideal order, but it is

not clear how people and ideas fit into that order, and this tension between ideal and reality underpins all of the following chapters. The dates that (loosely) bookend this survey—the beginning of the First Crusade at the opening, and the end of the Albigensian Crusade in France at the closing—are chosen to illustrate how ideals and institutions could be transformed in unexpected ways through unexpected choices. Within this chronological framework, the following chapters will focus almost exclusively on the 'Latin West', the region from Hungary to Iceland, and Sicily to Scandinavia, where the religious rites of Rome prevailed and Latin functioned as the language of thought and learning. The Byzantine culture of the 'Greek East', centered on Constantinople but influential throughout the Mediterranean and the Balkans, also transformed itself markedly during this period, but for reasons of space will be treated only in those instances where its scholars, emperors, and soldiers had direct contact with the West. Similarly, this book can only treat the Islamic world of the Mediterranean by way of comparison.

Chapter 1 introduces the political order of Western Europe through four chronological narratives concerning, respectively, the German Empire (including northern Italy), the Mediterranean kingdoms of northern Iberia and of Sicily, France and England, and the 'peripheral' polities of Northern and Eastern Europe. It is hoped that this will allow the reader to situate the Latin West in time and space, and also to demonstrate the dilemmas that lords and their subjects confronted as they tried to adapt received ideals to the realities of governance. With this basic political background established, the remaining chapters proceed thematically. Chapter 2 begins with the weight of numbers—that is, demographic statistics—before surveying how a burgeoning population fed itself, re-organized itself, and made its elites rich during a period of demographic explosion and relative economic prosperity. The spiritual life, whose contours were profoundly re-shaped by these changes, serves as the topic of the third chapter, a survey of religious ideas and their institutional framework. Europeans expressed their religiosity with increasing fervor throughout the twelfth century, created new structures for their piety, and seem to have felt increasing anxiety about threats to the ritual purity of the Latin West. Chapter 4 revisits the notion of the 'Renaissance of the Twelfth Century' through a consideration of its intellectual production that emphasizes the collision of a vast array of traditions, some internal to Europe, some originating in the Muslim world of the Mediterranean. The emphasis throughout will be not 'rebirth' or 'progress' so much as cultural encounter and the manipulation of traditional ideas in new institutional and political contexts. The final chapter seeks to tie together the social, political, religious, and economic history of the period through an analysis of the crusading movement. Inspired by religious enthusiasm and a profound vision of the political order, the Crusades articulated quite clearly what the Latin West thought it ought to be. Their failure showed that vision was unrealistic.

Some of the twelfth-century people who left sources to us referred to themselves as 'moderns'. Contrary to a popular misconception, they had an acute awareness of the past, and their belief in the Last Judgment did not stop them from thinking about change in the world. If we allow our subjects the luxury of self-definition, we must reject any simple notions of progress (or resistance) to modernity, and with it the idea of 'renaissance'. It is clear that some of the most important developments of the twelfth century have firm roots in earlier periods, and the fruits of others, such as scholastic philosophy, were most fully realized in later ones. But this book does unapologetically insist that something with long-term implications for subsequent history did happen between 1095 and 1229. What emerged was the *possibility of Europe,* and that possibility expressed itself in difficult choices. By 1229, a few frameworks had been established and sometimes claimed as definitive, such as the philosophical method of the schools, canon law, or (perhaps) the French monarchy, but these were still adapting and adaptable. It is hoped that some of the latent possibilities of the twelfth century will show that anxieties about difficult choices can be historically instructive.

Chapter 1: Varieties of Political Order in the Latin West

On November 27, 1095, according to several contemporaries, Pope Urban II addressed a Church council at the French town of Clermont. The historian Fulcher of Chartres insisted that a grim spiritual climate prevailed across Christendom: 'With Henry reigning as so-called emperor, and with Philip as king in France, manifold evils were growing in all parts of Europe because of wavering faith'. Christianity in the west lay in disarray, unscrupulous knights pillaged at will, and 'no one was spared of any suffering'.[1] Violence, disorder, and slack piety threatened the physical and spiritual well-being of everyone—other chroniclers share at least the perception that the carnage had reached unprecedented levels.[2] Having already held several synods throughout France, Urban II convened this council to deal with some immediate problems, including disputes between local bishops, the recent, scandalous marriage of the king of France to the wife of the count of Anjou, the moral reform of the clergy, and the need to free bishops from the control of secular rulers.[3] Unfortunately, his speech survives only in second-hand (at best) accounts, and the various chroniclers who recorded it differed on many details; they reconstructed his words according to what happened next, which shaped what they thought he *ought* to have said. During the two decades that the speech percolated in the minds of assorted writers, it took on new layers of meaning, but there can be no doubt that whatever Urban II said, it struck a chord and reveals a great deal about the Christian world order as he and his contemporaries conceived of it.

According to Fulcher's version, Urban II began with local issues, and he exhorted the knights of France to stop destroying church property and to put aside their private warfare. He chided the clergy for their worldliness and asked them to be true shepherds rather than mercenaries and so to restore the world to its proper order. After he had addressed Western Europe's endemic violence, he turned his attention to the wider geopolitical and religious scene:

> For, as most of you have been told, the Turks, a race of Persians, who have penetrated within the boundaries of Romania [the Eastern Roman or 'Byzantine' Empire] [...] in occupying more and more of the lands of the Christians, have overcome them, already victims of several battles, and have killed and captured them, have overthrown churches, and have laid waste God's kingdom.[4]

Muslim armies from the East had recently assaulted the Byzantine frontiers with increased vigor, and so had threatened the very existence of the empire. After the Seljuk Turks annihilated their army at the Battle of Manzikert in 1071, the emperors had struggled to keep the invaders from the gates of their capital at Constantinople. A desperate Alexius I Comnenus appealed to the pope for some kind of military aid, though no extant source explains precisely what sort of aid he requested (most scholars assume that he had in mind a small mercenary strike force[5]). In response, Urban II exhorted the knights and clergy assembled at Clermont 'to strive to help expel that wicked race from our Christian lands before it is too late'. And there was something else: 'remission of sins will be granted for those going thither, if they end a shackled life either on land or in crossing the sea, or in struggling against the heathen'.[6] Those who fought the Turks would help their own bids for salvation; that is, it would help cure some of Western Christendom's own ailments.

It has been customary to associate Urban II's speech with the 'calling of the First Crusade', but properly speaking he could have called anything of the sort. He had no word for 'crusade', and, although previous popes had toyed with the idea of sending military aid to the East, the concept was not fully articulated or even understood. Urban II and the chroniclers who re-remembered his speech were talking about very novel things. The speech at Clermont, and subsequent retellings of it, came at a turning point in a series of negotiations about the just war, the role of penance in Christian life, the need to quell violence within Western Europe, and the Latin Church's proper relationship with its Greek counterpart in the East.[7] Rather than any antecedent of the modern term 'crusade', he used the Latin *peregrinatio*, 'pilgrimage'. Subsequent versions, written at ever further remove from the actual speech, introduced new elements, including sensational charges that Muslims coercively circumcised Christian infants and let the blood run into baptismal fonts.[8] Despite the different accounts of Urban II's speech, it is clear that he and those who followed him tried to solve several of Europe's most pressing problems through an armed pilgrimage to the center of the Christian world. The solution was to mobilize a fragmented political order to action by appealing to their spiritual anxieties and engendering a sense of apocalyptic fervor.

As pope, Urban II held considerable secular authority in a politically divided Italy, where he fought for precedence with the German 'Roman' emperor, the urban aristocracy of Rome, the king of Sicily, and the nobles of wealthy northern cities. But he also represented the unity of Christendom, an ideal of a unified West trying to heal itself through the repatriation of Jerusalem. By appealing to this idealized unity, he managed to inspire a successful expedition to Asia Minor, and ultimately, Jerusalem itself, led by powerful magnates like the duke of Normandy (son of the King of England), the counts of Blois, Flanders, and Toulouse, and many other warriors from the high and low nobility of France, the Rhineland, and southern Italy. At considerable expense and inconvenience to themselves, these feudal lords put aside local warfare and headed, through a number of routes, toward Constantinople and the Holy Land, where they in fact conquered Jerusalem and massacred its inhabitants in 1099.

With the benefit of hindsight, we can detect in Urban II's speech tensions between the local and the universal, the ideal and the real, the secular and ecclesiastical that would characterize Western Europe throughout the long twelfth century. These tensions were on display 134 years later, when a penitent Count Raymond VII of Toulouse, a descendant of one of the pilgrim-warriors of the First Crusade, humbled himself at Notre Dame in Paris to finalize the Treaty of Paris. Representatives of the papacy looked on. Count Raymond and his immediate ancestors had been the primary political targets of another series of military campaigns launched by a pope. In 1208 Pope Innocent III, by scholarly consensus the most important pontiff of the High Middle Ages, had called for armed intervention in the south of France, which was thought to be infected by heretics. The local nobles had failed Christendom by allowing these dissidents to flourish. The kings of France prosecuted the conflict, now known as the Albigensian Crusade, with varying degrees of enthusiasm, often through commanders taken from the northern French nobility, and Louis VIII had more or less settled the issue when he occupied

Avignon (nominally allied to Raymond) in 1226. Three years later his widow Blanche of Castille (acting as regent for the 14-year-old Louis IX) presided over the end of the conflict. It addressed the alleged root cause of the struggle—the so-called Cathar or Albigensian heresy—by requiring Raymond to promise obedience to the papacy, to expel heretics from his territories, pay indemnities to bolster the institutional church and especially its monasteries, and to establish a university at Toulouse where leading theologians could promulgate orthodox doctrine.[9] Given that the precise nature of the heresy and the actual threat it posed has been questioned by recent scholarship, it is fair to say that the most significant consequences of the settlement were geopolitical. The kings of France had previously ruled over much of southern France as distant and sometimes nominal overlords, and the southerners resisted them culturally, politically, and during the crusade, militarily. The destruction of Raymond's main fortresses, combined with previous French conquests in Gascony and Provence, effectively made Louis IX the true ruler over a region corresponding more clearly than ever before to the modern borders of France. When Raymond's heirs died childless two decades later, all of his lands reverted to the French king, giving him direct control of more of France than his counterpart in 1095 could have imagined.

In that same year of 1229, Frederick II, the king of Germany and Sicily as well as Holy Roman Emperor, wore his crown during a solemn ritual at Jerusalem's Church of the Holy Sepulchre. He had recently taken the city by treaty while on a crusade that had not been sanctioned by the current pope, Gregory IX, who was not at all impressed by Frederick's conquest. A ritual that ought to have been the fulfillment of Urban II's dream had instead, like the Albigensian Crusade, revealed deep fissures in the Christian order.

In 1229, as in 1095, the Church insisted on purity and unity, and political and spiritual motives intermingled, but now, in France and elsewhere, new political players asserted themselves, and they needed to confront new political realities. Gregory IX claimed to speak for a unified Christendom just as Urban II had. The kings of France, and their counterparts in Iberia, England, and even Eastern Europe, however, presided over states whose growing organization encouraged a particularism that provided a real challenge to the papacy's universalizing vision of Europe. Neither vision triumphed in the short term, but the tension between the two must inform any clear understanding of the political life of the period. This chapter explores the continuing negotiation between these visions of Europe through a series of narratives that, for lack of a better term, can be called 'political'.

None of the twelfth-century polities discussed here correspond geographically or conceptually with a modern nation-state; straight, solid lines on maps do no justice to their true nature. Modern historians perhaps lack the conceptual vocabulary to discuss twelfth-century political life, and recent debates point out the sometimes muddy relationship between contemporary terms and the relationships they describe. Should we speak of 'government' in a vaguely modern sense, or rely on the more slippery 'lordship'?[10] Was there any semblance of public authority, or was all authority essentially private, the special possession of great men, acquired by violence and to be passed on to heirs along with other possessions?[11] Can one rightly distinguish between 'Church' and 'state' in the Middle Ages?[12] These questions, and many others, intersect with any narrative history of the states of twelfth-century Europe, but it will be useful to emphasize three essential problems. First, kingdoms, duchies, counties, city-states, and other polities struggled to achieve the kind of basic territorial integrity and continuity that the modern world tends to take for granted.[13] The most sensible maps of twelfth-century Europe eschew distinct territorial boundaries and instead vaguely indicate the possible geographical extent of a particular realm. From Wales to the eastern Baltic region, borderlands were fluid and subject to negotiation and contestation. Secondly, secular and ecclesiastical leaders advanced increasingly sophisticated theories of power and its legitimacy. The received models, such as that of the Roman Empire, could not address the realities of the twelfth century; neither popes nor emperors could truly realize their pretensions to universal rule. Kings and philosophers constructed bases for rule drawn from classical, Christian, and more immediate precedents. In England, for example, John of Salisbury claimed to have gleaned a vision of the body politic from a non-existent work of the ancient writer Plutarch, while a handbook for the royal treasury insisted that efficient royal administration reflected the sacred qualities of kingship (see below, Chapter 4). Third, rulers relied increasingly on written documents to administer their territories, wrote down their laws, and created additional institutions to extend and centralize their authority.[14] The development of the exchequer in England, the *cortes* in León, and new methods of fiscal accounting in lands as disparate as Flanders and Sicily, as well as records like Philip II Augustus of France's 'Ordinance of 1190' (regulating the collection of revenues and the system of courts), bear witness to this veritable revolution in government. Of course, all these trends influenced each other: as French kings, for example, sought to expand their royal domain, they deployed a theory of sacral kingship through which they would, years later, come to embody the French nation even as they required novel means of fiscal exploitation and administrative efficiency to expand through military conquest.[15]

Rulers and subjects throughout Europe confronted these problems in often idiosyncratic ways. The complex set of responses to widespread political fragmentation, which occurred on the continent in the ninth and tenth centuries after the Carolingian Empire dissolved, has often been subsumed under the amorphous term 'feudalism'. In the last few decades, however, many medievalists have insisted the term has no specific or even useful meaning in this context.[16] For historians who use the term (including the present author), 'feudalism' refers to a political order in which some aristocrats, called vassals, ruled over territory that they held from other aristocrats, called lords or suzerains. In return for the land they held (which historians refer to as a 'fief', even if the term was rare in medieval practice), vassals promised homage and fealty to their lords. It usually implies a politics marked by personal relationships and highly localized authority and units of jurisdiction.

This order of things should not be oversimplified as merely localism or thinly veiled anarchy. Most regions of Europe possessed a clear notion of a political community that regulated the behavior of kings, lords, and subjects alike. And although most politics was 'personal' in the sense that governance depended on an individual's charisma (and often on his direct presence in his territory), it was not therefore 'private'. Relationships among the powerful were negotiated publically through an elaborate system of symbols and rituals.[17] Whenever kings held a feast or celebrated a holiday, they made a political statement, and especially when they wore their crowns at such an event. Rituals often took place in the context of public assemblies of great men, where the political community would gather in force to represent itself collectively, as when kings declared a general peace (a kind of ritually ensured ceasefire among the nobility) or celebrated the coming-of-age of a family member. Political power was not simply exercised through administrative mechanisms; it was performed.[18]

Through this shared political language, overlapping communities gradually grew up and created different opportunities for collective action, though they were certainly structured hierarchically, with ordained kings at the top of the hierarchy. Such a complex set of relationships could prevent kings from establishing institutions that modern readers might associate with stable government, and they were certainly incompatible with the goals of the new types of civic organization that appeared in towns. They did, however, represent a system within which people could settle disputes, and within which normative notions of justice could develop.[19] It has also been argued that the political order depended on complex scriptural interpretations, and that twelfth-century exegetes wrote egalitarian sentiments, designed to protect Christians from arbitrary oppression by lords, into their biblical commentaries.[20] A complicated set of factors determined the privileges and duties that accompanied political life, and, as a result, what a lord or subject could do, or what he could not do, would be negotiated, and when it was decided, it would be demonstrated through ritual performance.

Because of all these considerations, the political map of Europe in 1229 was taking on some of its modern characteristics, but its polities were defined by contemporary realities that long preceded those that accompanied the emergence of the modern nation state. Institutions that seem to prefigure modern government, like England's exchequer, seem like mundane responses to immediate conditions when seen in their broader contemporary context. Borders, even when they closely approximated those of the twenty-first century, tended to be ill-defined sites of negotiation rather than true national boundaries.

The German Empire, the Papacy, and Northern Italy

Urban II presided over a Christendom that was concluding a centuries-long process of re-organization following the collapse of the empire of Charlemagne (King of the Franks, 768–814) and his heirs in the late ninth century. In the aftermath of that collapse, which resulted from dynastic accident, the division of kingdoms among heirs, and foreign invasions from east, west, and south, public authority and most semblance of centralized administration disappeared from Central and Western Europe. In their place, highly localized political relationships emerged. East of the Rhine, Carolingian kings of East Francia, who gradually became identifiable as German kings, were replaced by the Saxon (919–1024) and then Salian (1024–1125) dynasties. What is usually termed the 'German kingdom' of the early Middle Ages consisted of several duchies (rendered *ducatus*, *regna*, or *provinciae* in Latin), each populated by a self-defined clan (*gens*) acutely conscious of its independent identity, the most important being Franconia, Lotharingia (Lorraine), Swabia, Saxony, and Bavaria. All of these were theoretically subject to the king. Taken together, the people, the region, and its language could be referred to by the Latin *Teutonici* or, later, *Alemani*, but there was little consistency in this regard.[21] Otto I, 'the Great', had claimed and received the title of 'Emperor of the Romans' in 962 (after which point modern historians begin referring to the 'Holy Roman Empire'), and his successors attempted as best as they could to follow his example. German kings periodically claimed the throne of Italy, also a part of the former Carolingian Empire, though Charlemagne himself had never controlled the region south of Rome. In 1033, Emperor Conrad II had integrated Burgundy, centered around Arles in southern France, into his domains, and so gave the empire a third constituent kingdom. Few German kings troubled themselves unduly with Burgundy, but since the imperial title depended on papal coronation, they swept into Italian politics whenever their domestic fortunes allowed.

Voltaire's famous quip that the 'agglomeration which called itself the Holy Roman Empire was neither Holy, nor Roman, nor an Empire', is singularly unhelpful for understanding twelfth-century political culture in Germany and Italy; it makes sense only in terms of Enlightenment assumptions about the proper structure of nation-states. When imperial clerks and apologists used the phrases *sacrum imperium, imperium Romanum,* or (after the 1150s) *sacrum imperium Romanum* in royal documents, they made territorial, political, and theological claims which resonated with accepted history and which possessed great explanatory power. They asserted a widely understood ideal of authority, ordained by God, stretching back (it was supposed) to Caesar Augustus, and they recognized the political reality of a geographically and ethnically diverse realm. The imperial ideal evoked holiness, Roman-ness, and the contemporary empire itself in a conscious struggle with competing visions of the world order.[22] Nearly all of the German kings sought to control the wealthy and strategic cities of northern Italy and then to enter Rome itself for an imperial coronation. When a king called himself the 'King of the Romans', his friends and enemies knew precisely what he meant. That the imperial ideal often did not mesh with reality did not make it any less central to political life.

In the twelfth-century context, 'Germany' refers to a sphere of influence stretching from the North Sea in what is now the Netherlands to Bavaria in the southeast, while further flung regions like Frisia and Carinthia, though under German political influence and generally part of the imperial dominions, were and are often seen as outliers to a central core. Germany and the empire were held together by consensus of the magnates and by traditions inherited from the Romans, Carolingians, and Ottonians, and quite often by the external threats like that of the Magyars in the tenth century. Moreover, the extent of this polity shifted constantly, as kings extended their dominion throughout the twelfth century by encouraging nobles, dukes, and townsmen to emigrate to the regions beyond the Elbe. They presided over an eastern frontier where mostly German-speaking Christians intermingled and eventually converted Slavic-speaking pagans. To the south, they periodically claimed the throne as kings of Italy, where they ran up against papal authority when trying to impose their will on the increasingly independent city-states of the Lombard region, some of which were becoming major Mediterranean trading powers. The polity at the center of these geopolitical conflicts itself was an inherently unstable but still powerful synthesis.

The challenges of imperial rule, 1095–1125

Medieval German kings had three primary objectives, and they did not realize any of them for long. First, they sought to assert their royal prerogatives throughout their subject duchies, often through tight control of the church at the local level. They also attempted to control the cities of northern Italy through a combination of diplomacy and force, for reasons that were at once symbolic, economic, and military-strategic. This region was for all intents and purposes the key to receiving an imperial coronation by the reigning pope. Finally, they claimed universal authority within their territories as heirs of the Roman Emperors and as divinely anointed rulers. Many dukes and local lords of the German lands, as well as the popes, opposed all of these endeavors when they could, but they acknowledged the honor due to a representative of the tradition of Caesar or Charlemagne or Otto the Great, and they recognized that an effective monarch could bring stability. The popes, for their part, frequently found themselves hostage to Roman city politics, and, as far back as the 740s, had appealed across the Alps for military support in order to make good their secular and ecclesiastical claims in Italy. What had started as a symbiotic relationship had deteriorated into civil war in the 1070s. Although the twelfth century saw alternating periods of conflict and compromise, the two sides rarely co-operated.

In the 1150s, Bishop Otto of Freising, a historian and uncle of the German king Frederick II, boasted that 'this is the very apex of the law of the Roman Empire, namely that kings are chosen not by lineal descent but through election by the princes'.[23] Kings routinely ensured succession of their sons by having them elected and consecrated while the father was still alive, but all the nobles and bishops of the German lands accepted the principle of elective kingship. In the early twelfth century the election procedure was not strictly codified, and hotly contested elections led to serious conflict on several occasions; succession depended on a combination of local authority and family connections that could result in some semblance of a princely consensus.[24] As a general rule, however, an effective king with a reasonably competent son could assure the latter's election. At his election, the king took on the title 'king of the Romans', with or without papal approval. Although the popes retained the privilege of bestowing the imperial crown, the kings insisted that the authority of the imperial office, the *imperium*, came from election.[25] In order to assert that authority, however, they needed the support of their nobility and of the Church. These dilemmas came to a head for King Henry IV (r. 1056–1106) at the time of Urban II's speech at Clermont in 1095.

Even though the idea of crusading had probably occurred to him already, Henry IV did not answer Urban II's call. He was trapped in Verona, bogged down with unsuccessfully trying to impose his will on northern Italy. Pope Urban, the long-time papal ally Duchess Matilda of Tuscany, and her new husband, the young son of the powerful Duke Welf IV of Bavaria had joined forces against him. Not only did several Lombard cities revolt against Henry IV, but his own son Conrad joined the enemy and was crowned king of Italy in 1093. To make matters worse, Pope Urban II had also excommunicated Henry, a lingering consequence of what scholars usually call the 'Investiture Controversy'.

From the beginning of his reign, Henry IV had, like most of his predecessors, tried to control his kingdom by carefully choosing and sometimes manipulating bishops and archbishops. In so doing he assured that he would have loyal servants at the local level who could check the power of dukes and counts, and also administer what were often wealthy ecclesiastical estates. The imperial Church system became a component and an extension of royal power. The king, as the 'anointed of God', was obliged to look after God's Church and intervene on its behalf when necessary. At the end of the eleventh century, an anonymous propagandist went as far as to argue that 'the royal power is greater and higher than the priestly and the king greater and higher than the priest, as being an imitation and emulation of the better and higher nature or power of God'.[26]

Occasionally, imperial intervention helped the papacy, most notably in 1046 when Emperor Henry III (1017–1056) deposed rival papal claimants and established Clement II securely at Rome. Over the course of the eleventh century, however, the papacy became increasingly uncomfortable with imperial control over bishoprics and monasteries as part of a larger concern with 'reform' of the Church. This entailed improving clerical morals and prohibiting clerical marriage, ensuring that clerics paid no money for their offices, and, ideally, ending the practice whereby kings endowed bishops with the symbols of their office. At their most extreme, the reformers denounced any interference by kings (as well as counts, dukes, and other laymen) in ecclesiastical appointments, and the ritualized demonstration of that interference through investiture, as an assault on the purity of the Church: 'Now everything is done in such disorder that the first are last and the last are first, so that the sacred canons are rejected and the whole Christian religion trampled underfoot', wrote one of the radical reformers.[27]

In 1073, Henry IV and the newly consecrated Pope Gregory VII had clashed over their rival conceptions of earthly and spiritual power, and particularly over the former's attempts to keep a friendly, anti-reformist bishop in the archbishop's throne in the key Lombard city of Milan. When Henry rejected the reformers' candidate for the archbishopric, who had been duly elected, Gregory excommunicated and deposed him. As a result, his position in Germany collapsed and he made a justly famous display of penance at the castle of Canossa in 1077 where he was reconciled with Gregory. In the aftermath, Henry, though weakened, recovered enough to remain a threat to subsequent popes, while Gregory died in exile in 1085.[28] In the long term, the reformers would succeed in identifying the ecclesiastical and secular spheres of authority as radically distinct, and bishops and monasteries would gradually come to identify more with the interests of the wider Church and the papacy than with their kings.

In 1095, then, a once-again excommunicated King Henry IV was stuck in northern Italy after attempting to subdue the Lombard cities he regarded as part of his patrimony. Even this king, who periodically styled himself 'Augustus', could not cross the Alps and return home for fear of being taken prisoner, while his rival Pope Urban II prepared to command a united army of Christians in the Holy Land (Urban ultimately chose to remain in Italy during the First Crusade). In 1097, Henry returned to Germany, where he tried to pacify his enemies and reassure his allies. But the kingdom was subject to inherently entropic political forces, as demonstrated by a rash of local revolts in the 1090s. The popes and their allies capitalized on the disorder to weaken Henry's position still further. At Mainz in 1103, he attempted to rein in local violence by having the great men of the realm swear to bring, 'peace to the Church, clergy and monks, and to the laity, to merchants, to women lest they be abducted, and to the Jews [this last group having suffered grievously during pogroms associated with the First Crusade in the 1090s]'.[29] At this time he prescribed strict death sentences or mutilation for those who engaged in local warfare—his anonymous biographer singles out 'those who had squandered their goods on soldiers so that encompassed by a large force of knights they might advance in the world'.[30] In this regard he followed the example of the 'Peace of God' movement through which bishops attempted to regulate private warfare for about the last century.[31] When Henry IV implemented it, he also advanced an ideology in which the king protected his people and checked aristocratic violence. He also belatedly answered the call of 1095, promising to atone for his past transgressions against the Church by travelling to Jerusalem. Just as Urban II had done, he tied domestic tranquility to holy war in Palestine.

By Christmas of 1105, Henry IV was his son's (also Henry) prisoner, and he counted only one major bishop as an ally. Forced into what was essentially an abdication, he surrendered the imperial insignia to his son. He would escape, but his effective rule was over. In letters from the last years of his reign, Henry alternated between pathetic protestations of his ill treatment and defiant assertions of his imperial prerogatives. '[T]o you', he wrote the king of France, 'I have thought it necessary to lament my calamities and all my woes and to mourn them. And I should even have fallen to your knees, were that possible without prejudice to the majesty of the Empire'.[32] He died in 1106 never having renounced his right to choose and invest bishops.

His son Henry V would not renounce that right either, and despite his initial cooperation with Pope Paschal II, he invaded Italy in 1111. Eventually the three-front opposition of papacy, German princes, and Italian cities brought Henry V to negotiations with Pope Calixtus II in 1119, resulting in the so-called Concordat of Worms three years later. This agreement represented the end of three years of often highly complex negotiations, but in its recorded form it is brief, vague, and obsessed with compromise. King and pope promised to help each other, and Calixtus even granted 'true peace to you and those who are or have been of your party during this discord'.[33] Its content is intuitively pleasing to modern readers: the king renounced the right of investing bishops with the symbols of episcopal authority (ring and crozier), and allowed for free elections by the clergy and people of the dioceses. He would, however, be present at such elections and effectively be allowed to break ties in the voting. In return for renouncing investiture, the kings received assurance that bishops, in their capacity as secular lords, would owe homage to the king and would receive a scepter, symbolizing their secular authority from the hands of the king. The spiritual aspect of the priesthood was insulated from symbolic contamination by laymen, while the royal proprietary interests were protected. The notion that episcopal duties were divided between the secular and sacred had informed similar debates in France and England, but their severability was not obvious. Bishops often came from the families of great lords, and their territorial strength aided their spiritual mission. At Worms the parties accepted the reality that imperial bishops were vassals of the king—junior partners owing homage and fealty to their royal lords in return for the power and jurisdiction that came with a bishopric. In the long term, however, the reforming popes succeeded in thwarting the kings' claims to be quasi-priests and in identifying the pastoral responsibilities of bishops as distinct from the business of governing a kingdom.

Structures of government and political challenges for the German emperors

Although textbooks tend to focus on the actions of kings, popes, and bishops, it is clear that peasants and townspeople experienced power in important new ways during this period. According to Thomas Bisson, the conflicts in Saxony during the age of the Investiture Crisis resulted in 'a massive failure of public authority in Germany'.[34] New, oppressive lordships sprang up and a long-term trend toward decentralization began. Henry V died without an obvious heir in 1125, leading to a change of dynasty under the elective system. The next two German kings, Lothar and Conrad III, maintained the *status quo* effectively and often revisited the policies of their predecessors. Lothar supported Pope Innocent II against an anti-pope installed by a rival party in Rome, led a mostly successful invasion of Italy, and for his efforts was crowned emperor in 1133. Conrad presided over rapidly escalating conflicts between great lords before helping to lead the unsuccessful Second Crusade (1145–1149), which failed miserably before the gates of Damascus. During their comparatively nondescript reigns, the governing patterns of political culture and royal administration continued to develop throughout the German kingdom. We can discern these patterns most clearly through the diffusion of real power to regional lords, the growth of towns as economic forces and political players, and the rise of an administrative class.

Throughout the century, counts and dukes secured regional power bases, almost always to the detriment of the kings' authority. The prevailing entropic political forces, however, broke the old duchies into new jurisdictions and created new power centers within them. By 1115, for example, there were effectively three dukes in Swabia, and other regions underwent a similar fragmentation of ducal authority. This trend continued throughout the twelfth century, and by 1190, the establishment or promotion of Austria, Styria, and several duchies, their number had effectively doubled. Meanwhile, princes in the east of the kingdom persevered in the colonization of the Slavs, and in the process founded new principalities, which altered the political dynamics of the kingdom. While some eastern princes established great power bases for themselves, the general trend was toward the fragmentation of jurisdictions. Bishops and archbishops, as feudal lords, joined in this trend and established great ecclesiastical principalities within duchies. The archbishops of Cologne, Trier, and Mainz, in particular, exercised immense political and military power.

While the dukes, regional princes, and bishops engaged in this balance-of-power politics, German and Italian towns asserted themselves more independently. Most major towns sought to free themselves from feudal obligations to ecclesiastical and secular lords alike, and the lords sought support by granting liberties (usually in the form of freedom from feudal dues and tolls) to the towns. In the middle of the century Trier, Cologne, and Mainz all had their own seals, meaning that they, through their ruling classes, were operating more or less independently. In Italy, the major towns gained even greater *de facto* independence in the decades after the Investiture Controversy, during which they could ally with church reformers to throw off imperial jurisdiction, increasingly taking on the privileges and functions of lordship. In 1115 the leaders of Bologna had the imperial palace there destroyed. Milan, Pisa, Genoa, and other important trading cities became effectively independent communes by the time of Lothar III; in the 1160s, Frederick Barbarossa failed in his bid to dominate the area. Enriched by economic growth and structurally transformed by demographic shifts, Lombardy presented the emperors with entirely different challenges than those faced by Henry IV and his predecessors.

That the towns could go their own way while emperors were distracted across the Alps speaks to the continuing need of emperors to affirm their rule in person. German kingship was itinerant kingship, and the kings, as they had since Charlemagne, travelled incessantly. The 'capitals' of the constituent kingdoms of the empire—Aachen,

Milan, and Arles—served as venues for the ritualized display of royal power, above all through coronations, but the administrative center followed the person of the king and his retinue of between 300 and 1000 (which may occasionally have reached 4000). This mass of humanity and governmental machinery frequented a few favorite royal palaces and also took advantage of the hospitality that major cathedral towns owed the king. Henry IV was constantly moving across a wide array of territory; his favorite stops included destinations as far removed from each other as Worms, Goslar, Regensburg, and Verona. His son Henry V stayed often at cathedral towns on the Rhine, while Frederick Barbarossa regularly visited palaces scattered from Altenburg, in formerly Slavic lands, to Kaiserlautern, west of the Rhine.[35] In addition, stops at cathedral towns were invaluable in stressing the sacred character of kingship. Kings celebrated major holidays not only at Aachen but at other major cathedrals like Regensburg and Magdeberg, where they also might, irrespective of the season, assert their sacral kingship through an elaborate crown-wearing ritual.

Archbishops, bishops, and other clerics in the court augmented the king's authority both symbolically and through their roles as territorial magnates and administrators. As trained, literate professionals they created a new kind of ruling elite. Rainald of Dassel, who ran Frederick Barbarossa's administration as royal chancellor and became Archbishop of Cologne, embodied the confluence of ecclesiastical power, secular government, and literate culture at the imperial court. 'Well-spoken, and most literate, eloquent, foresighted and extremely wise', he rose from relatively undistinguished beginnings to become a star student in the schools of Paris and then an architect of Frederick's policies and military leader in his own right.[36] At the beginning of the thirteenth century, Piero della Vigna would provide similar services to Frederick II.[37] Despite the grand political ambitions of some of the chancellors, the imperial chancery typically engaged in the mundane business of drafting the royal documents through which the imperials exercised their will. Over the course of the twelfth century, the imperial court became increasingly an engine of literate administration: the royal chancery of Frederick I issued charters at double the rate of his immediate predecessor Conrad III.[38] This trend, however, needs to be seen in terms of experimentation with different types of documents (which often had a vexed relationship to business carried out orally) than with an inexorable modernization of government.[39]

In addition to writing as a technology of power, the emperors used a highly diverse, and somewhat ill-defined, social group known as *ministeriales* to exercise their will and authority. Initially comprised of men of servile status, *ministeriales* could have military, administrative, or judicial functions and were known for their loyalty to the emperors (they were among the last supporters of Henry IV before his forced abdication). They formed the backbone of German government and became a reliable class of governmental functionaries not entangled with messy aristocratic relationships. Over the course of the twelfth century, the *ministeriales* more and more became assimilated to the knightly classes of Germany.[40] In addition, although they could be helpful to imperial ambitions, they were employed by bishops, towns, and dukes as counts as well. As a result, they could be used to thwart the centralizing ambitions of the monarchy. When Frederick I ascended to the throne in 1152, however, he recognized that the *ministeriales*, as well as the literate bureaucrats who created and kept records, were potential vehicles through which he could extend the reach of imperial power.

Frederick I and the travails of the imperial ideal

Before Conrad III died in 1152, he had named his nephew, Duke Frederick of Swabia, as his heir, passing over his eight-year-old son (another Frederick) in a move designed to keep a stronger, though more distant, member of his Staufen family on the throne. Once elected, Frederick I 'Barbarossa' ruled practically, accepting the new realities and allowing great princes to exercise their power; for the most part, he avoided making dangerous enemies at home. When confronting the pope, he was willing to make bold, even rash, claims for imperial powers, but here too his ambition gave way to what could feasibly be accomplished south of the Alps. His Italian schemes, however, still ended in failure.

At his court, Frederick 'Barbarossa' joined the practice of government to lofty principles of imperial authority. He surrounded himself with trained scholars, many of them from the schools of Paris, and fused German custom with the apparatus of Roman law. His chancellor aforementioned Rainald of Dassel perfectly embodied the contradictions and possibilities of the court. A cleric from a comital family who enjoyed trading manuscripts of classical authors like Cicero with his friends, Rainald never embraced the principles of church reform. In 1148 he opposed the Council of Rheims prohibition on clerics wearing aristocratic clothing (including ostentatious furs), and he saw no moral difficulty in leading knights into battle. According to Otto of Freising, Rainald and his fellow courtier Otto the Count Palatine 'possessed a pleasant and imposing presence, nobility of family, an intellect strong in wisdom [and] unperturbed spirits'.[41] Under Frederick and Rainald the imperial court formulated, copied, and issued written documents that helped shore up Frederick's position on both sides of the Alps. But the scholars also turned the court into a hub of literary activity, much of which centered around Rainald himself. The so-called Archpoet of Cologne, a self-styled parasite who sought preferment in the chancellor's circle, wrote a panegyric for Frederick titled 'Hail, Lord of the World'. The Archpoet also described the court as a center for drunken womanizers like himself in one of medieval Europe's greatest poetic exultations of wine, sex, and ambition, the so-called 'Archpoet's Confession'. Numerous other poems from the period celebrated Frederick's exploits, especially those in Italy.[42]

Frederick's advisers also insisted that the empire was truly a Roman one, and that the emperor was in no way inferior to the pope. Ritual and representation were crucial to this project. Through Rainald, Frederick insisted that the papal palace at the Lateran remove a painting of Lothar III holding Innocent II's stirrup in a gesture of feudal subjugation. The court perfectly understood that the visual arts mattered to their program: 'It began with a picture, the picture became an inscription, the inscription seeks to become an authoritative utterance'.[43] The chancery at the same time began using the term *sacrum imperium* as a matter of course, and in 1184 he summoned princes from 'the whole Roman world' to celebrate the knighting of his two sons. While the court boldly asserted the imperial ideal, there were few direct threats to Frederick's rule in Germany. He established himself at the top of a chaotic set of feudal relationships in which the most powerful nobles could begin to acquire extensive principalities, mitigating the chaos by regulating the nature of those relationships. At Roncaglia in 1158, Frederick laid out the obligations of fief holders and established rules such as those forbidding the subdividing of counties (which presumably would have threatened stability).[44] Through the granting of privileges and shrewd marriage arrangements, Frederick managed to make this system work for him throughout most of his reign.

Frederick's occasional difficulties with his great princes can be illustrated through the example of Duke Henry 'the Lion' of Saxony. In 1156, Frederick brought Henry, from the rival Welf family, into his good graces by granting him the additional duchy of Bavaria (at the same time creating a new duchy in bordering Austria to check Henry's power).[45] King and duke enjoyed good relations, and Henry ultimately acquired a number of lordships throughout the empire.

He controlled lands from the Alps to the Baltic and helped drive German settlement in Slavic lands. Although as a duke two times over Henry recalled the traditional system of power in Germany, he in fact operated within an entirely new geopolitical setting. Through negotiation, marriage (and, on one occasion, divorce), colonization, and simple bullying, Henry presided over a set of lordships that stretched from the Alps to the Baltic. He furthermore encouraged German settlement in Slavic lands, all the while enjoying good relations with Frederick. It has been suggested that Henry regarded himself as a quasi-king, and there is some iconographical evidence supporting this—in a beautiful gospel book Henry is depicted in majesty, crowned by God's own hands.[46] Eventually, for reasons that scholars do not entirely understand, Henry ran afoul of the Emperor. Henry clearly had made a habit of encroaching on the rights of lower lords, and they appealed to Frederick to move against him. In the end, after complicated judicial proceedings Henry was declared an outlaw, relegated to smaller principalities after an exile, and watched his duchies be granted to his rivals.[47] Although Frederick thus acknowledged the feudal rights of regional lords, he emphatically positioned himself as the head of the political order.

Frederick handled Henry the Lion the way he did because his Italian policy demanded stability in Germany, and that Italian policy in turn reflected his vision for imperial rule. He sought no less than the re-imposition of imperial rule in northern Italy, and would march across the Alps eight times during his reign. At the outset events appeared to follow the old pattern, according to which the German king provided military muscle for the papacy against its enemies, and in return was crowned emperor. In 1152, Pope Eugenius III faced two determined enemies: the Roman populace, as organized in its commune, and King Roger II of Sicily, who in principle held his kingdom as a papal fief. While early medieval crises in Rome tended to center around rival noble families in the city, Eugenius III had to deal with a rather novel challenge. In 1143 and 1144 the commune of the city of Rome declared itself a revived Roman Senate and continued to rebel against the papacy for a decade. They approached both Conrad III and Barbarossa, offering them the imperial title in return for their support, not only for their political designs against the papacy but before their vision of the political order in which the secular Roman Senate created imperial power. This senatorial model, now competing with imperial and papal ones, vividly demonstrates how creatively antiquity could be intruded into twelfth-century politics, but it had limited relevance to contemporary Rome.[48] The emperors, at any rate, had thrown their lot in with a sacred vision of kingship, even though they understood it differently than the popes did. They rejected the Roman overtures and helped the papacy restore order. By the late 1140s the Roman rebellion had become intertwined with the reforming interests of the charismatic religious figure Arnold of Brescia, who took Church reform to extremes unimagined (and unwanted) by the papacy. He preached against the ambitions of popes and other clerics for secular control—universally accepted by contemporary political culture—and mixed Roman patriotism with profound spiritual energy. But this project ignored too many political realities, and the 1153 Treaty of Constance doomed it. At Constance, Frederick promised never to ally with the Romans, the king of Sicily, or the Byzantine emperor, while Eugenius III assured Frederick of his imperial coronation. Once crowned in 1155, Frederick captured Arnold, handed him over for execution, and the new Pope Hadrian IV enjoyed a period of security.

Frederick could not follow up his successful coronation with further military action because the army of 1154–1155 was too small (and not particularly interested in a summer campaign in central Italy), and because German affairs called him home. Feeling abandoned, Pope Hadrian IV allied himself with the King of Sicily and ensured that when the Emperor came again three years later, it would be as an adversary. In 1158, Frederick promulgated edicts at Roncaglia which confirmed his claims to imperial rule over northern Italy. In these edicts, Frederick's practical interests in controlling Lombardy (he stood to gain huge revenues there), his conception of the emperor as the heir of Rome, and the increasing importance of the revival of Roman law (which was invoked by Frederick's Italian supporters) all come to light. He made good on his claims through decisive military action, culminating in 1162 when he conquered the recalcitrant city of Milan, razed it to the ground, and had its stones incorporated into new fortifications at rival Pavia. Despite this triumph, he could not sustain his advantage against Pope Alexander III (elected in 1159), a shrewd canon lawyer who himself had political interests in Lombardy. Alexander III allied himself to a group of cities that ultimately become the Lombard League, and for the next two decades imperial and papal claims to authority over Christendom played out over the course of three more imperial expeditions. In 1176 the League, led by Milan, defeated the Germans decisively at Legnano, and Frederick tempered his ambitions in Italy thereafter. In treaties at Venice in 1177 and again at Constance in 1183, the emperor, while claiming tribute and affirming his lordship over Italy, granted the communes increasing autonomy over their own affairs. Frederick, however, remained one of the most powerful rulers in Europe, and the neutralization of Henry the Lion made his position in Germany stronger than ever. He was a natural choice to help lead the Third Crusade after the fall of Jerusalem to the Muslim leader Saladin in 1187. But Legnano and its aftermath forced him to try new strategies in Italy, and he implemented one of them by betrothing his son to the daughter of the king in Sicily. When he died crossing a river in Asia Minor in 1190, Germany was at peace but heavily involved in the politics of Western Europe and the Mediterranean.

Henry VI, Frederick II, and the fracturing of Germany

Since Frederick's son Henry VI had already been crowned king, the succession was a foregone conclusion. The king of Sicily, however, had died in late 1189, and Henry's wife Constance had a legitimate claim to be the queen there. In the long run, the rival candidate Tancred (who had papal support) was unable to resist Henry VI's German army. Henry was crowned as king of Sicily on Christmas Day, 1194. Back in Germany, a combination of *ministeriales* and loyal princes and bishops kept a semblance of order, but Henry's death in 1197 at age 32 left many open questions, not least of all the succession to the German kingdom. Although Henry had tried to impose the principle of hereditary succession, and had at any rate ensured the election of his son Frederick II in 1196, a group of princes elected Henry's brother Philip of Swabia (apparently regarding him as a more plausible Staufen candidate than the toddler Frederick). Meanwhile a rival group of electors led by the archbishop of Cologne offered the crown to Otto of Brunswick, the Welf son of Henry the Lion. The resulting, highly destructive quarrel between three claimants was far more than a clash of personalities. Not only was one of them a small child, but the dynastic feud overlapped economic concerns, struggles within the German Church, and, of course, the role of Italy. Moreover, 1198 brought a new pope, Innocent III, who brought a bolder vision for the role of the papacy in the world than had been seen since the eleventh century. He saw the disputed succession as a fracture in Christendom that required his intervention. As a result, the rivalry between Welfs and Staufens became another arena for the struggle between papal and imperial authority.

Frederick II had been born in Sicily, where his claim to the throne was not seriously disputed despite Innocent's claims to be his feudal lord, leaving Philip as the Staufen king in Germany. Otto, however, secured papal support by renouncing his claims to ecclesiastical authority in Germany and acknowledging Innocent's political authority in parts of Italy. In the end, Philip won the support of the majority of German princes, including important bishops, and thus brought Innocent III to the negotiating table. However, he was murdered before he could be crowned emperor. With the field more or less open, Otto of Brunswick was crowned Otto IV in 1209. When Otto IV, however, returned to traditional imperial policy in Italy, he lost papal support as well as that of some of the German princes. Thus Frederick II, already well ensconced as king of Sicily, was elected king of Germany in 1211 and crowned the following year. When Otto IV suffered a disastrous military defeat against King Philip Augustus of France at Bouvines in 1214, Frederick II stepped in with full papal support. He had a formal coronation at Aachen in 1215 after which Pope Innocent III definitively legitimized Frederick II's rule at the Fourth Lateran Council.

At first, Frederick II spent his time in Germany trying to settle the matter of the disputed secession, and adopted conciliatory policies toward the Welfs and the papacy. After 1220, however, he spent precious little time in the German part of his inheritance, and he definitively broke with the old pattern whereby the emperors shored up their rule in Germany before crossing the Alps. He would focus primarily on Sicily, Italy, and on two occasions, Egypt and the Holy Land for the remaining three and a half decades of his rule, and his reputation as a multi-lingual polymath savant, though largely a romantic invention of the twentieth century, has some basis in the cultural achievements of his court in Palermo. His crusading adventures, moreover, seemed to invert the proper order of things. He did not accompany the Fifth Crusade, and thus incurred the anger of the papacy. When he managed to acquire Jerusalem by treaty on his own, he received scant credit for it. As far as the history of Germany is concerned, his reign was not without enormous consequence. When Frederick II's dreams of a unified German-Mediterranean empire died, Germany began the trajectory toward fragmentation that would characterize its political order until the nineteenth century.

Multicultural Kingdoms and the Mediterranean World: Sicily and Iberia

The Kingdom of Sicily, comprising not only the island but also the southern end of the Italian peninsula, was far removed geographically from the Staufen homelands of Swabia, but nonetheless central to Frederick II's ambitions. It also lay at the heart of the multicultural Mediterranean, where Arab, Byzantine, and Latin civilizations met. Still claimed in principle by the Byzantine Empire, and potentially within the orbit of the Holy Roman Empire, the island had an Arab-speaking Muslim majority in 1100, and the papacy claimed to be its feudal overlord. Its rulers combined Greek, Arabic, and Norman administrative traditions in an attempt to keep it unified despite repeated periods of fragmentation. Although less urbanized than northern Italy, the area was wealthy and comparatively well administered, and Sicily has served some historians as a kind of model of a bureaucratic medieval kingdom. Given Italy's early modern experience of disunity, the Sicilian kingdom has been seen as an abortive experiment in nationhood, an example of the path not taken. More recently, scholarship has presented the region as a laboratory for cultural conflict and assimilation, if not tolerance.[49]

To the west, on the Iberian peninsula, the Christian kings of León, Castile, and Navarre had long looked across an unstable frontier at the Islamic world as they attempted to conquer territory from the remnants of the Abbasid caliphate. In Iberia as in Sicily, kingdoms with diverse religious and cultural groups pushed for consolidation in the face of decidedly entropic forces. Both provide cases where the development of state structures occurred alongside the cultural and political expansion of Western Christendom.

Roger II and the Norman kingdom of Sicily

In the middle of the eleventh century, the Byzantine emperors still claimed much of the southern Italian peninsula, where local governors had managed to maintain fairly effective control of the southernmost regions of Apulia and Calabria and exerted moderate influence over cities like Amalfi and Naples. The local populations included Greeks who followed the rites of the Byzantine church, Italian-speaking Catholic Christians, usually called 'Lombards', and, increasingly, adventurers from Northern Europe, collectively referred to as Normans (but who counted in their ranks Bretons and others from various parts of France). The politically disunited island of Sicily hosted a Muslim, Arabic-speaking majority. The papacy, the Byzantine and Holy Roman Empires, and Muslim rulers in North Africa all sought influence in the region, which was prone to episodes of acute fragmentation; southern Italy's position near the exact center of the Mediterranean world made it impossibly difficult for any of the major regional powers—Christian or Muslim—to control completely. As a result, a dynamic mix of Eastern and Western influences came to shape the government and cultural expression of what would become the Kingdom of Sicily. Its rulers confronted the challenges of multicultural Europe while exploiting the possibilities it offered.

By the year 1000, adventurers, most of them from the duchy of Normandy, were operating in the area, often as mercenaries for various Byzantine officials, but occasionally as their enemies. In 1060, they fought on behalf of one Muslim warlord in a dispute with another. Gradually, they established permanent bases for themselves and began to play a role in local politics. Normans were effectively ruling Apulia by 1042, and in 1053 they defeated Pope Leo IV and his southern Italian allies at the battle of Civitate. The papacy then changed its policy: in 1059, Nicholas II declared two Norman nobles to be, respectively, the prince of Capua and the duke of Calabria, Apulia, and Sicily, and established these new polities as papal fiefs. This tied papal fortunes to those of the Sicilian Normans for nearly 150 years. The key political realities for the Norman rulers of Sicily would be their theoretical subjection to papal overlords, the fragmented and multicultural make-up of their population, and the tendency of their vassals to assert independence at the local level. From time to time, the Byzantine emperors also made their interest in recovering their old possession known.

Initially the Normans seemed poised to take on the role of papal military ally that had fallen to the emperors since the Carolingian period, but this relationship was riddled with ambiguity. Duke Robert Guiscard of Apulia came to Pope Gregory VII's aid in 1082, but in the process sacked Rome. Over the next three decades, the Normans rid the southern mainland of Byzantine rule and wrested control of Sicily from the Muslims. In the first decade of the twelfth century, then, a Norman duke, Roger Borsa, ruled Apulia and Calabria, while his technically subordinate cousin Roger II became the count of Sicily.

On the mainland the political order soon disintegrated, and no leader maintained firm, centralized rule anywhere other than on the island of Sicily. There, Count Roger II (count 1105–1130, king 1130–1154) effectively subjugated the majority Muslims and then could turn his attention to the mainland. After the death of Duke William of Apulia and Calabria in 1127, Roger II claimed the inheritance of the entire duchy, which was confirmed by Pope Honorius II in 1128. Two years later, the always opportunistic Roger II pledged fealty to an anti-pope, Anacletus II, apparently in return for a royal title that rested on a historically dubious argument: 'it was certain kingship had always existed in [Palermo], governing all Sicily' and therefore 'it was right and proper that the crown should be placed on Roger's head and that this kingdom should not only be restored but should be spread wide to include those other regions where he was now recognized as ruler'.[50] Roger II took advantage of the papal schism between Anacletus II and Innocent II, whose claim drew the support of luminaries like Saint Bernard of Clairvaux and thus ultimately prevailed. Despite Innocent II's victory, the popes never delegitimized the crown established by an anti-pope. The kings of Sicily, for their part, never looked back and always regarded their crown as legitimate even as they periodically acknowledged papal suzerainty.

Once established as king, Roger II turned his attention to pacifying his barons and resisting foreign invasions. By 1140 he had turned back one invasion by Emperor Lothar III, another by Pope Innocent II, and put down papal-inspired revolts in several peninsular cities. At the treaty of Mignano in 1139, Innocent II formally gave Roger II the kingdom as a fief. As the sole and secure ruler of the new kingdom he then built a strong, efficient, and relatively centralized government that superimposed Norman innovations onto Greek, Arabic, and Italian precedents, while absorbing influences from around the Mediterranean.[51] One of his chief advisers early in the reign, George of Antioch (d. *c.* 1151), perfectly illustrates the sort of multicultural professionalism that helped make Sicily a leading example (for many traditional scholars, at least) of bureaucratic kingship. A Greek-speaking Syrian Christian, who also knew Arabic, George served as the finance minister to a North African sultan before coming to the court at Palermo in the second decade of the twelfth century. There he became an intimate of the king, a *familiaris regis*. While this last title often has a vague connotation when applied to members of medieval courts, in Sicily it implied a very specific status as a royal adviser and administrator.[52] He served as a diplomat and military leader, but also helped organize the office that handled documents relating to land tenure in the kingdom, known by the Arabic title *dîwân* (which was rendered as *duana* in Latin). Some 20 years before his death around 1151, he was given the office of *ammiratus*, which stands etymologically somewhere between the Arabic 'emir' and English 'admiral'. Other officials in Roger II's administrations had titles drawn from both Greek and Arabic precedents.[53]

As many as 80 per cent of Roger II's charters were composed in Greek by ethnically Greek notaries, and it is generally assumed that Arabic charters were produced, though none have survived. That many of his Latin charters bear his signature in Greek reflects the continuing importance of Greek administrative procedures in the Norman Kingdom. His ideology of power also drew heavily on the East. In a mosaic produced during the last decade of his reign, Roger II wears the costume of a Byzantine emperor crowned by Jesus Christ, and Byzantine insignia figure prominently on his coinage alongside his Latin titles. A gold coin from the 1130s bears the Arabic inscription claiming that Roger ruled 'through the grace of God [Allah]' on one side, and a cross accompanied by the name of Jesus on the reverse.[54] His stunning royal chapel, the Cappella Palatina at Palermo, similarly integrates Norman architecture with the arches characteristic of mosques and a Byzantine dome, and is adorned with spectacular Greek mosaics.

Despite Roger II's shrewd manipulation of the governmental mechanisms and symbols of the Byzantine and Islamic worlds, in the long term his kingdom became increasingly Latinized as well as Christianized; the Roman, Latin rite came to predominate in churches. Greek monasteries and bishoprics lost support during the twelfth century and, despite contemporary suspicions that he secretly practiced Islam, Roger II executed an Arab royal official who had converted to Christianity but was suspected of having relapsed in his religious devotion.[55] Before and after Roger II's death, Palermo's Muslims revolted; 1160–1161 marked a particularly bloody episode. The kings' interest in Byzantine and Arabic civilization seems to have been both practical and ideological, but it was not the product of any great cultural sensitivity. The historian Romuald of Salerno assured his readers that Roger II 'labored in every possible way to convert Jews and Muslims to the faith of Christ, and endowed converts with many gifts and resources'.[56] By 1200, Latin-Greek-Arabic tri-lingual administrators had largely disappeared from the court at Palermo, and Latin became the dominant language of royal business.

These recurring tensions are symptomatic of the fundamental problems faced by Roger II and his successors. Holding the kingdom together required sound economic policy, continual diplomacy with the papacy and the emperors, constant vigilance over a restive aristocracy, and an ability to deal with intercultural conflict. Although Roger II built up an effective monarchy, he did not resolve any of these difficulties for the long term. After his death, his son William I (much later to be known as 'William the Bad') began his reign by protecting the geographical integrity of the kingdom through diplomacy and military campaigns against his external enemies. In 1156, however, he faced a major crisis. Frederick Barbarossa had come to Rome a year earlier, and a Byzantine army was operating along his eastern flank in Apulia, and there were revolts there and in Capua and elsewhere. Barbarossa, however, showed no interest in the south after his coronation, and William managed to defeat the Byzantines militarily. With the international situation thus secured, William could use the force of kingship, along with the loyalty of barons who had received fiefs from his father, to defeat the rebels.

In the aftermath, William largely withdrew from political life and so left the administration in the hands of officials who were competent but susceptible to intrigue. A series of *familiares* came to power in turns, all the while acknowledging that an Eastern-style absolute monarchy remained in place. In 1160, the hated chief minister Maio of Bari was assassinated, and for the next decade a series of palace factions conspired against each other. These factions coalesced around one of a number of prominent ministers including two Englishmen who had become bishops, a Frenchman, and a Muslim convert to Christianity. William I died suddenly in 1166, leaving his wife Margaret of Navarre as regent for the infant King William II. To help rule the kingdom, Margaret invited an entourage of clerics from northern France, including her young relative Stephen of Perche, who became the royal chancellor and archbishop of Palermo. She convinced Stephen to stay in Palermo by contrasting the riches he and his followers could obtain there compared with the 'poverty of northern Europe'. But these foreigners aroused even more resentment: the nobility felt threatened by the concentration of power in the royal administration, while the Greeks rebelled in Messina, as did the Muslims in Palermo. In the end, Stephen's right-hand man, a canon from Chartres cathedral named Odo Quarell, was publicly dismembered while 'the Greeks were busy slaughtering everyone from north of the Alps they could find'.[57]

By the end of William II's reign in 1189, his conciliatory policies toward vassals and ethnic minorities had achieved peace within the kingdom's borders. The Spanish Muslim traveler Ibn Jubayr (1145–1217) visited Messina and Palermo at the end of 1184 and praised William II as 'admirable for his just conduct, and for the use he makes of Muslims', who worked in his court while keeping their true faith secret. He continued that 'one of the remarkable things about him is that he reads and writes Arabic' and summed up William's rule with delicious ambivalence: 'the king, to whom [Palermo] is his world, has embellished it to perfection and taken it as the capital of his Frankish kingdom—may God destroy it'. Ibn Jubayr also described a thriving though somewhat insecure Muslim community in Palermo where there were 'countless mosques' and teachers of the Qur'an', and where Muslims lived in peace but strictly segregated from their Christian neighbors.[58]

William II also stayed on good terms with his feudal lord, the pope; his father had paid homage to Adrian IV in 1156, and the son continued to support Alexander III against various anti-popes. Still, William II continued the practice, illustrated by the prominence of bishops and archbishops at the royal court, of exercising relatively tight control over the kingdom's Church and its revenues. Although their fortunes were officially tied to those of the papacy, the Norman kings of Sicily avoided the disastrous church–state conflicts that their contemporaries in Germany, England, and elsewhere had to confront. William II made peace with Frederick I Barbarossa and then attacked Byzantine and Muslim possessions in the Mediterranean, with varying degrees of success. He also used marriage as an effective diplomatic tool, wedding himself to a daughter of Henry II of England and matching his aunt Constance with the future Henry VI of Germany. Such high-profile betrothals spoke to the increasing prestige of the monarchy. The Norman kings had demonstrated that a regional monarchy could make strides toward geographic cohesion and relatively efficient government despite its feudal and cultural tensions, and Sicily was ready to play a larger role in European affairs.

Frederick II and Sicily's place in the Mediterranean

The childless William II's death at age thirty-six in 1189 exposed the problems inherent in his kingdom's internal structure while underscoring its position in Mediterranean geopolitics. Uncomfortable for several reasons with the claims of William II's aunt Constance to become queen, a group of nobles and royal *familiares* elected Count Tancred of Lecce, a grandson of Roger II, to be king. Fearing the practical threat of encirclement by the Empire, and also the theoretical implications of a true Roman emperor ruling most of the Italian peninsula, Pope Clement III supported Tancred, who ruled effectively for a time. Tancred, however, had to confront a not insignificant minority of nobles on the mainland who favored Henry VI, which limited his actual sphere of influence. To make matters worse, the Muslims of Palermo rose in revolt against him at the same time. Finally, Henry VI marched into southern Italy in 1191; despite some military success, Tancred was never able to eliminate the threat, and when he died in 1194, Henry VI easily conquered the kingdom. As noted above, upon Henry VI's death in 1197 his son Frederick

II was passed over for the German crown, but he had no rivals for the Sicilian crown, which he formally received at the age of three in 1198.

Frederick II's minority saw the disintegration of the kingdom into near anarchy under the nominal regency of Pope Innocent III. He came of age in 1208 and had only started to re-establish royal authority in Sicily when his election as king of Germany in 1211 (of which Innocent III approved) drew his attentions to the north. After 1220, however, he returned to Sicily, which would be his main focus and base of operations for the next three decades. Although he had to a certain extent tolerated the decentralization of German administration as the price of uncontested rule, Frederick II always sought to impose strong royal authority in Sicily. There was some cross-fertilization between the governmental apparatuses of the two distinct kingdoms; Frederick II brought expert bureaucrats northward with him to help him rule Germany, and issued Sicilian charters from a special office there. Once back in Sicily, he assumed control over the Church and issued a series of statutes that outlined his vision of royal authority.

In the 23 years following his coronation, the barons of Sicily, along with some military adventurers from Germany, had taken advantage of Frederick II's minority and subsequent absence to resist central authority and encroach on royal rights and possessions. Upon his return, Frederick II showed how effectively strong personal kingship could overcome the tendency of feudal regimes to disintegrate. After Pope Honorius III crowned him emperor in 1220, he travelled throughout southern Italy repairing the instruments of royal power. Later that year, he issued assizes at Capua that attempted to turn back the clock to 1189 and the 'good customs' of William II.[59] They confirmed the king's control over the instruments of government, while invalidating some of the privileges that his nobles had usurped during the period of disorder. They also re-established the military basis of his power by determining how many knights were owed him under the feudal system. Frederick also quashed the stirrings of urban autonomy in some of the towns. In 1221 he finally arrived on the island of Sicily, where he had similar successes. Although the Norman administrative mechanisms had survived the period of disorder, Frederick II augmented them with considerable personal involvement; instead of running the kingdom from Palermo as his Norman predecessors had, he followed the German tradition of ruling from an itinerant court.

In the person of Frederick II, then, the bureaucracy that had emerged in the twelfth century met a king with a lofty conception of his sacred duty. With the help of expert lawyers, some of whom were drawn to the university he founded at Naples in 1224, he worked on legislation that would codify his vision of kingship into a practical model for government. The fruits of Frederick II's legislative efforts are the Constitutions of Melfi, issued in 1231, which incorporated elements of Roman, Norman, Byzantine, canon law, and other various traditions into a practical means of restoring effective rule in Sicily.[60] The constitutions applied only to Sicily, which was not truly part of the empire—despite Frederick II's insistence on calling himself Augustus in the tradition of Roman emperors—and they vividly demonstrate the complex relationship between ideals and practical concerns that pervaded contemporary political life. Frederick II's program for Sicily, while not exactly systematic, was all-encompassing, and covered not only matters of dispute resolution and land-tenure, but relations between religious minorities, adultery, and heresy.

Frederick's itinerant court attracted top-rank intellectual stars, such as the scientist and astrologer Michael Scot (a Scotsman who had trained at Paris and Toledo), and he certainly had a penchant for asking grand questions about life and the universe. He understood at least the basic elements of Arabic and seemed enthralled with certain ideas of Aristotle, which has led some scholars in the past to portray the court as a haven of multicultural intellectual endeavor. This romantic notion, however, has given way to a view in which the Latinization of Sicilian culture seems to be more significant than the persistence of some aspects of Greek and Arabic learning.[61] This makes sense insofar as the Roman and canon law that provided him with so many of his ideals were of Latin provenance. If not the man of letters he has sometimes been made out to be, Frederick certainly had an agile mind, and wrote his own work *On the Art of Hunting with Birds*, which itself provides an excellent example of his practical attitude toward Latin letters.[62]

Frederick felt a profound sense of Christian calling which was incompatible with the unregulated presence of Muslim and Jewish minorities in the kingdom. He required Jews to wear distinctive clothing (following the church's Fourth Lateran Council, discussed below in Chapter 3), and restricted relations between them and Christians. In 1224, seeking an end to the nearly perennial revolts by Sicily's Muslims, he deported nearly all of them from the island and settled them in Lucera, an inland town in Apulia. This last measure was essentially practical, but it was part of a larger religious outlook that included Frederick's sincere commitment to crusading. After nearly a decade's worth of delays, Frederick embarked for Palestine in 1228. By this time, he had arranged a marriage to the queen of the Latin Kingdom of Jerusalem that gave him a plausible claim to the kingship there. Pope Gregory IX (1227–1241), however, was quite reasonably suspicious of Frederick's commitment in light of his failure to take part in the Fifth Crusade (1217–1221) and subsequent delays. He had excommunicated the emperor a year earlier, meaning that Frederick's crusade was not officially sanctioned by the Church. What followed mortified some observers: rather than march on Jerusalem or some other military target, Frederick negotiated with the Egyptian sultan al-Kamil (1180–1238), who was glad to hand over control of Jerusalem in exchange for a promise of non-aggression and certain military concessions. The disgruntled chronicler Philip of Novara complained that '[H]e made his truce with the Saracens in all particulars as they wished it'.[63] Frederick, for his part, exulted that

> by a miracle rather than by strength, that business [the recovery of Jerusalem after its re-conquest by the Muslims in 1187] has been to a conclusion, which for a length of time past many chiefs and rulers of the world amongst the multitude of nations, have never been able till now to accomplish by force, however great, nor by fear.[64]

On March 18, 1229, the excommunicated king wore his imperial crown in an elaborate ceremony at the Church of the Holy Sepulchre in Jerusalem, demonstrating his rule over Christendom as spectacularly as one could imagine.

Few were impressed with the display. In fact, allies of Gregory IX had invaded southern Italy and scored a major military victory just before Frederick's entry into Jerusalem. The emperor was forced to hurry home before any of the internal problems of the Latin Kingdom of Jerusalem could be addressed. According to Philip of Novara, when Frederick left the port city of Acre, a group of local butchers 'pelted him most abusively with tripe and scraps of meat', and he fled 'cursed, hated, and despised'.[65] In the end, Frederick managed to turn back the papal threat, make peace with Gregory IX, and establish a firm rule over Sicily that would last for nearly two decades. But the crusading adventure of a king of a strong regional monarchy graphically illustrates how far European politics had strayed from the universalizing vision of Urban II at Clermont.

The transformation of medieval Iberia

Urban II's crusading ideal also found expression on the Iberian peninsula, where Christian rulers coexisted with but also fought against an established Muslim presence. Although they were almost completely removed from imperial politics and dealt with only occasional ideological interference from the papacy, kings and counts in Iberia faced a highly complex and shifting political environment. To the south, they encountered the Muslim territory of al-Andalus, which had political and commercial ties to North Africa (and ultimately, via the gold trade, to sub-Saharan Africa), while the county of Barcelona, in the far northeast, was in the political and ecclesiastical orbit of southern France. Scholars crossed the Pyrenees to take advantage of the classical learning preserved through Arab intermediaries in al-Andalus, while pilgrims periodically flooded the famous route from France to the shrine of Santiago de Compostela. Like southern Italy, Iberia lay at a major cultural crossroads.

Since Muslim armies had conquered the Christian Visigothic kingdom of Spain in 711, the seemingly straightforward division of the peninsula into Islamic and Christian spheres had masked internal rivalries and considerable diversity in customs on both sides of the highly fluid religious divide. Al-Andalus, which in the year 1000 encompassed roughly two-thirds of the territory of modern Spain and Portugal, was a multicultural society characterized by often tense but generally peaceful accommodation of members of the other Abrahamic religions. Jews and Christians (who remained a majority throughout the Middle Ages in some regions) had the status of *dhimmis*, or subject peoples, according to which they paid special taxes and were prohibited from proselytizing. Historians have sometimes overstated the degree of harmonious cohabitation (referred to as *convivencia* in modern Spanish) there, and pogroms against Jews and Christians were not unheard of, but Al-Andalus reaped profound cultural benefits from its richly textured religious fabric.[66] Many communities of subject Christians, now generally referred to as Mozarabs, adopted the Arabic language and the sumptuary customs of the Muslims, while Andalusian culture explicitly blended traditions. Aristotelian and other ancient ideas were passed back and forth and synthesized by all members of all three Abrahamic faiths. Such blending could play out in more mundane ways. The Jewish poet Joseph the Scribe, for instance, wrote love poems that combined the emerging Romance vernacular with the local Arabic dialect on a line-by-line basis.[67] All the great towns of Iberia with the significant exceptions of Barcelona and Toledo were under Muslim control throughout the eleventh century. With perhaps 75,000 inhabitants in the year 1100, Muslim Córdoba was larger and grander than any city in Christian Spain.

The Christian kingdoms tucked up against the Pyrenees began their attempts to expand southward as early as the late eighth century, but the so-called *Reconquista* became a recognizable movement only after the collapse of centralized Muslim rule in al-Andalus in 1008. As al-Andalus broke up into the dozens of so-called *taifa* kingdoms, local Christian kings and nobles made militarily convenient alliances with Muslims against their fellow Christians, while Muslim rulers routinely sought Christian assistance against their co-religionists. All sought to expand and consolidate their holdings without great regard for religious considerations. In addition, Christian kings generated considerable revenue by taking tribute money from the *taifa* rulers. In 1085, Alfonso VI of Castile captured the ancient Visigothic capital of Toledo, which marked a major turning point. By the first decade of the twelfth century, the kingdoms of León, Castile, Navarre, and Aragon, along with the counties of Portugal (created in 1096) and Barcelona, were all trying to expand southward.

The *Reconquista* had started as *ad hoc* actions by individual princes, but it gradually took on the characteristics of a crusade against infidels. The career and legend of Rodrigo Díaz (1043–1099), better known today as El Cid, demonstrates this transformation. He initially fought with King Sancho II of Castile against *taifa* kings and served as Afonso VI's tribute collector in Seville and Córdoba, but ran afoul of Alfonso VI because of slander by other vassals. He then fought for the Muslim rulers of Saragossa and greatly impressed them with his gallantry; he occasionally found himself fighting Christians, thanks to the complex alliances that proliferated during the period.[68] By this point in the late 1090s, the Muslims, now unified under the North African Empire of the Almoravids (or Mubarit), had embarked on an urgent, religiously tinged attempt to roll back the recent Christian advances. Rodrigo provided effective resistance to them along the coast and conquered Valencia. Despite his success, the progress of the *Reconquista* slowed as a result of Almoravids, who re-captured Valencia shortly after Rodrigo's death in 1099. The prose chronicle of his life, written perhaps in the 1140s, mentions crusading only obliquely, but the ecclesiastical authorities were beginning to link Iberia with Jerusalem. In 1118, Christian warriors in Iberia were granted the same indulgences as those in the Holy Land, and the First Lateran Council in 1123 granted similar privileges to soldiers 'traveling to Jerusalem or Spain'.

Because of this complex ideological and political background, it is nearly impossible to narrate a straightforward history of twelfth-century Iberia. Several distinct kingdoms pursued often distinct trajectories and developed distinct institutions, and the predilection of royal parents for the name Alfonso muddies the waters even further (one must keep track of no fewer than six Alfonsos!). Modern historians have often viewed the political history of the period with a view to the eventual formation of a united Spanish kingdom during the early modern period. Nothing in twelfth-century Iberian history made that inevitable. One can, however, focus on a few representative moments and trends that show the conditions that allowed for the possibility of unification much later. First, the experience of northern Spain in the twelfth century graphically illustrates the continuing role of family dynasties in geopolitics. Alfonso VI managed to unite León and Castile and was regarded as a true leader of a revived Spain— he dared to style himself 'Emperor of Spain' late in life. However, he died without a male heir in 1109. That same year his daughter Urraca entered into one of the most famously unhappy marriages in medieval history to King Alfonso I 'the Battler' of Aragon, who due to impotence, sterility, or lack of interest could not produce an heir. As a result, any hopes that the three greatest kingdoms of Christian Iberia would be united were dashed—the marriage ended within a few years, and the former spouses fought against each other until 1117. The fact that the bride and groom shared a common great-grandfather made the marriage technically incestuous and therefore relatively easy to dissolve. Both Aragon and León-Castile recovered from this incident. Alfonso I conquered Saragossa for Aragon in 1118, and Urraca scored major victories against the Muslims and successfully passed the crown to her son (from her first marriage) Alfonso VII (1126–1157). This Alfonso claimed his grandfather's imperial title, but on his death the kingdoms of León and Castile were divided between his sons.

Aragon's dynastic fortunes were similarly vexed. Alfonso I apparently never resolved whatever issue prevented him from siring children with Queen Urraca, and died without issue after a highly successful and expansionist reign in 1134. For reasons that are not clear, he willed his kingdom to three religious orders, namely the Templars, Hopsitallers, and the Knights of the Holy Sepulchre. Realizing the impracticality of the will and fearing a power vacuum, the Aragonese nobility fetched Alfonso's brother Ramiro out of a monastery (with appropriate papal dispensation). Ramiro (II) bravely answered the call by serving as king just long enough to get married and father a girl named Petronilla. He then retired back to his monastery. The regents betrothed the infant Queen Petronilla to the Count of Barcelona, and once the marriage was consummated in 1161, they produced an heir, Alfonso II, who created what is known as the 'Crown of Aragon' from the union of the old kingdom and Barcelona. Meanwhile, the duchy of Portugal, which had initially been created for the son-in-law of Alfonso VI, was transformed through a process not entirely understood into yet another kingdom by 1140.

The six kingdoms of Christian Iberia had to resolve these rivalries and familial struggles in order to confront the recurring threat posed by Muslim al-Andalus, and thus a consideration of dynastic politics leads naturally to the linked problems of self-defense and expansion. León, Castile, Aragon, and Portugal all captured important cities in the 1140s, and during that same decade, Iberia became practically, as well as symbolically, tied to the crusading movement.[69] In 1147, Alfonso I Enríquez of Portugal conquered the Muslim city of Santarém just as a fleet of crusaders bound for Jerusalem gathered in England. Through a local bishop, Alfonso implored the contingent of English, Flemish, and German soldiers to avenge the insult that the Muslims of al-Andalus had inflicted on Christianity, and they obliged after minimal disagreement.[70] The northerners distrusted Alfonso, but he had wisely given them free rein to plunder the city as an incentive for their cooperation. They besieged Lisbon and exchanged religious insults with the Muslim defenders for several months before the city capitulated in late October. On November 1, a group of clerics solemnly transformed its main mosque into a Christian church.[71] It is not clear if Pope Eugenius III had prior knowledge of the decision to divert the crusading army to Lisbon, but he certainly approved. On the other side of the peninsula, soldiers and sailors from Aragon, Castile, and Barcelona, as well as the Italian city of Genoa, conquered the cities of Almería and Tortosa throughout assaults that exuded crusading fervor. Eugenius III explicitly encouraged this expedition in the second version of his papal bull calling the Second Crusade.[72]

Despite such runs of success, the *Reconquista* seems inevitable only in retrospect; the Muslims even threatened to re-take Toledo on several occasions. Between the 1140s and 1170s, a new North African dynasty motivated by intense religious fundamentalism, the Almohads (or Muwahhids), displaced the weakened Almoravids and sought to recover al-Andalus for a strictly interpreted brand of Islam. Whenever conditions in North Africa allowed, the Almohad caliphs vigorously attacked the Iberian Christian states, which likewise took advantage when those caliphs were across the straits of Gibraltar. But the Christians often cared more about immediate balance of power politics than the long-term prospects of conquering al-Andalus, and did not hesitate to attack each other. Not even Abu Yusuf Yaqub's crushing victory over Castile at Alarcos in 1195 inspired the Christians to

unite, as León and Navarre allied with him a year later. Alarcos, however, caught the attention of the papacy, and Pope Innocent III began
asking for a Christian counter-attack in increasingly strident terms.
In 1212, a large contingent of crusaders answered the call and crossed
the Pyrenees from southern France. They joined Alfonso VIII of
Castile's already considerable army of men from Castile, Aragon, and
Navarre, and destroyed the Almohad army at Las Navas de Tolosa on
July 1. The North Africans had effectively lost their ability to pressure
the Christians in Iberia, and al-Andalus would, until its final destruction in 1492, be a weak client state limited to the region around
Granada. After this battle, Innocent III withdrew crusader privileges
from fighters on the peninsula, as if to acknowledge that crusading
energies were now needed elsewhere.

Although they did not leave as clear a written record of their
progress as their Sicilian counterparts did, the rulers of Iberia did
attempt to impose new methods and institutions of government.
Like most contemporary kings, they focused primarily on collecting
revenues, controlling their often restive nobility, and managing the
power of their growing towns. Because of the ongoing concern with
al-Andalus, however, they also had to manage the settlement of newly
conquered territories and preside over a religiously divided society.
In a few important documents surviving from León, Aragon, and
Catalonia, the kings can be seen addressing these problems, in some
cases by seeking out the approval of their nobles and townsmen. King
Alfonso of León, when he succeeded to the throne in 1188, called
a court of 'the archbishop and the bishops and the magnates of my
kingdom, and with the citizens chosen from every city' to lay down the
foundations of royal rule. The process may be as significant as what
was actually decided, since it demonstrated that kings found it expe-
dient, if not essential, to consult with their disparate constituencies
when determining policy. In the record of this meeting, sometimes
regarded as the first example of what would become the parliamen-
tary *cortes* of the later Middle Ages, Alfonso notes his promise 'that
I will not make war or peace or alliance without the counsel of the
bishops, nobles and men of good standing through whose counsel I should rule'.[73] In domestic matters, Alfonso provided for royal
courts to hear cases between private individuals and referred to established royal officials, some of whom, like *alcades*, had titles derived
from Arabic antecedents. That same year, Alfonso II of Aragon issued
similar statutes based on a meeting with great men at Girona, in
which he emphasized his role as protector of his subjects while also
binding himself not to abrogate certain rights.[74] These 1188 courts
established an important precedent, and by the thirteenth century

all of the Iberian monarchs were holding similar assemblies. In 1228, James I of Aragon held a court in which the great men of Aragon confirmed his succession.[75] Such assemblies began as practical vehicles through which the royal will was made known, but gradually became institutions with a decidedly representative character.[76]

At roughly the same time, jurists at the court of the counts of Barcelona (who, after 1164, were also kings of Aragon) compiled a set of laws for the county now called the *Usatges of Barcelona*. While it is not entirely clear to what end they were collected or how important they were to the legal practice of twelfth-century counts, they provide an encomium of the problems faced in ruling a county with an expanding frontier and increasingly important urban life marked by religious tension.[77] As such they are rife with ambiguity. For example one entry in the compilation reads '[L]et Jews who are beaten, wounded, captured, incapacitated, and even killed be compensated according to the ruler's will', while another orders '[L]et Jews swear to Christians but Christians never swear to them'.[78] Many of the customs in the *Usatges* seek to maintain peace within the feudal order, such as prohibitions against deserting one's lord in battle or committing adultery with the lord's wife.[79] Some confront seemingly trivial points of honor with a view to tempering the potential for violence in a knightly society: 'if one spits in another's face, let him make compensation of twenty sous to him or suffer his retaliation'.[80] But the *Usatges* also offer guidance on technical matters such as the inheritance and parceling out of fiefs among the nobility.

The *Usatges of Barcelona* thus represent thoroughly 'feudal' customs that point haltingly toward the importance of central legislation and written law at a moment when Iberian political life was still characterized by both expansion and fragmentation. Kings in Aragon-Catalonia and elsewhere depended increasingly on written documents to centralize their rule and to reinforce the importance of kingship itself.[81] After the Christian victory at Las Navas de Tolosa in 1212, the border with al-Andalus stabilized along a frontier that would remain relatively constant until the fifteenth century, while kings like James I of Aragon (1213–1276) and Alfonso X of Castile and León enjoyed reigns long enough to make significant strides in centralizing their governments.

Competing Monarchies in France and England

Across the Pyrenees, the kings of France similarly sought to expand the reach of their authority. Their main antagonists, however, were not Muslims but the great regional magnates who were nominally their vassals. That one of those vassals, the king of Normandy, was also the king of England for most of the twelfth century meant that each of the kingdoms that flanked the English Channel would develop along lines determined in part by the other. When Duke William of Normandy became king of England by right of conquest in 1066, he remained subject to the king of France for his lands in Normandy; he and his successors spoke French and administered their continental possessions separately (William even bequeathed his kingdom and his duchy to different sons). The period plays a pivotal role in the traditional histories of both countries as well as in the comparative study of the origins of modern states, as scholars have sought twelfth-century origins for French absolutism and English constitutional monarchy. Although there can be no question that both kingdoms made strides toward centralized administration, the goals of the kings and their subjects, and their methods for achieving them, had little to do with those of Louis XIV in seventeenth-century France or the early English parliamentarians. But considered in terms of contemporary political culture, the differences between the two countries were striking, and provide great insight into the ways kingship and government were exercised and constrained.

After the Norman Conquest in 1066, English kings enjoyed a measure of control over their government and their nobles that was exceedingly rare. They inherited a relatively sophisticated and centralized administration from their Anglo-Saxon predecessors, and ensured the loyalty of their aristocracy by installing loyal Normans as their barons (after essentially eliminating the Anglo-Saxon nobility). They were efficient and ruthless administrators in their own right, as William I 'the Conqueror' (1066–1087) demonstrated through his commissioning of Domesday Book, the famous inquest of property throughout the kingdom. Still, they repeatedly confronted a series of major dilemmas. The Church often interfered with their drive toward administrative and jurisdictional centralization, the nobles required careful consideration and could not be taken for granted, and their commitments on the French mainland made enormous demands on their attention and resources. In some ways, the French kings faced even more daunting challenges. At the beginning of the twelfth century, several of their great regional princes—the duke of Normandy and the counts of Flanders, Champagne, and Anjou—rivaled them in wealth and power, while others, like the dukes of Aquitaine and the counts of Maine and Blois, exercised considerable local autonomy. They directly ruled over only a small region around Paris called the Île de France, which did not itself generate enough wealth to extend their reach. The kings of France, however, did have an air of holiness about them that no other noble in France had. By aggressively asserting the prerogatives of kingship, they enhanced their political position throughout the long twelfth century, until by 1229 they ruled securely over a diverse kingdom whose boundaries were beginning to conform to the 'hexagon' of the modern period.

The dilemmas of the early Norman kings of England

On November 2, 1100, King William II ('Rufus') was shot by an arrow and killed while hunting in the New Forest of southern England. Contemporary accounts differed as to the details; the consensus view held that his death was accidental though richly deserved, for William was detested by a wide variety of constituencies, including some very prominent clerics (the Archbishop of Canterbury had been exiled because of the king's anger in 1097). There are still some scholars who suspect that William's younger brother, who took the throne as Henry I (1100–1135), had a hand in what was effectively a political assassination, but most seem content to regard William's demise as a case of friendly fire.[82] Whatever the particulars, Henry I seized the opportunity, and his actions in the following months and years offer a telling glimpse into the political life of the period. As his first move, Henry marched to Winchester to take control of the royal treasure housed there. He then made clear to a group of nobles there that he was claiming the crown as the son of William the Conqueror. His brother Robert Curthose, Duke of Normandy, also garnered some baronial support for a claim to the throne, but he was off on the First Crusade, and nothing in the prevailing understanding of succession meant he would have an obvious claim over that of Henry. Therefore, Henry caused no great scandal when he had himself crowned king by the bishop of London at Westminster Abbey a mere three days after William II's death.

At the time of his anointing, Henry was busily stressing that his claim to rule was legitimate. Perhaps on the very day he was crowned he issued a charter promising to curb the alleged abuses of William II and to rule in accordance with feudal custom and right order. The so-called 'Charter of Liberties' or 'Coronation Charter' lays out the foundations of English royal power and provides clues as to its perceived threats. The first chapter of the charter notes that he was crowned 'by the common counsel of the barons of the whole kingdom of England' and abolishes 'all the evil customs by which [it] has been oppressed.' In particular, he renounced some of William

II's extortionate policies toward the church as well as his opportunistic exactions from the aristocracy. William had, for instance, levied heavy fines (known as 'reliefs') on the sons of nobles who wished to inherit their fathers' fiefs; Henry, in a somewhat ambiguous clause, promised that heirs would receive their lands 'by means of a just and lawful "relief" '.[83] The charter also refers back to the rule of his father William I and to laws of the Anglo-Saxon King Edward the Confessor (1042–1066), and thus demonstrates the importance attached to custom and precedent in Norman kingship. The 'Coronation Charter' makes clear that England was a feudal monarchy in which the king had to take care to look after the interests of nobles and the Church (which was also a major fief-holder).

Henry had good reason to get internal affairs in order rapidly, for Robert Curthose invaded England in the summer of 1101, hoping to rally enough support to outclass Henry in battle. In the end, Robert did not have the resources to mount the necessary campaign, and Henry effectively purchased his acceptance of the succession by promising him an annual payment of either £2000 or £3000, depending on which source one believes.[84] Peace between the brothers would not last; Henry clearly spent the next years preparing his own invasion of Normandy, which commenced in 1104, after he somewhat tendentiously accused Robert of violating minor provisions in the 1101 agreement. At the battle of Tinchebray in 1106, Henry defeated and captured Robert, and once again unified kingdom and duchy. That the brothers William II, Henry I, and Robert Curthose all sought, at various times, to control both territories suggests that they saw England and Normandy as forming a common inheritance, even if they remained distinct entities. For the next 30 years of his life, Henry set about confronting the dilemmas of ruling the Anglo-Norman realm. He needed not only to hold together a diverse realm but to keep his nobility in check, avoid conflicts with the Church that could weaken his authority, raise adequate revenue, and dispense justice over a complex and interlocking set of jurisdictions. Traditional models of kingship could not adequately encompass everything he sought to accomplish.

Retaining control of Normandy was itself the first great challenge. Its barons had a history of restiveness and they required careful observation. Although in some quarters the English kings' habit of spending a lengthy period of their reign abroad has been presented as a major failing, it was in fact essential to proper lordship. Henry secured Normandy through brute force when necessary, but also through marriage alliances and strategic castle building. He benefitted from having vassals with lands on both sides of the Channel and thus a vested interest in both kingdom and county. Robert of Beaumont, for example, was the count of Meulan in Normandy and of Earl of Leicester in England thanks to royal largesse.[85] Henry's French counterpart for most of his reign, Louis VI (1108–1137), watched the expansion of Norman power carefully, and countered when he could. Louis and Henry used alliances and raids to chip away at each others' borders but made peace when it suited them, as in 1113 when a treaty was struck. Two years later, however, Louis responded to Henry's support of the count of Blois (then in revolt against the French king) by allying with the count of Flanders and some major Norman nobles in attacking the borders of the duchy. The kings' respective attempts to control their vassals clearly overlapped, and in this case, Henry's position was seriously threatened. As Louis VI's biographer Suger of St Denis put it, Henry, despite having success early in his reign, 'now found himself disturbed by a different and luckless turn of events, like someone falling from the top of the wheel of fortune.'[86] But such swings of fortune were almost inevitable given the combination of balance-of-power politics and internal dissension that the Norman kings of England faced on the continent. In 1119, however, Henry recovered his position by combining his military and diplomatic skills. First, he made peace with the count of Anjou by marrying his son to the count's daughter, secured the allegiance of some lesser nobles, and then embarked on a scorched-earth campaign. This culminated in a great triumph at the battle of Brémule, which for the most part put an end to the immediate threat and led to a peace that more or less held for the rest of his reign. As part of the agreement between the kings, Henry's son William Aetheling paid homage to Louis for Normandy (a ritual which Henry himself had assiduously avoided performing). Then in 1120, all of Henry's future plans were upset when William, along with some 300 members of the royal court, was drowned in a shipwreck (the famous 'wreck of the White Ship'). Fortune's wheel, here manifest in the precariousness of dynastic rule, rendered military and diplomatic success moot in the long term, at least from the heartbroken Henry's point of view.

Ecclesiastical chroniclers were quick to view disasters like the shipwreck in terms of divine will, and they carefully monitored how the Norman kings treated the Church, and hence what punishment or reward they deserved. The historian Orderic Vitalis reported that William Aetheling and his friends hurled insults at the priests who came to bless the White Ship as it cast off, and they drowned shortly thereafter.[87] According to Suger, Henry's fortunes had improved in

1119 because, 'although a wanton man, he was a generous donor to churches and a liberal giver of alms'.[88] Possible supernatural interventions like these notwithstanding, ecclesiastical policy represented another great challenge for Henry and his successors. William the Conqueror had cultivated a good relationship with the Church. While he zealously guarded his feudal rights over Church lands, which he regarded as fiefs, he supported the general principles of the reform movement (so long as the king directed their implementation) and he had even carried a papal banner when he invaded England. William II, on the other hand, seems to have cared little for reform, and routinely plundered ecclesiastical revenues. He appointed the brilliant and pious reformer Anselm, previously abbot of Bec in Normandy, to be Archbishop of Canterbury, only to quarrel with him over the control of the English Church. Frustrated by William's habit of leaving abbacies and bishoprics vacant (so he could exercise the royal prerogative of collecting their revenues during the vacancies), and thwarted in his attempts to call a reforming council of the English Church and consult directly with the papacy, Anselm chose exile rather than obedience. After his accidental death, which was widely seen as an act of divine retribution, his successor Henry I invited Anselm back to England. Henry dearly needed the archbishop's political support to make good his claim to the throne, but quickly fell out with him over lay investiture. Apparently emboldened by his experience at Roman council, listening to Pope Paschal II condemn investiture as well as the paying of homage to kings by bishops, he fought bitterly with Henry over ecclesiastical liberty. Because bishops and abbots held vast tracts of land all over the country—Henry claimed half of his kingdom was at stake—the king could not realistically give up the rituals through which he signified his control over them.

Compared to the conflicts between Gregory VII and Henry IV in eleventh-century Germany, the subsequent dispute was rather tame.[89] In 1107, they brokered compromise similar to the one that would be worked out at the Concordat of Worms. The popes gave ground on the issue of bishops performing homage for their fiefs, while Henry renounced investiture of the priestly symbols of episcopal office. While the agreement did draw a clear line between ecclesiastical and secular affairs, in practice Henry and his successors managed fairly careful control over the Church. They would continue to have a say in episcopal elections, and generally succeeded in having their preferred candidates elected. Not only did bishops serve as secular lords, they also played an important role in Henry's administration, serving as counselors, judges, and legal consultants to the king. Although Henry sometimes brought talented bishops into his court, he more often gave his most successful servants choice ecclesiastical positions. His royal chancellor Roger le Poer became bishop of Salisbury in 1102, and many other bishops served at court in various capacities. Some even had military responsibilities, contrary to the spirit of the reform movement. This cross-fertilization between ecclesiastical and secular government would have seemed entirely natural, and neatly illustrates the importance of gifted and educated men for a royal administration increasingly dependent on the written word.

Scholars are divided as to whether Henry I or his grandson Henry II should be credited with creating the literate bureaucracy of high medieval England, but the first Henry undoubtedly made some important contributions. It has also been suggested that neither king created quite as efficient and extensive centralized administrations as has been suggested by scholars looking for the origins of modern administrative organization.[90] Certainly the kings and their clerks were trying to do something other than run a modern-style nation state, and their methods sought to accommodate local custom and immediate needs more than to apply coldly rational principles to government. In order to advance and extend the king's lordship, they used tools at their disposal and refined others.

One such tool was literacy. In 1130 Henry's chancery employed four scribes who produced perhaps 4000 Latin documents, according to a recent estimate.[91] These documents included formal charters that made a grant of property or privilege to a person or institution, as well as much shorter writs that offered succinct instructions for how to implement the royal will. One such writ, for example, sought to ensure that local knights would perform their feudal service to the abbot of Abingdon Abbey. After a brief greeting, it reads simply:

> I will and I firmly order you to perform my guard service concerning Windsor as you were accustomed to do in the time of my brother [William II], and as Abbot Faritius orders you; and you are to be obedient to him. And it displeases me greatly that you do not carry out his order concerning this, as you ought to do.[92]

The writ was thus highly personal. It was a kind of substitute for the king's presence, appealing to memory and custom even as it fixed an obligation in written form. Significantly, this particular writ was preserved by the monks of Abingdon, who included it in their official chronicle.

Henry also employed scribes to keep track of the revenues coming into his court. His military campaigns depended on a steady cash flow, which he acquired from the productivity of the estates he personally controlled, as well as tolls, fines, and other fees. In the first half of his reign, Henry established the practice of auditing his accounts with the help of a checkered cloth laid on a table, around which his clerks counted and recorded the income. Though this practice would ultimately be incorporated into a standing treasury—the Exchequer—under Henry it represented an occasion rather than an office. The early exchequer has often been romanticized as a precursor of modern, rationalized fiscal governance, but recent research has suggested it was subject to corruption, somewhat haphazard in its practices, and not entirely efficient.[93] It is nonetheless important as an original adaptation to the challenges of twelfth-century kingship. The exchequer was originally itinerant like the rest of the royal court, but it came to reside more and more at Westminster, where it would carry on its business whether the king was present or not. Its account records were committed to writing each year in what are called Pipe Rolls, but only the roll of 1130 survives from Henry I's reign.

At the exchequer, the king's agents at the local level, the sheriffs, reported on their revenues and were audited as carefully as possible. The office of sheriff had originated in the Anglo-Saxon period and represented, for some, a kind of intrusion of the centralizing monarchy into the communities of the various shires. While they collected fines, tolls, and other revenues, they also presided over shire courts that heard local disputes. Ideally, a sheriff was a person trusted by the king to represent his interests, and to serve as his eyes, ears, and voice; many royal writs, in fact, concerned the activities of sheriffs. In addition, Henry sent other officials out to the shires, most notably the 'justices on eyre', itinerant judges who set up courts whose decisions were legally equivalent to those of the king's own court. These justices heard the most important cases and, again, showed the tendency of Norman kings to extend their authority through trusted proxies.

Despite all of these innovations, Anglo-Norman kingship was still personal kingship. Henry's queen, Matilda, served effectively as a regent in England while he travelled around Normandy, and he felt comfortable leaving administration in the hands of trusted servants, but the importance of having a strong king was painfully evident at two key moments. The first was the death of William Aetheling, which left England without an heir and Henry to grow old surrounded by some twenty-three illegitimate children who could not succeed him. The second moment was the king's own death, which left a disputed succession. He had named his daughter Matilda, the widow of Henry V of Germany, and current wife of Geoffrey, count of the important French county of Anjou, as his heir, but his nephew Stephen had seized the throne and acquired just enough baronial support to establish himself as king. The ensuing civil war made it impossible for Stephen to pay adequate attention to the dilemmas of Anglo-Norman kingship. That Henry had exercised kingship as robustly as one could hope is affirmed in the historian Henry of Huntingdon's observation that contemporary observers were divided into groups according to their opinions of his character: the first thought that he 'was eminently distinguished for three splendid qualities', those being wisdom, skill in warfare, and the acquisition of wealth; while the second group 'attributed to him three vices', namely avarice, cruelty, and incontinence, particularly when it came to his sexual appetite.[94] Effective kings in such a turbulent age could not help but combine a diverse set of attributes.

Louis VI and the growth of Capetian France

As Henry I sought to extend his authority over the relatively well-defined territories of England and Normandy, King Louis VI of France (1108–1137) and his son Louis VII (1137–1180) sought to improve their position relative to that of their great vassals, including Henry himself. At the beginning of his reign, as noted above, Louis VI directly controlled only a small fraction of the territory he theoretically ruled as king—the 'royal domain'—and that area itself could be profoundly unstable. Local nobles engaged in private warfare and created a general atmosphere of fear. The contemporary writer Guibert of Nogent (c. 1060–c. 1125), wrote that a castellan named Thomas of Marle, 'a robber of paupers and pilgrims to Jerusalem', resisted royal authority, sought to consolidate his power, and committed countless crimes (related in stomach-churning detail) against the defenseless.[95] It has been calculated that, in his time as a warrior, first as a prince and then as a king, Louis VI responded to some 27 documented cases of local violence or oppression.[96] The biographer Suger insists that Louis VI could repay violence for violence. When he attacked a disruptive vassal named Ebles of Roucy, 'the plunderers were themselves plundered and the torturers were tortured with the same or even more pain than they had used to torture others.'[97] Louis VI's primary task, then, was to bring peace to the royal domain while simultaneously keeping an eye on his most dangerous vassals. Before his reign was half over, he had largely succeeded in bringing peace to the area around Paris.

He had several assets to help him consolidate his gains. First, the French crown had been safely in the hands of his Capetian dynasty since the tenth century. Most Capetians had the good fortune of long reigns, so succession disputes were rare, and at any rate Louis VI had been designated king in his father's lifetime (possibly to guard against a rival reviving the memory of Frankish elective kingship). In addition, despite periods of relative weakness, and some rather disreputable and much-censured sexual misbehavior by his father Philip I, Louis VI's forebears had managed to create an air of sacrality about them; they had relatively few major disputes with the Church. Because authority in France was so fragmented, the French kings had never attained the level of control over bishops that the English and German kings had, and therefore lay investiture was a less pressing issue. Louis VI tended to negotiate with the Church regarding episcopal appointments rather than to make bold claims of theocratic kingship in order to get their way. Although France had its own version of the Investiture Controversy under Philip I, by Louis VI's reign it had been essentially resolved, and he enjoyed mostly amicable relations with the papacy.[98] The French kings demonstrated the sacred character of their kingship frequently and ostentatiously. The great royal abbey of St Denis, just outside Paris and rebuilt in the middle of the twelfth century, testified to royal holiness through its new Gothic elements. As early as the reign of Robert II 'the Pious' (996–1031), the Capetians had been thought to have the power to cure skin diseases—either scrofula or leprosy, depending on the source—as a reverberation of the healing powers of Christ. This power was also imputed to English kings, but they were apparently less successful at it.[99]

The French kings also had more concrete, and more easily documented, means of securing their domain. Philip II had established small administrative units called *Prévôtés*, to allow for more orderly and manageable organization at the local level. These units were administered by royal agents, *prévôts*, who collected revenue, looked to royal interests, and tried to ensure some modest consistency in the meting out of justice. During the reigns of Louis VI and his son Louis VII (1137–1180), the *prévôts* would prove an effective means of extending royal power. But nothing was quite so effective at representing royal authority than the presence of the king himself, and French royal court was constantly traveling. Louis VI benefitted from a small core of trusted advisors, literate men with connections who

helped regularize the business of government. Under mostly competent leadership, the production of written charters increased during
the century: whereas an average of 5.7 royal charters per year survive
from Philip I's reign, the figure increases to 14.0 for Louis VI, and
28.1 under Philip II 'Augustus' (1180–1223).[100]

Despite early difficulties with local uprisings in the royal domain,
the Capetians always had their eye on the rest of France, and they
intervened when they could, generally with a view to checking the
power of the great princes, especially the dukes of Normandy, as Louis
VI did repeatedly in the 1110s. Louis also intervened in a succession
dispute in Flanders in 1126. In 1137, just before his death, he married the soon-to-be Louis VII to Duchess Eleanor of Aquitaine, which
loosely joined the royal domain to much of the territory of southern France (though Eleanor's lands were not formally integrated into
those of Louis). Louis brought Eleanor with him on the Second Crusade, where she was rumored to have had dalliances with at least one
other man. Partly for this reason, but also because she did not produce an heir, Louis had the marriage annulled in 1152, leading to
one of the more significant instances of dynastic politics impinging
on the conjoined history of France and England.

Henry II and the Angevin Empire

In the 1150s, England was recovering from a period of widespread
instability resulting from Henry I's death without a male heir. His
nephew Stephen of Blois had more or less seized the kingship from
Matilda, who, as Henry's legitimate daughter, had the better hereditary claim. Matilda and her husband Count Geoffrey 'Plantagenet'
of Anjou were unable to dislodge Stephen from England (despite
having their allies capture him at one point), but they did conquer Normandy. For most of the 1140s, the Anglo-Norman realm
was divided, and England itself slipped into the period of civil war
that historians still generally refer to as 'the Anarchy'. Stephen failed
at solving the dilemma created by being king and duke of a cross-
channel dominion, and he could not control an aristocracy eager to
reassert some of the privileges that had been compromised by Henry
I's expansion of royal power. He showered the Church with liberties in his coronation charter to ensure its support, but the bishops
took sides and several major sees were controlled by his political enemies. Contemporary chroniclers leave no doubt as to the level of local
violence that accompanied Stephen's weak and constantly distressed
kingship.

By 1153, Henry I's grandson, Henry Plantagenet, had come of age and become a legitimate threat to Stephen. Well established as duke of Normandy and count of Anjou and Maine, Henry still needed time and support from disaffected English nobles to make good his claim to the throne. When Henry invaded England in 1153, Stephen resisted, and a renewal of civil war was possible, but after the death of his eldest son he quickly agreed to a truce. The Treaty of Winchester excluded his son from the royal succession and granted Henry the throne as soon as Stephen died. He accommodatingly did so nine months later, and Henry II began his reign amid a political climate of general exhaustion, but with promise. He was the greatest prince in northern France. At this point, traditional dynastic politics intervened in a somewhat bizarre way, for just as Henry II was planning his invasion of England, in 1152, Louis VII had his marriage to Eleanor of Aquitaine annulled. She almost immediately was re-married to Henry II. While in retrospect this seems like a huge blunder on Louis VII's part, it must be remembered that she had not produced an heir (otherwise her allegedly scandalous behavior might have been tolerated), and contemporary observers seem to have thought that Louis made the right move. But when Henry II and Eleanor were crowned in 1154, they together controlled half of France as well as all of England.

The 'Angevin Empire', as historians usually call it, consisted of the Anglo-Norman realm Henry II claimed from his grandfather through his mother Matilda, the counties of Maine and Anjou that he inherited from his father, and the sprawling duchy of Aquitaine that he effectively married into. The empire, however, was not institutionally integrated. Each duchy and county had its own administrations, and as such it was united only by the person of the king. So although many of the dilemmas Henry II confronted were similar to those of his grandfather, they were on a much larger scale. In England, he tried to re-establish the relatively centralized administrative infrastructure of Henry I that had deteriorated during Stephen's reign, and tried to assert the royal will through a maze of competing jurisdictions. He standardized the process of issuing writs, and improved the workings of the exchequer; a nearly complete set of Pipe Rolls survived, allowing scholars to reconstruct the monies going in and out of the treasury in any given year. Together, these efforts have garnered him the status of the 'father of English common law', though scholars debate how self-consciously he tried to develop the kind of legal system implied by that term. He certainly sought a more active role for the king in all aspects of his rule and laid firm foundations for impersonal government.[101] This led him to assert the primacy of royal courts, sometimes at the expense of local and ecclesiastical ones, and this famously brought him into conflict with the Church. It would be impossible in the space allowed here to convey the true scope of his activity in law and administration, but a few documents from the 1160s, along with their respective contexts, can illustrate his goals and failures.

In 1166, Henry II issued the Assize of Clarendon a set of twenty-two statutes that concerned themselves with maintaining the peace by regulating judicial procedure. In this assize, written and oral, custom and innovation, personal lordship and impersonal institutions, sit uneasily together, and so it offers a cross-section of the competing impulses that characterize contemporary rulership. The very first chapter of the assize provides for what can, with some justification, be described as a provision for a grand jury of indictment. 'Twelve of the more lawful men of the hundred [a local territorial unit whose precise extent varied]' along with 'four of the more lawful men of each vill' were to be designated to determine if there were any suspects of the crimes of robbery or murder in the area. This harbinger of modern legal process, however, is followed by the directive that the possible criminals so identified be subjected to trial by ordeal (in this case, immersion in water). Even in the late twelfth century, trials by ordeal, also known as 'judgments of God', were becoming distrusted, but their appearance here would probably have made perfect sense to legal thinkers at the time.[102] What is most significant here is that Henry's sheriffs and other officials would be performing standard procedures for all his subjects. According to one modern historian, it thus 'brought royal justice into the heart of English society'.[103] Henry made this entirely explicit in Chapter 8 of the Assize, which summons all men to attend county courts irrespective of any local privileges they have. While some of the provisions of the Assize seem mundane, they all point to an intrusion of a centralizing monarch into local justice.

Henry issued several other important assizes in his long reign, including one at Northampton in 1176 that confirmed the Clarendon statutes, adding additional details to the workings of the jury. People in and around the king's administration recognized the significance of these developments and even wrote treatises about them. Both the *Treatise on the Laws and Customs of England,* attributed to Glanville, and Richard Fitzneal's *Dialogue on the Exchequer,* which details the operations of the royal treasury, date to this period. The increasing complexity of judicial process and royal finance depended in part on written documents, and hence on educated clerks who could read and write them. Henry's itinerant court thus attracted a school-trained, literate elite who rubbed elbows with knights and other more unsavory elements, such as jesters and parasites. Several commentators wrote scathing critiques of the court as a den of iniquity, but it was essential to the projection of royal power as well as to the everyday business of government. Many, though by no means all, of the literate elite at court were clergy.[104] Bishops, who controlled extensive territories as feudal lords, also served the English kings as administrators. The enmeshment of ecclesiastical personnel in the business of government led to inevitable crisis after Henry appointed his royal chancellor, Thomas Becket, as Archbishop of Canterbury in 1162. Thomas had been a loyal royal henchman who had served in a military capacity despite being in minor clerical orders, and showed no inclination toward the reform movement. But once ordained as a priest and consecrated as archbishop he dashed Henry's hopes that the greatest secular position in government and the highest ecclesiastical office would be joined in the person of a cooperative friend; he resigned the chancellorship soon after his consecration. Becket, for reasons that were probably both practical and ideological, advanced the principles of ecclesiastical liberty and took them further than many others had, to the conclusion that clergy existed outside the realm of royal justice.

Whereas the great crisis of Church and state in Germany had centered around lay investiture and competing theories of the world order, the conflict between Henry II and Becket stemmed from the incompatibility of two of the most important developments in twelfth-century political life: the extension of royal jurisdiction on the one hand, and the increasing identification of the clergy as a distinct and more pure group in society on the other. Henry revealed this incompatibility when he sought to bring the clergy fully under the umbrella of royal justice in criminal cases, even though the Church held that clerics were, because of their ordination, subject only to ecclesiastical jurisdiction. Practically speaking, this meant that Henry II wanted clerics accused of criminal offenses to be tried in the royal courts, while Becket argued they should be tried only in ecclesiastical ones.

In 1164, Henry laid out his position on the place of the Church in his kingdom in the Constitutions of Clarendon. The constitutions cover a great deal of ground, but they all insist that the king had the right and duty to regulate ecclesiastical affairs. Disputes over the control of local churches, even if both parties were clerics, belonged in the royal, rather than ecclesiastical courts, and those clerics whom the Church found guilty had to be handed over to face royal justice. Henry also explicitly rejected certain aspects of the papacy's claim to universal authority by refusing to allow bishops to appeal to Rome on matters of canon law without royal approval. All these claims were based on appeals to privilege.[105] The very term constitutions (*consuetudines* in Latin, rendered literally as 'customs'), in contrast to the term 'assize' which would be used in 1166, stresses the traditional nature of Henry's claims. But by putting the customs in writing, Henry was announcing a new vision for English government; far from merely imagining an idealized past, the constitutions opened possibilities for the future. It is thus impossible to see either party in the dispute as a revolutionary or a reactionary—each was combining tradition and innovation for immediate rhetorical and practical purposes.

Thomas Becket stunned his supporters by initially agreeing to the Constitutions of Clarendon (his name appears first on the witness list). Shortly thereafter, however, he had a change of heart and repudiated them, then lived in exile from 1164 until 1170. Meanwhile, the English Church debated the issue. Many bishops took Henry's side, some for theological reasons, some because Becket came to be regarded as self-aggrandizing and unreasonable. Becket himself, though he had mundane interests in defending ecclesiastical liberties, such as protecting the revenues of the manors he controlled, saw himself as a defender of absolute and eternal principles against the messy business of royal government: 'the Lord is never found to have said "I am custom"; but he said "I am truth" '.[106]

The king and archbishop attempted to reconcile in 1170, and Becket returned from exile only to be murdered, allegedly because an exasperated Henry bellowed 'will no one rid me of that meddlesome priest?' Four knights went to the cathedral at Canterbury, found Thomas at prayer, and murdered him in extravagantly messy fashion: as the high-born assailants insulted him for his humble origins, they hacked away at his head for a good while, until one of them scooped out the brain with the point of a sword. It was an act of rage tinged with symbolic meaning; the knights probably thought nothing of violating sacred space in defense of royal prerogatives.[107] The crime, however, mortified nearly everyone, including perhaps Henry himself, and Henry spent four years negotiating forgiveness, which was granted after a humiliating penitential ritual at the Norman town of Avranches in 1174. Perhaps predictably, part of the settlement involved Henry promising to undertake a crusade to the Holy Land, a promise he never fulfilled. Henry's penance satisfied Pope Alexander III, who desperately needed support in his dispute with an anti-pope. Although Henry would never again make grandiose claims to jurisdiction over the Church, he did maintain relatively effective control over his Church for the remainder of his reign; the next two archbishops of Canterbury were monks noted more for their piety than their political acumen.

In the last decade of his life, however, Henry was overwhelmed by the challenges of holding the Angevin Empire together, especially given that his sons began to revolt in earnest and to take sides with the young king of France, Philip II 'Augustus'. A clerical observer in the late 1180s created a (probably fictional) dialogue in which Henry II lamented that his sons had rejected his affection, left him old, unloved, and vulnerable. 'My friends and neighbors oppose me, and I have found that the servants and allies I thought I had are in fact cruel enemies and unfaithful sinners'.[108] He was forced to do homage to Philip Augustus in 1183 for his continental lands, and in 1189 he, for all intents and purposes, surrendered before dying alone and in a state of abject self-pity.[109] Although Henry had brought about a new phase in English royal government, he could not completely prevail over the structural weaknesses of an 'empire' held together by feudal obligation and dynastic accident.

Philip Augustus and France's coming of age

Although the preservation of the Angevin Empire was probably beyond the resources of Henry II and his successors, its demise was hastened by Philip Augustus's relentless efforts to weaken it and to expand the French royal domain. Philip built on the administrative apparatus of his predecessors, maximized revenues, and entered into shrewd alliances to assert his royal lordship over many parts of France where kings had previously had only a marginal presence. Most historians regard his reign as among the most successful in French history, for by the time he died in 1223 he had nearly doubled the size of the royal domain and evicted the English kings from the bulk of their continental territories. He also far surpassed even his greatest vassals in wealth, power, and prestige. That he was willing and able to violate basic principles of the prevailing political morality helped him to dispossess his rivals, and to construct a model of kinship that began to displace the feudal order.

Philip Augustus was crowned king at the age of fourteen as Louis VII's health deteriorated. At the coronation, Philip and his handlers explicitly articulated his vision for France: a king supported by and superior to great vassals. Henry II's son and heir, Henry 'the Young King', carried Philip's crown, while the count of Flanders carried his sword and then waited on the new monarch at the subsequent banquet.[110] Afterward, he wasted no time in starting to rule in his own right, casting off his regent and confronting enemies foreign and domestic. Noted by contemporaries and historians alike for political savvy and ruthlessness, he put both on display in 1180 when he issued an edict against the Jews in Paris. According to Philip's biographer Rigord,

> the Jews were arrested in their synagogues all over France at his order on the fourteenth of February [1180] and despoiled of their gold, silver and vestments, just as the Jews themselves had despoiled the Egyptians on their exodus from Egypt. By this was signified their coming expulsion, which followed in time by God's disposition.[111]

The 'coming expulsion' arrived in 1182, but he brought them back in 1198, in part so he could tax their financial activities.[112] When he confiscated Jewish property, he not only acquired a massive influx of cash for his treasury, he made a point about his kingdom. It was to be pure, Christian, and unified under his person.

Philip Augustus simultaneously expanded the royal domain, often at the expense of his vassals, capturing key parts of Flanders, establishing control over regions adjacent to the royal domain, such as Valois, while quelling rebellions far to the south. Although he initially allied with Henry II, conflict with the English king was inevitable, since Philip's plans to strengthen the position of the French crown inevitably involved weakening the Angevin Empire. By 1186, he had enticed Henry II's sons Richard and John to ally with him against their father. As the price of his support, Philip required that Richard perform homage for the continental lands he would inherit, and thus there was no question about the relative positions of the two monarchs when it came to Normandy and the other French territories. But before he could move against Richard (which he almost certainly intended to do), the two of them took vows to prosecute the Third Crusade together with Frederick Barbarossa. After Jerusalem fell to the Muslim army of Saladin in 1187, the papacy had implored Europe's royalty to recapture it as the quintessential act of Christian kingship, and Philip made careful arrangements for his expedition. Rigord reports that the king provided that his *baillis*, royal financial and judicial officials that he had instituted by 1184, would see to the king's interests throughout the kingdom, and set down strict rules for their conduct. Before Philip could fight for Christendom in Palestine, he made sure to establish his personal rule back home by deploying trusted administrators. In a testament usually called 'the Ordinance of 1190', which is included in Rigord's biography, he explicitly commanded that because 'the royal office exists to provide for the needs of subjects by all means and to place the public before (the king's) private interest [...] we have decided on the counsel of the Most High to set down how the necessary business of the kingdom should be managed in our absence'.[113] He established the 'Saladin Tithe', a general tax on the kingdom to fund the crusade (which was collected with only moderate success at best), and left his mother, Adela, and Archbishop William of Rheims, as co-regents.

Although piety suffused all elements of his kingship, Philip Augustus prosecuted the Third Crusade rather unenthusiastically and played a passive role as Richard captured the important stronghold of Acre. As soon as the siege was over, Philip hastened back to France, where he contrived with Richard's brother John to deprive him of his kingdom and thus dismantle the Angevin Empire. After he struck a truce with Saladin and headed for home, Richard fell into the hands of his political enemy the duke of Austria, who handed him over to Emperor Henry VI, who in turn held him for ransom. Philip almost surely conspired with Henry to set an extortionate ransom, the payment of which would cripple Richard's treasury. Once Richard returned from captivity and subdued John, Philip gained little headway in his military campaigns against Normandy. But another dynastic accident, the premature death of Richard in 1199 and the succession of the mostly ineffective John, allowed Philip to extend his kingship further than would have been conceivable to most of his predecessors. Richard had explicitly recognized Philip as his feudal overlord, and Philip invoked feudal custom and royal privileges against John to devastating effect. First, he weakened John's control over his continental subjects by asking them to appeal to the royal court at Paris, thus subverting local jurisdiction, much as Henry II had sought to do in England.[114] Second, exercising his feudal rights relating to the marriages of his vassals, he summoned John to that court in 1202 to answer charges that he had improperly married Isabel of Angoulême, who was already betrothed to another of Philip's vassals. When John failed to appear, Philip declared John's fiefs in France to be forfeit. In a military campaign that benefitted greatly from John's indecision, Philip seized Normandy in 1204. Maine, Anjou, and much of Poitou fell soon afterward, leaving John in possession only of Gascony in the far south. Rather than install new dukes and counts, however, Philip simply appropriated these territories into the royal domain, which greatly increased royal revenues, while effecting greater administrative and conceptual unity to the French kingdom.

John, whose difficulties in England will be discussed below, spent the next ten years trying to recover Normandy, but Philip Augustus had both the resources and the political acumen to dash any hope of reuniting the Angevin Empire. As John fell out of favor with the papacy and rival claimants to the imperial title fought in Germany, Philip made and unmade alliances, and got into the good graces of Pope Innocent III. His son Louis (VIII) stymied John's military advance in the south just before Philip crushed John's continental allies—the disputed emperor Otto IV and the count of Flanders—at the Battle of Bouvines. This pitched battle may have been the logical culmination of years of policy and gradual weakening of English power, but it stood as a potent symbol of the newly assertive French monarchy.

Philip also looked to extend his authority in the south, and there he found that Innocent III and he had shared interests. The area around Toulouse, and particularly the town of Albi, was perceived by the Church to be infested with dualist heretics now known as Cathars. Alarmed that the local secular authorities seemed content to tolerate the dissenters, and frustrated that several preaching tours had done nothing to solve the problem, Innocent III called upon the French nobility to effect a military solution, which led to 20 years of wars, collectively referred to as the Albigensian Crusades. Philip initially proceeded cautiously and let others do the fighting for him. The crusaders' victory over Count Raymond of Toulouse (thought of as too soft on heresy, if not a heretic himself) shifted the balance of power in the south, as friendly nobles were installed in Raymond's fiefs. When Philip Augustus died in 1223, his son Louis VIII intervened actively in the south and ended up thoroughly triumphant. A combination of conquest and treatises brought the lands of Toulouse and much of the south of France into the royal domain, just as war with King John had secured the old Angevin dominions. The crusades did little to eradicate heresy; that job was accomplished largely through the establishment of inquisitorial procedures in the 1230s and afterwards. To summarize the results of this bloody conflict, one can hardly improve on the French historian Achille Luchaire's assessment that 'everyone, from Innocent III on, had worked, struggled and suffered, without realizing it, for the benefit of the king of France'.[115]

Although Philip Augustus was at best a lukewarm crusader, the wars in the south allowed him to present himself as a defender of

Christendom and a king who purified his kingdom. It is therefore entirely fitting that his reign began with the expulsion of the Jews and ended with a large-scale war against heresy. He avoided major conflicts with the Church and effectively integrated the role of ecclesiastical protector into his job description in a way that assured the loyalty of his bishops. At the same time, he created and expanded institutions of government that allowed him to assert sacred kingship more effectively than ever before. Much of this, of course, served his territorial ambitions, since warfare became ever more expensive during his reign and it required careful accounting and collection. He also made some strides in building an infrastructure to convey his lordship, most famously perhaps by paving the streets of Paris.[116] His achievements, perhaps, can be overstated. During his reign, the county of Barcelona, of which French kings were traditionally overlords, became effectively independent. In addition, Philip secured the realm in part by favoring his great lords, and in some areas he depended for his authority on chains of feudal relationships rather than his own administration or power. Still, he had put in place the germ of a vision of kingdom that would culminate in the reign of Louis IX, a crusading king who would be made a saint by the end of the century.

Magna Carta and the community of the English realm

As Philip Augustus and his courtiers began to articulate a vision of a unified France centered on a 'most Christian king', the Angevin Empire disintegrated. With no coherent ideology to bind, say, Anjou to Aquitaine, let alone Aquitaine to England, it is not clear what, beyond a series of accidental dynastic conjunctures, John had to hold together.[117] Still, some historians argue that a more effective king than John could have ultimately created a cohesive maritime empire, and that Philip's total triumph was contingent on specific events and far from inevitable.[118] This remains a minority view, and in the event the English kings, despite overseas holdings in Ireland and Gascony, became gradually more English and disengaged from their continental political moorings. In the long run, this probably encouraged the political and cultural consolidation of England, which still included a diverse collection of Anglo-Saxon, Norman, British, and even Norse people and customs.

Historians have long argued over the relative effectiveness of the two brothers, Richard and John, as monarchs. Richard famously spent only six months out of a ten-year reign in England; that he could do so neatly illustrates the strides the Anglo-Norman and Angevin kings had made in creating impersonal structures of government. When he died, he left John an efficient system of revenue collection, but rapid inflation meant that John constantly struggled to fund his military campaigns. Richard also bequeathed to him a determined enemy in Philip Augustus. Moreover, John seems to have had a penchant for making bad situations worse. Although a few have claimed that John had some administrative talent and perhaps more military aptitude than is usually allowed, he certainly failed to address the main dilemmas of English kingship as they have been identified in this chapter. He quarreled with Pope Innocent III—who, as the most assertive and influential pope of the High Middle Ages, made for a staggeringly poor choice of an opponent—when he refused to accept the election of the learned Stephen Langton to be archbishop of Canterbury. In 1208, his kingdom was placed under interdict, which halted the administering of the sacraments of the Church. The contrast with the sacred kingship of Philip Augustus could not be sharper. Nor, as we have seen, could he hold together the possessions he inherited. Finally, his nobles, already chafing at the expansion of royal power, increased their hostility in response to these failures. John's military expenses had led to a fiscal crisis that he could not fix despite increasingly harsh and creative exactions from his nobility. He exceeded the bounds of feudal custom repeatedly, particularly by experimenting with wildly unpopular general taxation. After Bouvines (which negated any positive effects of John's 1213 reconciliation with Innocent III), they saw little reason to acquiesce in John's government, and perhaps sensed an opportunity to assert some of their old prerogatives, such as a wider jurisdiction for private baronial courts, that had been eroded under Henry II.

In May of 1215, after several months of negotiations, a group of barons renounced their loyalty to John on the grounds that he had not respected their customary rights, and open violence broke out soon thereafter. The king desperately tried to shore up his support through various means, including a somewhat pathetic promise to undertake a crusade. In the end, however, he sought to calm the situation by promising to abide what were regarded as traditional customs. After a series of military reverses, these customs were committed to writing at Runnymede in Magna Carta, the 'Great Charter', a document that has had to bear a whole universe of interpretations as to its significance. One of the interpretive extremes is neatly demonstrated by the monument erected at Runnymede by the American Bar Association, 'to commemorate Magna Carta, symbol of freedom under

law'. According to such an interpretation, the charter laid the foundation for modern liberties by enshrining individual freedom as a legal
principle. At the other end of the interpretive spectrum, historians
have denied that it could have intended such a transcendental reach,
and that instead Magna Carta was a reactionary grasp for power by a
landed aristocracy concerned only to recover its place in a fundamentally elitist system. Obviously, the most useful analysis lies somewhere
in between.

The barons who forced John to agree to these customs had private
interests, and appealed to the person of the king to secure them. This
had always been one of the duties of the king, but John had failed
to balance the interests that always competed within the feudal order.
This was, perhaps, the essence of personal kingship, and it is why most
noble rebellions, like those that occurred under Stephen, tended to
coalesce around a rival claimant to the throne.[119] But in 1215, the
barons rebelled on behalf of a political community of the realm that
would be identified in the first clause of the charter as 'all the free
men of our kingdom'.[120] As a result, they anticipated new attitudes
toward the political order even as they vehemently sought a return
to what they thought were the 'good old days' before the unbridled
growth of centralized power. The king, however, was still regarded as
the dominant feudal lord in the realm.[121] As such, he had obligations,
but this assertion was not new; in fact, some of the clauses are taken
directly from Henry I's Coronation Charter, which also made explicit
reference to 'evil customs'.

Most of the charter directly addressed the problems that caused the
relationship between the king and his barons to sour between 1199
and 1215. In clauses 2 through 9, John promises to adhere to traditional limitations on his power over the aristocracy. He renounces
the charging of excessive 'reliefs' (the fees that allowed an heir to
take possession of an inherited fief) from his vassals and pledges not
to force widows to marry against their will. Clause 9 makes sure that
barons in debt will not have their property seized unjustly. The charter
did not, however, relentlessly attack the instruments of royal government. In Clause 18, John explicitly promises to have royal justices hear
cases in the counties. The innovations of Angevin kingship that per-
tained to the public order were thus retained. Some novelties, such
as general taxation, were also considered: in Clause 14 it was stipulated that the king would summon the great men of the kingdom 'to
obtain the general consent of the realm for the assessment of an "aid"
[an emergency tax]'. Magna Carta recognized other constituencies
beyond just the barons. Burgesses in the towns had their traditional

rights protected, and merchants benefitted from Clause 35, which sought to standardize weights and measures throughout the kingdom.

Looking forward to modern conceptions of the political order, commentators have focused primarily on two principles that one can reasonably (but with considerable risk of anachronism) distill from the charter. By requiring the king to obey certain written customs, the charter effectively placed the king under the rule of law. Contemporaries presumably still thought of law as an extension of royal power rather than a limitation of it, but here they made clear that the king had to act within carefully circumscribed limits. The best known example of this principle is Clause 39, which, it is fair to say, anticipates the Fifth Amendment to the United States Constitution:

> No free man shall be seized or imprisoned, or stripped of his rights or possessions, or outlawed or exiled, or deprived of his standing in any other way, nor will we proceed with force against him, or send others to do so, except by the lawful judgment of his equals or by the law of the land.

This and other clauses clearly required the king to follow some basic principles of fairness in the administration of justice. In addition, three of the clauses strongly suggest that the king would need, at least in some instances, to govern in consultation with a group of his subjects. Clauses 12 and 14 involve consent for taxation, while Clause 61 requires that 25 barons be elected to a council, and that council was to ensure royal compliance with the charter. It would take many years, and considerable changes of circumstance, before such a council became anything like a modern parliament, but it demonstrated that a king in dire straits might well need one.

This brings up the point that Magna Carta was produced by a monarchy beset by a serious crisis, and it did not even resolve that crisis. John's new ally Innocent III gladly declared the charter void, John abrogated it, and civil war began a few months after Runnymede. In terms of its immediate impact, it was a spectacular failure, and the dilemmas of English kingship continued. The crisis and attendant violence ended not because of shared assumptions about government, but because John died in 1216—clearly the personal qualities of a king still mattered. For the next few decades, however, the charter effectively provided a new set of possibilities for royal government. Henry III reissued it in 1216 and 1217 with the most objectionable clauses purged, and in 1225 he convened a council of nobles in order to secure the assessment of a new tax. But the old problems of English kingship remained; in 1230 Henry III, after over a year of planning, invaded western France with no success whatsoever.

Christianization and the Kingdoms of Northern and Eastern Europe

The kingdoms discussed so far, even those that took over territories previously ruled by Arabic-speaking Muslims, all had some connection to the old Roman Empire, and had been Christian for a significant part of their history. In Scandinavia and Eastern Europe, on the other hand, missionaries, kings, and peasants worked to bring new lands into Latin Christendom. Settlers, often directed by kings and inspired by bishops, brought the ideas and institutions of the twelfth century to these areas and created frontier societies where diverse cultural traditions interacted and were synthesized. In the case of Eastern Europe, especially in the Baltic areas, secular and ecclesiastical leaders explicitly tied this expansion to crusading, and Christianization went hand in hand with the formation of new polities. The Scandinavian kingdoms, along with Hungary, Poland, and Bohemia, have long been peripheral to twelfth-century studies in the Anglophone world, but in recent decades they have attracted greater scholarly interest, and many of their primary sources are now available in translation. Recent studies, moreover, have emphasized that what happened on the edges of the Latin West reflected some of the most important concerns of people in the more established, 'central' regions. In subsequent chapters we will find Hungarians attending school in Paris and Norwegians fighting Muslims in the Holy Land. Although the polities of the north and east possessed some unique features, they shared challenges, and in some cases, historical trajectories, with emerging countries like France, England, Aragon-Catalonia, and Sicily.

Scandinavia's entry to Latin Christendom

In 1110, King Sigurd of Norway helped besiege and capture the city of Sidon in what is now Lebanon, after a military action that helped solidify the First Crusade's conquest of Jerusalem in 1099. In the two years it took him to reach the Holy Land, he had visited Henry I's England, Louis VI's France, both Muslim and Christian parts of Iberia (where he joined the duke of Portugal in a successful siege of Sintra and an unsuccessful one of Lisbon), as well as Norman Sicily. An Old Norse chronicler even made the chronologically impossible claim that Sigurd had assisted in Roger II's coronation (which did not in fact take place until 1130). After Sidon, he lingered in Jerusalem with its Latin king, Baldwin I, acquired a relic of the True Cross on which Christ was crucified, according to the crusaders. According to the chronicler, 'then that holy relic was given to King Sigurd with the stipulation that he and twelve compurgators should swear to promote Christianity with all their might and establish an archbishopric in Norway'.[122] Although the archbishopric at Trondheim would not be established until the 1150s, Sigurd had clearly demonstrated that his Norwegian kingdom was to be a part of Christendom. He had been entertained by important kings and participated in the expansion of Christendom in three different areas: Scandinavia, Iberia, and the Holy Land.

By 1100, in part under the influence of Christianization, dozens of small territories ruled by local chieftains were in the process of being consolidated into three loosely organized kingdoms of Norwegians, Danes, and Swedes, though their boundaries bore only the vaguest resemblance to the countries that today bear their names. The Danes periodically subjugated the other two groups, but any political balance could be easily upset. For three centuries, Scandinavia had been important to the history of the Latin West and beyond in several ways. Most important in the earlier period had been the Viking expeditions that both traded with and raided territories stretching from Spain to Ireland to Russia. Norseman had established trading colonies at Dublin, York, and various Baltic locations, founded the duchy of Normandy in 909, and formed the state of Rus in far Eastern Europe; coins from ninth-century Baghdad, discovered in medieval Swedish tombs, testify to the range of Viking commerce. They settled Iceland in the tenth century and reached Greenland and then Newfoundland by 1000. From 1016 until 1035 the Danish king Cnut ruled over a North Sea Empire that eventually included Norway, Denmark, and England. Cnut's empire disintegrated after his death, but Scandinavians of various sorts enjoyed a wide cultural reach throughout the twelfth century.

Christianization, urbanization, and the development of kingship went hand in hand in all three kingdoms, though at different paces. In 1104, the Danish Church was granted an archbishop at Lund (in modern Sweden but then under Danish rule). A papal legate established Trondheim as the center of an independent Norwegian Church in 1154 and gave it jurisdiction over Iceland, the Faeroe Islands, and even Greenland. Trondheim participated in a large web of cultural influences, especially English ones; its cathedral bears a striking resemblance to the Gothic masterpiece in Lincoln. In 1164,

Uppsala became the archbishopric for Sweden, which was only then uniting its two constituent peoples, the Götar and the Svear, into a single polity.[123] Around that same time, the practice of anointing and crowning kings in a religious ceremony of the sort common in the Latin West was established in Norway, which also developed a tradition of sacred kingship around the cult of the sainted Olaf II (1015–1028). Danish and Swedish kings were first crowned in the sacral fashion in 1170 and 1210, respectively.[124] Scandinavia did not have the same history of strong kingship as other parts of Europe, and even in the early twelfth century it was not uncommon for countries to be ruled by co-kings, but by the end of the period hereditary rule was being introduced.

The kings of the north apparently sought many of the same goals as their counterparts in England, France, and elsewhere: centralized rule based on written records, a symbiotic relationship with their national Churches, control over nobles at the local level, and occasional consultation with assemblies of nobles and clergy. The state of documentary evidence, however, makes it difficult to outline the stages of these developments as clearly as in England, Barcelona, or Sicily. The earliest written law codes for Norway, for example, date to the middle of the thirteenth century, and legislation seems to have been a regional, rather than a national, concern. Warrior nobilities coalesced as identifiable classes by this time, though royal control of them seems to have been relatively weak. In addition, bloody succession crises, such as that which saw Norway descend into full-scale civil war after the 1130s, militated against national unity. Until stable monarchies could arise, the Church would remain the greatest force for cohesion in all three of the kingdoms.

Our best sources for law and culture come from Norway and Iceland, but the latter had no kings, so its records are not entirely instructive for the Scandinavian kingdoms. Perhaps their most distinctive element of justice and governance was the *thing*, a regional assembly of free farmers that met to vote on legal cases and on policies, sometimes on a yearly basis. *Things* were initially entirely oral proceedings in which the community made group decisions, settled disputes, and meted out punishment (the most common of which was outlawry). Encouraged by kings, the *things* in Norway became gradually more regular and took on the responsibility of making law, while in Iceland, which had no kings, the large assemblies known as Althings became essentially representative assemblies of free farmers. The most famous vote of the Icelandic Althing was its decision to adopt Christianity in the year 1000.[125] Over the course of the

High Middle Ages, the kings began to turn the *things* into instruments of royal authority. In the Icelandic sagas (based mainly on stories about tenth- and eleventh century Icelanders written down in the thirteenth), and the written collection of laws called *Grágás*, which were probably first redacted in the mid-twelfth century but exist in thirteenth-century copies, there is excellent evidence for law and dispute resolution.[126] Both sagas and the *Grágás* emphasize peacemaking, feuds, and adultery, but they are not especially relevant to the political trajectory of the Scandinavian kingdoms.[127]

Although these kingdoms did not develop as quickly as their southern counterparts, Scandinavia did become thoroughly integrated into the political life of the Latin West by the early thirteenth century. Pope Innocent III saw fit to place Norway under interdict in 1198, and the Danish king acquired rights over the thriving commercial city of Lübeck in 1201. The Danes would play a major role in the crusades to the eastern Baltic, as well as to the Holy Land, with a large Danish contingent joining Richard Lionheart and Philip Augustus in 1191.[128] Under King Valdemar II (1202–1241), Denmark expanded so aggressively eastward that its king took on the title 'King of the Danes and the Slavs'. Towns such as Visby on the island of Götland became important trading centers and linked Scandinavia to trading networks that extended to the Mediterranean and beyond.

Christian consolidation and expansion in Eastern Europe

Starting in the eleventh century, traders, missionaries, and land-hungry settlers (more or less in that order) turned the stretch of Baltic coast from the mouth of the Elbe river to what is now Estonia into a center of trade, Christianization, and cultural encounter. The German kings, as well as more recently established rulers, like the kings of Poland and the dukes (and later kings) of Bohemia, enlisted settlers from the west as well as armed force to expand the limits of Latin Christendom beyond the Oder and Vistula rivers. Here they encountered the influence not only of paganism but of Byzantine Christianity, along with polities like Kievan Rus, which looked not only to the Baltic but to the east and south as well. Novgorod, for example, was home to a magnificent cathedral of Holy Wisdom (consecrated in the 1050s), inspired by its counterpart in Constantinople. To the south, the Christian kingdom of Hungary took steps toward a centralized administration and a strong Church organization. The unifying visions of popes and emperors, along with the local ambitions of Christian kings and the growth of long-distance trade, combined to transform the region radically by the 1240s, when the Mongols would reach Hungary before turning back to Asia. Expansion here tended to follow a pattern in which trade routes and missionary work, aided by military conquest, were accompanied by the establishment of bishoprics, the control of which was often hotly disputed.

Several different rulers interested themselves in the Baltic region, including the kings of Germany, Denmark, and Poland (which probably had its first proper coronation of a king in 1025), as well as the dukes of Saxony. Emperor Otto I the Great had stopped the Hungarian invasions of the empire at the Battle of the Lechfeld in 955 and established several bishoprics to missionize the polytheistic Slavic population in the east, but a general revolt wiped out nearly the entire Christian presence there soon thereafter. In the 1120s, the once again thoroughly pagan land of Pomerania (east of the mouth of the Oder) was conquered by Poland and subsequently missionized by the German bishop Otto of Bamberg, who had been appointed imperial chancellor of Emperor Henry IV. In the middle of the century, the push to the west received a strong jolt when Pope Eugenius III endowed it with the character of a crusade. As early as 1107, in the aftermath of the First Crusade's success, a clerk in Magdeburg had linked the cause of converting the Wends (a term referring to the larger group of Slavs to which the Pomeranians belonged) to that of liberating Jerusalem.[129] In 1147, Eugenius III included the Wendish lands as one of three targets when he called the Second Crusade. The greatest saint of the era, Bernard of Clairvaux, took on the role of Eugenius III's propagandist, ensured potential crusaders they would receive the same privileges as those who went to Jerusalem, and forbade them to make peace until the Wends 'shall be either converted or wiped out'.[130] Enough Danes, Poles, and Saxons answered this call to form an imposing army, which had mixed results in the field and does not seem to have significantly added territory to Christendom. Some Slavs were baptized, but Christianity did not seem to have penetrated too deeply.[131] On the other hand, great lords like Henry the Lion of Saxony had flexed considerable muscle and established an important front of operations. Pope Alexander III followed up on this by calling another crusade to Estonia in 1171. While formally declared crusades made for effective rallying points, commercial ventures and royal encouragement of settlers would be the main instruments for the Christianization of the Baltic, a process not completed until the fourteenth century. The trading centers of Lübeck, Riga in Livonia, and Reval in Estonia played a primary role in the region's integration into the Latin West.

The political history of Poland, Bohemia, and Hungary is marked by the same tension between centralization and fragmentation evident in the rest of Europe, though they faced specific challenges. In Poland, entropic forces prevailed. After 1000, when Emperor Otto III had established an archbishopric at Gniezno at a famous meeting with the Polish duke Boleslaw the Brave (later King Boleslaw I), and Poland played an increasingly important role in regional politics. The kingdom began splitting up in the late eleventh century, and, after 1138, several duchies went their separate ways, with episcopal organization providing only a modicum of unity. After invasions by Czech and German forces in the 1130s, the Polish leaders found themselves in a subordinate position to the emperor.[132] The process of building a centralized state in Poland would be postponed until the later medieval period.

The duchy of Bohemia, although formally a part of the Holy Roman Empire, was somewhat more successful in maintaining independence and geographical integrity. Like the duchy of Portugal, it became a kingdom through a process that began in the 1150s, when Emperor Frederick I granted its duke a royal title. In 1198, Philip of Swabia supported Ottokar I's claim to be king of Bohemia, and the title became hereditary. Always closely tied to Germany dynastically, Bohemia's Czech rulers used German settlers to help establish control over and Christianize the area. The dukes managed to establish good relations with the Church and their nobility, and there are definite parallels with other parts of Europe. Clerks educated in Paris took up important positions in the Church and served at the ducal court. There was no major crisis of Church and state there, perhaps because the reform movement did not gain as much traction there as elsewhere. Clerical marriage seems to have been common throughout the century, and in 1197 a violent mob of prospective priests attacked a papal legate who tried to coerce them into making vows of chastity.[133] The dukes seem to have negotiated continually with their various constituencies, and to have been subject to restrictions on arbitrary actions through established custom.[134]

To the south of Bohemia, Hungary had been proudly Christian since the reign of Stephen I (1001–1038), though its kings and people were understandably troubled by the hoards of pious crusaders who periodically crossed their territory throughout the twelfth century. The Hungarian rulers extended their reach southward and thus came into contact and conflict with the Byzantine Empire and with the trading republic of Venice. The historian Otto of Freising, who passed through the kingdom during the Second Crusade, saw it as a barely

Christian territory on the edge of civilization: 'as it has suffered frequent inroads of the barbarians, it is not surprising that the province
remains crude and uncultured in customs and in speech'.[135] Otto also
noted a heavy presence of 'foreigners', and certainly a large number
of cultural groups, including some pagans and Jews, lived together in
the kingdom; there is even evidence that the kings resisted ecclesiastical directives to segregate or even persecute such populations.[136]
Few countries were as emphatically multiethnic as Hungary was at the
time, and membership in the 'Hungarian race' was determined not
by birth but by the fact of living in the kingdom; the many immigrants from places as far away as Flanders were full members of the
community.

Stephen I had left that community with a strong organizational
framework and a tradition of written law. He made effective use of
counts, who operated more as royal agents than independent power-
brokers; the counties could not be inherited. The counties were in
turn divided into smaller administrative units based around a castle,
giving the king a strong military presence in most of the country.
Stephen's successors, when not bogged down in external wars, continued to elaborate on his system and made additional strides in the
late twelfth century. Like the Bohemian dukes, they employed school-
trained clerks at their chancery and issued an increasing number of
charters. The sense of cohesion that these administrative techniques
and personnel gave the kingdom allowed it to survive both succession
crises and periodic foreign invasions.

Even the strongest Hungarian kings had to deal with the internal
crises that periodically faced their counterparts in England, Sicily, and
elsewhere. In the early thirteenth century, an increasingly assertive
nobility began encroaching on royal prerogatives, and ultimately pres-
sured King Andrew II (1205–1235) to grant them privileges in the
written document known as the Golden Bull of 1222 (reissued in
1231). Like Magna Carta, this document restricted the power of kings,
particularly as it related to the nobility, and guaranteed that if Andrew
II or any future king violated its terms, the barons would 'have the
right in perpetuity to resist and speak against us and our successors
without the charge of high treason'.[137] Despite its unique geographical position, the Hungarian political community clearly faced the
same dilemmas as those in the rest of the Latin West. The bull also
barred Jews and Muslims from royal office, perhaps reflecting the
barons' anxieties about the unique position of Hungary at a cultural
crossroads (as well as their resentment at royal officials in general).

On the international scene, to be sure, Hungary was poised between the Latin West, the increasingly unique culture of the Russian principalities, and the Byzantine Empire. It frequently involved itself in their wars as well, and its fortunes often rose as those of Byzantium fell. After the 1180s, when the rule of the Eastern emperors weakened somewhat, the Hungarian kings were able to establish a strong presence along the Dalmatian coast, where they were attacked by a diverted contingent of crusaders in 1204. The papacy had also long taken an interest in the kingdom's ecclesiastical affairs, but despite its apparent belief that it had granted the first royal crown to Stephen, there was minimal friction between Church and state there. In late twelfth and early thirteenth centuries, moreover, the cult of kingship in Hungary became increasingly centered on crusading. In 1192 the earlier king László I was canonized as a crusader in part because of an invented story that he had been chosen the chief military commander of the First Crusade before his untimely death. His successor, Andrew II, modeled his reign on László's legendary achievement, and inherited a crusading vow from his father Béla III (1172–1196). Even though Andrew's crusade of 1218 accomplished little (he arrived at Acre with a great army but prosecuted only one inconsequential campaign), he had joined the ranks of the longer-established kings of the Latin West in taking leadership of a military pilgrimage to the Holy Land.[138] Despite its peripheral status in much of modern scholarship, Hungary had definitively entered into the community of budding national monarchies, in part through its participation in the ideal of Christendom that Urban II introduced at the Council of Clermont. In the following century, however, the Mongol invasions would bring new pressures and inspire profound changes in its government and society.

Chapter 2: People, Economy, and Social Relations

Medieval chroniclers usually described political life as the experience of great men subject to a divine plan, but they also saw that the policies of the elites could have disastrous consequences for the rest of society. In his autobiography, Guibert of Nogent wrote that King Louis VI 'had unjustly thrown the people into turmoil' when he accepted a bribe from a faction of nobles around Laon, and as a result he had to sleep in guarded accommodations for fear of his life.[1] Documentary sources, such as the 'memorials of complaint' that record the grievances of peasants against violent and unscrupulous lords, preserved in a Barcelona archive, tell a similar story.[2] Some clergy noted disturbing trends: toward the end of the century the aging Peter of Blois excoriated aristocratic hunting parties that trampled the gardens of peasants with impunity, while the peasants themselves were punished with genital mutilation for daring to hunt in the royal forest. 'Certain princes of the earth', he wrote, 'think only about the immunity of their beasts, and as men groan under the anguish of servitude, stags, wild goats, hinds and hares exult in the right to total freedom.'[3] In criticizing English anti-poaching laws, Peter lamented the violence inherent in contemporary lordship and the social divisions between the landed aristocracy and the great majority of the population who depended for their livelihood on subsistence agriculture. When they violated their lords' hunting prerogatives, which supported a favorite leisure activity, peasants faced the brutal reality of lordship. Clerics generally acknowledged and approved of this social gulf even as they railed against its practical consequences. If the peasantry and other poor appear rarely in our narrative sources, privilege and social distinctions inform much of the religious and secular writing of the period. Nobles fallen on hard economic times are treated sympathetically in Old French romances, for example, while heroes looked down at and periodically beat invariably ugly peasants.[4] To be sure, conditions for many people changed little during the century, but for others population growth, migration, settlement patterns, monetization, and urbanization all combined to create different patterns of daily life and of relations between individuals.

Population

The central fact of social and economic life in the long twelfth century is remarkable population growth. This demographic explosion had begun to pick up steam about a 100 years earlier and would last, with significant regional variation, until roughly 1300. Any figures, of course, are conjectural and imprecise, the best guesses of scholars working with scattered evidence from monastic account records, manorial surveys (where they exist), archaeological sites, and rare, large-scale inquests like England's Domesday Book. On the basis of numerous post-war studies and revisions to them, one can reasonably estimate that in the mid-tenth century around 40 million people lived in the lands between Sicily and Scandinavia and between Russia and Ireland. By 1200, that number would balloon to perhaps 65 million, an increase of 50 per cent.[5] A careful study of Picardy indicates that that region had an average yearly growth rate of 0.68 per cent in the last decade of the twelfth century, a very rapid rate for a pre-industrial society.[6] Other areas grew as well, though less markedly. While the estimate of 50 per cent growth applies to England, Scandinavia, and Italy (and France grew by perhaps two-thirds), Eastern Europe, Russia, and Iberia grew by about 20 per cent.[7]

Faced with explaining the proliferation of human life, most scholars accept that regional climate change combined with improved agrarian technology to increase the food supply enough to feed considerably more mouths. Tree-ring studies, ice core and pollen samples, and geological evidence of glacial retreat demonstrate that most of Latin Christendom grew warmer and dryer from the tenth to the twelfth century, despite considerable variation and unpredictability.[8] Based on both documentary and anecdotal evidence, it has been suggested, even assumed, that the comparatively warm, dry climate led to a more favorable environment for agriculture, marked by longer growing seasons. Historians now disagree, however, as to whether improvements such as the horse collar and three-field crop rotation were causes or consequences of the need to feed more and more people; the relationship between these phenomena was clearly complicated. Despite long-term trends toward a gentler climate and demographic growth, the Europeans who reclaimed lands, moved their sheep to higher altitudes in response to receding glaciers, and migrated eastward, were responding to immediate crises and opportunities. Weather and other natural events were pressing challenges that required creativity and perseverance.[9]

Even during periods of demographic growth, however, death must have seemed to be everywhere. A staggering 43 per cent of the skeletons in cemeteries in Poland, Sweden, and Hungary in a recent study were of children aged 14 and under. Twenty per cent were under five years old, suggesting severe levels of infant mortality.[10] For those who survived childhood, however, a lifespan of fifty or more years was not unusual, and clerics who lived into their eighties or even nineties appear in the sources with some regularity. In the schools of Paris, certain lecturing privileges were restricted to masters over the age of 35 or even 40, indicating that medieval attitudes about the progression of life were not entirely different from modern ones (the law of the United States stipulates the presidents be at least 35). But as a general rule, non-elites who reached their twentieth birthday were nearly halfway through their life.

Although it is fair to say that daily life changed little for many European peasants during the period, these demographic changes gave rise (or were at least inextricably bound) to several major transformations in European culture and society. First, the more numerous inhabitants moved into new areas. On the local level, this meant the clearance of wasteland ('assarting'), or the draining of marshland and reclamation of the sea—most famously in Flanders but also in other regions including England, Iberia, Italy, and Poland. Across the continent, villages multiplied in the countryside, supplying landlords with sources for greater revenue.[11] On a larger scale, migration could entail directed movements of people into uninhabited or 'barbarian' areas, as occurred during the German *Ostsiedlung* ('eastward settlement'), during which German lords and Slavic princes alike encouraged the planned development of new villages under the auspices of monastic houses, the military order of the Teutonic Knights, and the minor nobility. Cultural changes, especially the expansion of the Germanic languages, ensued in their turn. Throughout Northern Europe, immigrants from points west followed upon the military conquest and merchant colonization of areas like Silesia and even Estonia, and Flemish peasants are documented re-organizing hamlets near the Elbe River by 1159.[12] Settlers from the northern Iberian kingdoms, as well as southern France, entered the formerly Islamic territory of Andalusia in the wake of the military successes of the *Reconquista*, marked especially by the victories at Toledo in 1085 and Las Navas de Tolosa in 1212. Despite the vitality of Iberia and Italy, the demographic center of gravity did gradually move northward across the Alps, with significant consequences for the making of the Latin West.

Second, Europe's population gradually redistributed itself into towns and cities. Statistical analyses and contemporary observers alike suggest that Europe and its culture became distinctly more urbanized in the century-and-a-half before 1229. Some areas, such as Italy and southern France, had a more or less continuous urban history stretching back to the Roman Empire, although the commercial centers of the High Middle Ages functioned in dramatically different ways from their ancient predecessors. Again, population figures must be treated with extreme caution, but it is clear that the number of towns with more than 5000 inhabitants, as well as the size of the largest settlements, grew significantly after 1100. London, for instance, probably doubled its population to 40,000 over the next 100 years (and a recent study suggests 80,000 is reasonable), though that figure itself was only a tenth of that estimated for contemporary Constantinople. A rough consensus holds that, by 1200, there were large towns with over 20,000 souls throughout Europe, including Lübeck, Prague, Kiev, Palermo, Paris, Bruges, York, and several cities in Italy, including Venice (itself perhaps 80,000).[13] Archaeology has confirmed the impression of urban growth: excavations of town walls suggest that the geographical extent of Cologne, Bristol, Northampton, Arezzo, and Bologna at least doubled.[14] Moreover, as permanent markets developed in towns, and as urban cathedral schools replaced monasteries as the leaders in intellectual production, culture and society owed ever more to town life.

Since the inhabitants of towns and cities, by definition, do not produce food for their own survival, their growth obviously required a substantial increase in trade, a development generally referred to as the Commercial Revolution of the Middle Ages.[15] By 1095, this revolution in the scale and methods of long-distance trade was well underway and spreading from the Mediterranean to the networks around the North and Baltic Seas. Already in the early medieval period, merchants from Italian cities like Venice, Genoa, and Pisa had profited from trade with Constantinople as well as the Islamic world. Frequently blurring the line between trade and piracy, Vikings had linked the Baltic to Baghdad through a series of connections that included commercial centers along the Volga River; coins minted under the Abbasid Caliphate have been discovered in Swedish tombs. From the eleventh to the thirteenth centuries, merchants became more organized and institutionalized in the towns, and represented a new category within their populations.

All these shifts had cultural consequences: social structures adapted to changed demographics, with the result that new opportunities were created in the towns as well as the countryside; Christians sought alternative ways of expressing their spirituality in light of changed social conditions; religious and other minorities experienced unprecedented levels of persecution (in the case of the Jews this has been directly related to economic change); and uniquely urban cultural forms, most famously the Romanesque and early Gothic cathedrals, took shape. Yet the overwhelming majority of Europeans lived in the countryside, in relatively isolated settlements.

Peasants, Lords, and Patterns of Settlement

Although medieval communities took on diverse forms, and no single model can accurately encompass the experiences of rural life that prevailed form Poland to Iceland, social organization in the countryside usually reflected people's need to produce enough food to feed themselves and to provide a surplus to their lords. Villages and other rural settlements devoted themselves, above all, to cereal cultivation. While this basic fact did not change during the twelfth century, villages, and their relation to law and lordship, were highly dynamic during this period; the traditional notion of pre-modern rural life as motionless and static does not do justice to the history of the high medieval village. Laws regarding villages varied widely, but almost everywhere in Europe settlements consisting of groups of houses surrounded by parcels (generally long strips, especially in the north) dominated the landscape.

Recent research has suggested a greater degree of geographical mobility among medieval peasants, especially during the High Middle Ages, than scholars previously allowed.[16] Peasants uprooted themselves when they needed to do so. It is assumed that they moved in search of better opportunities, in newly settled or reclaimed lands, but some of the reasons for people changing localities have eluded modern historians. Villages themselves tended to remain settled until drastic demographic changes, like those that would accompany the plagues of the fourteenth century, though archaeologists have not been able to locate a consistent rationale behind some of the recently discovered village plans.[17]

The standard scholarly estimate is that 90 per cent of Europe's population belonged to the peasantry, but there was significant social stratification within that group. Some peasants conformed to the common stereotype of farmers who struggled to feed themselves and family while their lords appropriated a hefty share of their produce. Others, however, were bonded servants with limited freedom and no property who permanently worked in the field or household of their lord. There were also a few who gained enough wealth that they could buy additional property and even speculate in land; these formed a distinct social group within their communities. Most participated, in one way or another, in a way of life structured around a village in which noble landowners siphoned the agricultural surplus of tenant farmers. The chief exception to this rule was the rural areas of Iceland, Scandinavia, the Pyrenees, and the Alps, where independent homesteads seem to have predominated.

Basic conditions of daily life

Medieval people identified themselves primarily with a family unit, though one would be hard pressed to provide a description of the scope, size, and function of the family that would apply to all parts of Europe, or across the entirety of the twelfth century. In strictly economic terms, a family's organization serves the basic interest of helping feed its members, and as a result it necessarily had followed different patterns according to immediate conditions. During the demographic explosion of the eleventh and twelfth centuries, smaller households based on nuclear families proliferated. It has been suggested that a typical household comprised between three and seven people grouped around a husband and wife, but there was a wide variety of family configurations. Considerable doubt also remains about the place of marriage in family relations. Couples were married by mutual consent but with considerable direction from their families; lords often took it upon themselves to approve possible marriage matches, but there was not a single understanding of what the lord's role was (they certainly never exercised the so-called 'right of the first night').[18] In general, twelfth-century people viewed marriage as a practical contract, often pursued with a view to procreation, and it may be that many peasant couples were not formally married.[19]

Within the household, the position and status of women varied from slightly ambiguous to emphatically inferior. Laws in many parts of Europe explicitly gave husbands the right (sometimes presented as a duty) to inflict corporal punishment on their wives, and women laborers were paid on a decidedly inferior scale to that of their male counterparts. The division of labor, however, was not as straight-forward as is often imagined; women did not work solely in the 'private space' of the house, but in the fields as well, and not only sewed clothing but slaughtered animals. Since marriage was viewed as procreative, it makes sense that laws made some provision for preg-nant women, offering them exemption from hunting and fishing regulations.[20]

Peasant houses varied considerably by region, but the typical dwelling in rural villages consisted of a single room that was shared by human beings and animals. As the population increased and placed new lands under cultivation, the layout and construction of houses adapted. There was a general trend toward more complex building techniques, including frame constructions and stone or rubble foun-dations, with stone houses also becoming more common (they had always predominated in southern regions, where timber was com-paratively scarce). In northern Germany, long, narrow houses were constructed with stalls for animals, grain storage areas beneath the roof, and occasionally even distinct bedrooms at the far end. Hearths were a nearly universal component of medieval peasant houses, but proper chimneys were rare during this period, meaning that smoke perpetually hung in the air. Archaeology also indicates that peas-ant houses had adjoining yards that offered space for outbuildings, gardens, and livestock.[21]

Most people derived the bulk of their calories from grain, which they consumed as gruel or as bread. They most often ate the rougher grains, such as millet, rye, oats, barley and spelt, with wheat being more common in France and England than elsewhere. The nobility apparently preferred wheat bread, but they were not its sole con-sumers. Recent studies have suggested that the meat consumption of the peasantry increased markedly after the eleventh century, perhaps making up for 40 per cent of an individual's calories. Villagers tended to boil meat when they had it, and they ate not only muscles but also every type of organ meat imaginable. Despite general improvements in diet, however, villages were highly vulnerable to the vicissitudes of weather, and drought or cold could easily lead to famine, as it did several times in the twelfth century.[22]

Men and women alike wore cloaks and tunics whose design was simple, functional, and for the most part not gender-specific. In the rural areas, tunics tended to be short enough to give one's legs room to perform the necessary agricultural tasks, and were complemented by trousers, and an over-garment, such as a cloak made from animal hide. There does not seem to have been great variation across Europe in this regard, taking into account obvious allowances for differing climates. Social groups that did not perform manual labor, such as the clergy and the nobility, may have worn clothes that hung to the ankle as markers of status. A German chronicle of the mid-twelfth century claims that peasants were only to wear dark-colored clothing, and limited the amount of material used to make them. As social distinctions became clearer, then, regulations arose to use clothing to accentuate them.[23]

Rural society and the agricultural surplus

The traditional understanding of the rural economy depends on the system usually referred to as manorialism, under which free or servile farmers owed rent and services to their lord, who could be a lay noble, a bishop, or an abbot. A manor consisted of the land held by a lord, which he rented out to peasants in return for a share of their agricultural produce, as well as service obligations on the lord's land. Many, but far from all, manors included a military fortification, perhaps a small keep, which both provided protection and symbolized the lord's military responsibilities. Typically, a peasant would work the lord's own land, the demesne, for a given number of days per year. In addition to these rents and services, lords had the privilege of assessing a variety of 'seigneurial dues' on innumerable aspects of daily life. Peasants might pay a fee at the time of their marriage, when they inherited their tenancies, or when their spouses died. They were required to press wine at the lord's wine-press, grind their grain at his mill, and in some places to bake their bread in his oven, all of which entailed fees. In some areas the fruits of peasant gardens, as well as the produce of domestic animals like eggs and honey, could be subject to dues as well. In areas where lordship entailed jurisdictional privileges, lords collected fines that they (in their capacity as manorial judges) charged petty lawbreakers. Together, the combination of legal, economic, and military prerogatives of the lord made up what historians call the 'ban', which Robert Fossier usefully defined as 'the power to enforce one's will'.[24] The system, if it can be called

that, was customary and subject to abuse, and records show that peasants tried to lodge complaints when their lords or, more commonly,
their lords' agents, committed random acts of violence against them
or unjustly expropriated their goods.[25] Despite considerable regional
variation, most agriculture can be said to have depended on this general model of seigneurial organization, and it would help drive, and
be transformed by, great changes in agrarian life over the course of
the twelfth and thirteenth centuries.

At the heart of these changes, of course, lay demographic growth
and the slight but noticeable redistribution of the population into
urban communities whose inhabitants did not produce their own
food. These two developments together required that landowners and
their tenant farmers produce a greater food surplus in order to feed
the larger number of non-productive urban residents. The means
by which this surplus was acquired, however, is currently a matter of
dispute among historians. Until recently, a consensus view held that
technological innovations, namely, the heavy wheeled plow, the horse
collar, and the switch to three-field rotation, improved agricultural
yields to the point that a larger, increasingly urban population could
be supported. The new plows were more effective at turning over soil
in the wet, recently cleared lands of the north, and rotating three
fields instead of having one of two (and thus half the arable land)
lie fallow each year increased productivity. These changes have been
collectively called an 'agricultural revolution'. Recently, however, this
orthodoxy has been challenged as some studies show that the spread
of the plows is very hard to track with any precision, three-field agriculture hardly became universal, and that grain yields (the amount
of edible grains produced by each seed planted) in the twelfth century were comparable to those in the ninth. Thus, more scholars are
coming to attribute the increase in agricultural surplus to the greater
efficiency with which lords extracted it from their peasants, as well as
to a probable long-term improvement in climatic conditions.[26] Lords
stretched the power of the ban wherever possible to increase revenues, and also used the available workforce to clear new lands, which
added to their surplus potential. As a result, lords had additional surplus for luxury items, which could stimulate long-distance trade, and
for patronizing cultural production.[27] Certainly technology played its
role, and in some areas agricultural productivity was decisive, but economic development of the countryside cannot be explained through
a reductionist emphasis on technology. An evolutionary approach,
showing the interaction of a broad collection of social and legal
factors, sheds considerably more light on the problem.

The agricultural surplus encouraged a more widespread use of money in the economy and this, in turn, catalyzed changes in rural social relations. Needing cash to participate in the nascent market economy, lords began collecting their seigneurial dues in cash rather than in kind, and also began converting service dues to cash payments. As a result, lords either used hired labor for their demesne land, or, more often, effectively eliminated the demesne by renting it out to other peasants, a practice that was itself possible because of demographic growth. Another consequence, however, was an increase in social stratification among the peasantry. By the thirteenth century, many peasants had acquired enough of a cash surplus to buy additional fields and equipment and created an acute wealth disparity in their villages.

Peasants provided the workforce needed to clear and reclaim land for agriculture and also to work the arable land thus created. Land clearance could provide a chance to improve their legal, as well as their economic, position. In areas of intense expansion into new parts of Christendom, as in the Slav regions of Eastern Europe and in Iberia, lords encouraged settlement by offering new privileges to the villagers there. German princes would send out a kind of village planner called a *locator* to oversee the establishment of new villages with uniform plots of land.[28] The settlers who followed, sometimes coming from points far to the west, even Flanders, received favorable terms for their willingness to help clear land and extend the geographic extent of the princes' rule. In these new settlements manorial ties could be much weaker than in traditional areas. In one case in Germany, newly settled peasants worked their land rent-free for ten years. Often, princes made their goals quite explicit and issued calls to peasants, advising that 'whoever was oppressed by a shortage of land to farm should come with their families and occupy the good and spacious land [...]'[29] The opening of new lands offered new models of rural settlement, which depended on granting villages freedoms that had not previously been afforded peasants in many parts of Europe. The reality of rural life for most peasants, however, was subjection in economic, if not always legal, terms to the nobles who owned the bulk of the land, and who depended on peasant productivity for whatever comforts their status afforded.

Aristocratic life

The late twelfth-century collection of laws called the *Usatges of Barcelona* defined a noble as a person 'who eats wheaten bread daily

and rides a horse'.[30] Nobles, at least ideally, enjoyed a higher standard
of living and a better diet than their peers, and their status derived,
at least by the late twelfth century in most parts of Europe, from their
membership in a landholding military aristocracy.[31] Since around the
year 1000, knighthood, the profession of warriors mounted on horseback, had been gradually fusing with the aristocracy to the point that it
became a defining mark of noble standing.[32] Great lords almost always
needed able mounted warriors for local conflicts, especially in tenth-
and eleventh-century France, and, as result, the aristocracy made for
a highly fluid group with sometimes vague boundaries. In Germany,
knighthood developed differently, since some of the most important
mounted warriors, the *ministeriales*, were in fact of servile status and
sought to become *de facto* nobles by being endowed with their own
free fiefs. Although *ministeriales* (and warriors of servile status in other
parts of Europe) took on some attributes of knighthood, they were
regarded as a distinct class, and were only one option for the magnates
and kings in need of loyal servants.[33] In England as well, knighthood
became an attribute of the aristocracy, but commoners played major
roles in the kings' military organization. Presenting themselves as
mounted warriors, however, became a near obsession among the
aristocracy, and the seals of kings and lesser lords all tended to depict
them on horseback or with other marks of the knightly profession.
By the end of the twelfth century, French and English kings received
spurs during their coronation rituals.[34]

Contemporaries were well aware that aristocratic ideals did not
always mesh with realities. In the romance *Erec and Enide*, the poet
Chrétien de Troyes presents Enide's father as an impoverished man
of noble blood who had fallen on hard times.[35] Peter of Blois vigorously protested that his father was from the *optimates*, or 'best men',
despite having few financial resources.[36] Relatively speaking, however,
the landowners enjoyed a higher standard of living than the peasants
who worked their demesne lands, and they took the social distinction
quite seriously.

Lordship arose to address local problems, especially those related
to security, which became acute in Western Europe after the dis-
solution of Carolingian authority in the ninth and tenth centuries.
The aristocratic household thus had the dual function of providing
defense for the lord and his family and servants, and of projecting
his lordly status and authority; scholars have disagreed over the relative importance of castles as symbols and as strongholds. The lord, his
wife, and his closest supporters would sleep in a single room, sometimes termed a 'great hall', by night, and during the day the hall

would become a site of justice and perhaps courtly entertainment. Ideally, the lords in their capacity as warriors would be absent for considerable stretches, during which times authority might devolve to their wives. There are high-profile examples of this happening on the level of royal government, as when Matilda, the wife of King Henry I of England, served effectively as his regent while he was away in Normandy.[37]

By the mid-twelfth century, fiefs were regarded as heritable, and families became more likely to embrace the principle of primogeniture, according to which the inheritance would pass in its entirely to the eldest son. As a result, younger sons uninterested in or unsuited to ecclesiastical careers had to find other ways of acquiring revenue-producing territory, such as loyal service to a king or great magnate, marrying an heiress, or both. William Marshall, who rose from relatively humble (but still technically noble) beginnings to become Earl of Pembroke under Henry II and regent of England during the minority of Henry III, presents an outstanding case of such social mobility. William came to the attention of Henry II through the prowess he showed in tournaments and in battle against the king of France, and was rewarded by being admitted into the royal inner circle and ultimately married to the daughter of the earl of Pembroke.[38] Henry II's most famous ecclesiastical servant, Thomas Becket, the son of a London merchant and a true commoner, used his considerable political and administrative talents to become a great landholder and ultimately the archbishop of Canterbury.[39]

The contempt felt by some aristocrats toward the 'men raised from the dust' is a sign of the rising self-consciousness of a military order based on at least pretensions to distinguished lineage. Clerics similarly sought to set themselves apart from the warrior aristocracy by rejecting the proclivities of knights, and above all their favored leisure sport, hunting. In fact, rejecting hunting became something of a litmus test of a cleric's commitment to reform, and the Third and Fourth Lateran Councils both explicitly forbid both hunting and its subgenre of falconry. But the defining aristocratic pastime was probably the tournament, at which young aristocrats closely simulated battle conditions in a series of contests, the most characteristic being an all-out *melée* between opposing sides of knights trying to capture each other. Although the stereotypical man-to-man jousting of the popular imagination was rare in the twelfth century, there was some opportunity for individual feats of bravery; William Marshall helped make his name through such contests.[40] Hunting and tournaments were privileges of an elite, whose wealth depended on the exploitation of arable land and also symbols of the prevailing rural order. By the early twelfth century, however, new elites and power structures were emerging in towns and cities which were to intrude on traditional visions of the social order.

Towns and Cities

In twelfth-century Rome, about 30,000 people lived within the old city walls that had once housed perhaps a million. Vast stretches of the medieval city's acreage consisted of ruins or pastureland, which perfectly illustrated the de-urbanization of medieval society in the heart of the old Roman Empire. Rome and many other cities in Italy and southern France had been continually inhabited since antiquity, but they functioned primarily as administrative centers rather than industrial or commercial sites. Between the eleventh and thirteenth centuries, all parts of Europe saw significant re-urbanization, which was the product of population growth and the companion of great economic and social change. With respect to size, organization, and function, medieval towns and cities differed radically from, say, nineteenth-century centers of industrial production like Manchester, so it is important to clarify what one means by 'town' or 'city' in this context. As a socio-economic entity, a city is a parasite, a center of population which cannot feed itself and thus must acquire its subsistence through trade. Therefore, the agricultural surplus discussed in the previous section was an absolute prerequisite for urban life. As a legal entity, a town had privileges that had the general effect of removing it from the system of feudal obligations that governed the countryside, privileges that generally made it easier to engage in commerce. The records of the town of Toulouse illustrate this shift neatly: in the early twelfth century a town scribe would sign documents as a 'scribe of the count', but by 1186 he styled himself the 'public scribe of Toulouse'.[41] Sometimes towns were granted these privileges at an identifiable moment in a charter from a local lord or a king, but often, as in Italy, they simply became customary over time and were only later codified in writing.

In terms of population, the threshold for a town, as opposed to a large village, seems to be about 2000, but the activities of the inhabitants matter as much as their numbers. The everyday job of a person in a large or small population falls into one of three basic categories. 'Primary' occupations feed mouths, and thus include farming, fishing, and hunting. In a medieval village these represented the largest part of the population. Villages also necessarily included members of the 'secondary' occupations, which served the interests of either farming or daily life: blacksmiths, shoemakers, butchers, bakers, and such. Only in towns, however, does one find a large numbers of 'tertiary' workers: merchants, bankers, lawyers, teachers, and so on. These professions do not feed people, and as a result depend on other people growing food for them, which they can purchase so as not to starve. To discuss towns is not simply to talk about population displacement, but about changes in the way Europe fed and organized itself, and these changes in turn had a great impact on religion and culture.

The contours of urban Europe

By the middle of the twelfth century, major towns were a fact of European life from the British Isles to Russia, which itself had over 120. The location of a town depended to some degree on the nature of its founding. Some gradually sprang up near fortified sites like the residences of counts, or other cultural centers like monasteries. Bury-St Edmunds in England depended for its existence entirely on its namesake abbey, and St Omer in France also originated outside a monastery's gates. The *Annals of St Bertin*, on the other hand, describe how Bruges grew up around the castle of the count of Flanders:

> In order to satisfy the needs of the castle folk, there began to throng before his [i.e. the count's] gate near the castle bridge traders and merchants selling costly goods, the innkeepers to feed and house them doing business with the prince, who was often to be seen there; they built houses and set up inns where those who could not be put up at the castle were accommodated [...]. The houses increased to such an extent that there soon grew up a large town which in the common speech of the lower classes is still called 'Bridge'.[42]

The importance of fortification cannot be understated; while historians may define towns by their population or legal privileges, contemporaries may have been most struck by their walls, which in most parts of Europe were a town's most important feature.[43] In the case of old Roman towns, even those that declined to the point of nearly disappearing had the advantage of being near the intersection of the old Roman roads or perhaps the fortification of an old Roman wall, and thus were logical places for settlement when trade began to pick up the High Middle Ages. At Cologne, Mainz, Troyes, and Metz, all former Roman towns, the medieval city's development depended on these elements of ancient infrastructure as well as an ecclesiastical institution (either a monastery or a cathedral). Ports like Lübeck, Visby (on the island of Götland off the coast of Sweden), and the older towns like Marseilles, Venice, and Genoa, owed their prominence to their harbors, while Milan lay near to the Alpine passes.

In the east, as well as in Ireland and northern Iberia, great princes could create towns almost out of whole cloth by granting urban charters, which could convince potential settlers to migrate. When some of the towns east of the Elbe received such charters, they were already established economic centers, but others were scarcely larger than villages. This kind of legal urbanization, whereby official town status was granted to an existing population center, could be an instrument of conquest. In 1139, Alfonso VII of Castile conquered the Muslim-ruled town of Oreja, and granted it a charter to encourage Christians to move there. Dublin had been a town in the economic, though not legal sense of the word since it had been a major Viking center, but received a charter from Prince John of England some years after it had been captured by an expeditionary force sent by Henry II.[44] Since new towns invariably adopted the legal customs of older ones, urbanization served as a way of unifying disparate parts of Europe, as families of town law extended for hundreds of miles.[45]

The extent of urbanization ought not to be exaggerated. Europe was still overwhelmingly rural, and, in terms of both population and economic sophistication, its cities seriously lagged behind those of the Byzantine Empire and the Islamic world. Moreover, areas of concentrated urban settlement were relatively few, including a stretch from the English Channel to the North Sea and up the Rhine, and northern Italy. Because of their unique legal features and economic importance, they had a role in shaping Europe's social and cultural character out of proportion to their relative size.

Town organization and government

In 1115, the people of Laon rioted. According to Guibert of Nogent, the men of the city began shouting 'Commune!' early one afternoon and then attacked the palace of the bishop Gaudry, who disguised himself as a servant and attempted to escape. As his friends and servants tried to fend off the mob with stones and arrows, Gaudry was hunted down. Guibert had held Gaudry's piety in low regard, and described his death rather graphically: 'one man by the name of Bernard [. . .] raised up a two-headed axe and savagely dashed the brains out of his holy yet sinful head'.[46] The corpse was subsequently mutilated. As for the perpetrators, Guibert had earlier told his readers,

> 'Commune', however, was a new name, and the worst possible one, for what it was: all those in a servile condition would pay their usual debt of servitude to the lords once a year, and if contrary to the terms of the agreement they were in any way delinquent, they would make regular payments as compensation; payment of all other taxes normally inflicted on serfs would be canceled. The people welcomed this opportunity to pay their own ransom, and handed over enormous piles of money to clog so many greedily gaping maws.[47]

Although Guibert was clearly shocked by the violence that could attend medieval social change, he did not realize the full implications of the term 'commune', since, far beyond merely freeing townsmen from seigneurial dues, it represented a form of town governance that gave power to the wealthy merchant of the city. 'Commune' tends to connote the sworn organizations of town elites that, over the course of the twelfth century, wielded a new kind of political power, and it has become a kind of shorthand for the legal framework of medieval towns in most parts of Europe. The bishop of Laon opposed his town's commune, but many other prelates encouraged them, since the details of a charter could benefit all parties. It was often, in fact, through the efforts of bishops or nobles that charters were secured to codify the relationship between the town and its overlord, generally in ways that encouraged trade. One of the most famous town charters, that of William Clito, Count of Flanders, for St Omer, is frequently cited as a summary of the kind of privileges that burghers sought. In this case, Count William granted the merchants freedom from a number of tolls and feudal dues, and regulated the repayment of loans.[48]

Kings also encouraged towns (and indeed Louis VI of France confirmed the St Omer charter), because a well-crafted charter could give them a direct source of revenue, free from the involvement of the local nobility. The charter for Lorris drawn up by King Louis VII of France, for example, exempted burghers from certain taxes and tolls, granted them free and secure passage to fairs, where they could buy and sell goods, and gave them a say in the selection of the king's provost, who looked to royal interests in the towns.[49] In Germany the emperors took an interest in urban development, and several imperial palace towns became important trading centers. Great princes also presided over urban growth, and they competed with each other for control of towns such as Lübeck, where Duke Henry the Lion of Saxony effectively seized it from Count Adolf II of Holstein in 1159 after his attempt to set up a rival town failed. Henry recruited settlers and traders from the Rhineland and sent representatives to rulers around the Baltic, offering them favorable trading arrangements.[50]

Even great lords like Henry the Lion, however, had to negotiate with the burgesses, who invariably acquired some kind of self-government. Communes generally included some kind of ruling council, whose members might be called *meliores* ('better men') or, in Italy, senators or consuls. These were elite bodies that are with good reason referred to as 'merchant oligarchies'. In Italy, such governments had been established well before 1100, and they successfully protected their liberties against encroachment by Frederick Barbarossa in the 1160s. The Italian merchant oligarchs to a certain degree had fused with the local nobility, and in no part of Europe were local aristocrats completely shut out of communes. In Venice, the doge effectively ran the city government, which had all the trappings of an aristocracy. This is worth noting if only to make clear that such communal bodies were a far cry from popular representative institutions. Still, by 1200, many towns had developed the basic institutions required for self-government, and written urban records survive from towns from London to Novgorod, where letters dealing with commerce survive on birch bark.[51] In Toulouse, the consuls had acquired considerable rights to act as judges and legislators in the 1180s and 1190s and could guarantee legal due process for its citizens.[52]

Merchants and craftsmen also began to regulate their professions in ways that overlapped with town governance, above all through sworn associations variously referred to as confraternities or guilds. Originally, guilds were groups of people who organized themselves to venerate a saint: confraternities devoted to the Virgin Mary were especially popular. The craft and professional guilds seem to have evolved gradually from these antecedents until they became a major force in town life and in the regulation of work and commerce. It is possible that as members of a specific trade began to occupy the same neighborhood, a confraternity that initially served a particular parish took on a professional character.[53] The earliest documents often do not use the language of guilds and confraternities and instead show merely that men of a trade were seeking basic privileges. A 1106 charter from the bishop of Worms lists 23 fishermen by name and essentially gives them control over the wholesale market; other men were allowed to catch fish, but they had to sell their catch to one of the 23.[54] Most of the earliest documents establishing or regulating guilds are grants of privilege from a bishop or king, which suggests that the professionals and craftsmen of the town still depended on traditional sources of authority for much of the twelfth century. That is, the urban environment required adaptation from the elites of the old order even as it spawned social structures that reflected new economic realities.

Guilds were comprised of the masters of each trade, and perhaps the most important thing they regulated was their membership. Young boys generally started as apprentices and then after years of training became journeymen (so named not because they travelled but because they worked for a day, or *journée* in French), whom the masters hired as needed for a fixed term, generally for a wage—they represent a major stage in the development of wage labor in the West. Upon completion of a 'masterpiece', the craftsman could formally join the guild. This tidy line of succession, however, may never have been closely followed, and by the end of the thirteenth century, hereditary could be the determining factor in guild membership. While guild statutes did make some stipulations about working conditions, they generally served the interests of the masters, who should be seen as producers and employers rather than workers.

Urban life

In twelfth-century sources, city life had acquired a number of meanings, and cities themselves had become powerful metaphors. After a visit to Paris in the 1160s, John of Salisbury gushed about Paris in a letter to his friend Thomas Becket:

> And there I saw such a quantity of food; a people so happy; such respect for the clergy; the splendor and dignity of the whole Church; the tasks so diverse of the students of philosophy—saw and marveled at it, as Jacob marveled at the ladder whose summit reached to Heaven [...][55]

Just a few decades later, however, the monk Richard of Devizes, in a passage that has become famous and widely quoted, complained that he did 'not at all like London', for it was a den of

> actors, jesters, smooth-skinned lads, Moors, flatterers, pretty boys, effeminates, pederasts, singing and dancing girls, quacks,

belly-dancers, sorcerers, extortioners, night-wanderers, magicians, mimes, beggars [and] buffoons.[56]

Both John and Richard had good points. Cities had turned themselves into centers of high and low culture alike, and by the end of the century, religious figures of both orthodox and heretical stripes were beginning to take notice of urban poverty. Moralists found plenty to be horrified at, and not just in the realm of sexual license (and indeed, the statutes of Arles and Avignon both acknowledged and regulated prostitution in the thirteenth century[57]). Usury, crime, and unfamiliar social arrangements, as well as new professions, caused considerable anxiety. The abundance of choices inevitably created fundamental moral dilemmas.[58]

The urban poor lived in cramped conditions, but in residences with fewer inhabitants than in typical peasant houses. Most dwellings for the poor were windowless, and often on the second floor of a building highly vulnerable to fire, though masonry structures became more common during the twelfth century; in the early thirteenth century, construction techniques allowed for taller buildings. The urban elites especially in northern Italy overlapped somewhat with the nobility, and at any rate their living conditions were somewhat better than those of the poor. They probably made use of available technology to provide fresh water, which was not an object of public works projects until the thirteenth century. Still, all members of society dealt with the constant dangers of fire, poor sanitation, wells that periodically were polluted, and massive piles of garbage and human waste. Over the course of the century, authorities clearly became aware of the problems presented by this state of affairs. Some municipalities, such as London, did establish public latrines by 1100.[59] After 1212 London required that its residences have roofs made of tile rather than thatch or straw, which indicates that large-scale fires were both common and greatly feared.[60] Given all the stresses associated with urban life, it is not surprising that low fertility rates prevailed in most cities, and they depended on a steady flow of immigrants from the countryside. Perhaps half of the population of some twelfth-century cities was born elsewhere.

Even if they were physically removed from the local warfare that could afflict the countryside, the cities were not without their political tensions, and one aspect of the urban landscape that would surprise many modern students was its intense fortification. Families of means constructed towers, often of great height to dominate their neighborhoods and protect their interests. Genoa and Pisa are said to have had hundreds, and, while they were most common in Italian cities, they also appeared in the Low Countries and parts of France. Like castles in the countryside, such towers, rising in exceptional cases to over 90 meters, served both practical and symbolic purposes. After visiting Genoa in the 1160s, the Spanish Jew and travel writer Benjamin of Tudela wrote that 'each householder has a tower to his house and at times of strife they fight from the tops of the towers with each other'.[61] When citizens or nobles used these towers for defense it generally meant a private dispute had escalated into violence, and that public forms of conflict resolution were not effective; they thus testify to the relative weakness of public authority in some urban areas.

Trade, Commerce, and Economic Growth

The cities of the twelfth century depended on the growth of trade and an economy based on the use of money rather than barter, which still played an important role in the exchange of goods. Initially the agricultural surplus of the countryside provided the basis of the urban economy, but as long-distance trade expanded, individuals and towns began to profit from importing and exporting, as well as the production of finished goods, especially textiles. Between the eleventh and thirteenth centuries, Europe experienced what has been called a 'commercial revolution', during which the diffusion of money, the increased growth of trade, and the development of institutions to support it transformed Western society. Although some European industries grew spectacularly, they did so only after the mechanics of commerce were created. Trade seems to have been the precursor to industry, rather than vice-versa.

The revival of coinage

In the early Middle Ages, with the exception of late eighth and early ninth centuries when Carolingian silver circulated fairly widely, the economy operated without the benefit of widely available hard currency. Precious metals were stored as treasure rather than sources of exchangeable specie, and local trade proceeded through barter and payments in kind. This changed during the eleventh century, as mints began to operate in earnest again; the royal mints in England produced some twenty million pennies around the year 1000. Mines in central Europe were exploited eagerly but became depleted by around 1050, just as Italian trade with the eastern Mediterranean was having a slight ripple effect in the west. Because most areas in the west, Italy included, lacked an obvious trade commodity, the net flow of precious metals could only be southward and eastward, to the Byzantine Empire and the Islamic world. Still, the economic recovery continued because the traders were resourceful when it came to finding solutions to the lack of coinage. Italian merchants frequently resorted to debasing currency with other metals like copper, and a Genoese document of 1156 promises that a debt will paid in either pepper or coin.[62] And, as will be discussed below, instruments of credit could also allow smaller amounts of cash to cover larger transactions. When new mines were opened in several parts of Europe (but most famously Freiburg, allegedly named after the freedoms granted to miners there) in the 1160s, another boom resulted, which not only stimulated the economy but caused severe inflation. The increased volume of coinage certainly had something to do with the three-fold rise in bread prices between 1180 and 1220, though increased demand because of the new concentration of people in towns also contributed. The greater availability of silver was accompanied by its minting into larger denominations than the traditional penny, as well as the appearance of gold coins, which had become extremely rare, especially in the north.[63]

These changes had profound consequences. Society needed an adequate supply of coin, for instance, if labor services were to be changed to cash payments and if rents-in-kind were to be converted to cash rents.[64] The increased use of money, and its potential for abuse, also alarmed some social critics, who invariably associated it with pollution and filth. A Latin lyricist of the mid-century wrote a satirical poem, 'Sir Penny', which conveys awe at the power of cold hard cash to effect both good and bad: 'The hand that holds a heavy purse/makes right of wrong, better of words/Sir Penny binds all bargains fast/Rough is smooth when he has passed.'[65] In this case, satire identified an issue that was also becoming prominent in canon law and other aspects of culture. As will be discussed below, anxiety over the role of cash in the new economy would result in a great deal of social critique of merchants and bankers, but also of Europe's Jews.

Trading areas and their goods

Coins are a tangible and traceable element in the growth of trade, and as such they were considered first here, but the true explosion in the use of the monetary medium took place relatively late in the twelfth century. Urbanization and economic expansion started at the local level at a scale far smaller than that of the long-distance trade of the Italian city-states. The most spectacular change in twelfth-century economic life may have been the linking of local trading networks into regional, and then hemispheric ones.

These regional economies tended to specialize in particular goods or products, although for many regions, including Picardy, southern England, the eastern Baltic, and German lands east of the Elbe, the primary export was surplus grain. Picardy, for instance, provided the grain supply that allowed Flanders to become the most urbanized region in Western Europe. Northern England raised sheep and shipped wool abroad, especially to Flanders, where the weavers of Bruges, Ghent, and other towns turned it into cloth (England had its own smaller and, at the time, less famous textile industry). Several regions in France began to specialize in wine, to the point that a visitor to Bordeaux gazed at miles and miles of vineyards and wondered what the locals ate (presumably grain from adjacent regions). Scandinavia and Eastern Europe were rich in furs and timber, and Poland became known for providing salt, which was in demand essentially everywhere. The Italian cities operated primarily as importers and exporters, passing on silks, spices, and other luxuries from the East (including as far away as China via central Asian intermediaries) and from Muslim Iberia and North Africa. Venice had some success marketing the armor it produced, and Piacenza made fustian fabric from Egyptian cotton. Constantinople served as the Mediterranean *entrepot* for many goods from Asia and the Islamic world, but Italians traded with Muslims in Tunisia and the now Christian island of Sicily. The Crusader port of Acre gradually became a trading center along with Alexandria in Egypt, while the Italians began to access the Asian trade through settlements around the Black Sea.

During the early Middle Ages, northern trade had focused on three major networks: those around the English Channel, the North Sea, and Baltic Sea. The south depended on the much more complexly interrelated networks of the Mediterranean, into which the Italian cities became linked as early as the ninth century. By 1100, trade revived in all of these areas. Rarely can we track the precise moment at which traders from one town arrived in another one far away, so again the model must be one of gradual evolution based on opportunism. Throughout the twelfth century, however, diverse regions were linked together through the exchange of both raw materials and finished products. People, as well as their goods, also traveled great distances, and foreign merchants became permanent fixtures in most major cities, with veritable merchant diasporas springing up across the Mediterranean. Venetian merchants established themselves all over the Mediterranean, of course, but they also made their way to London and Flanders by mid-century. The various regional networks interlocked to the extent that most of Christendom, as well as the Islamic areas of North Africa and the Middle East, became linked by trade. English families settled to do business in Genoa; Flemish cloth found its way to Sicily, Constantinople, Syria, Alexandria, and North Africa; silks and precious stones from points east were sold in Constantinople and then travelled to London via Regensburg, which itself sent merchants to Kiev. At Visby one could find textiles from Ypres along with goods from Constantinople that had come by way of Smolensk.[66]

As Henry the Lion's forceful takeover of Lübeck demonstrates, inter-city trade often spread through violence, and in Italy, papal and imperial power were brought to bear on urban politics. In 1168, the papacy effectively created the town of Alessandria to stymie Frederick Barbarossa's power there. The rival cities Venice, Pisa, and Genoa repeatedly fought to expand their trading empires at the expense of each other, and Genoa's quarter in Constantinople was destroyed in the 1170s. Pisa assisted Iberian monarchs in several stages of the *Reconquista* in return for trading privileges in the towns.[67] In 1201, a military expedition sent by the bishop of Bremen founded Riga and established a military order to help defend it. German conquest of the Baltic pagans, considered part of the 'Northern Crusades', was always accompanied by the establishment of trading centers.[68]

Historians have long debated the precise relationship between trading and the crusades, and they universally reject the notion that the Christian expeditions to the Levant were trade wars in disguise. Merchants from Pisa, Genoa, and Venice aided the crusades, and there is no reason to suspect their motives were venal rather than religious. They did secure some trading privileges in the Holy Land, but the ones that Venice had from Constantinople before the First Crusade, and which they forced the emperor to confirm in the 1120s, were more important to its merchants' operations. By the end of the century, however, Italians set up trading arrangements with both the Christians at Acre and their Muslim enemies at Alexandria.[69] But crusade and commerce joined together most spectacularly in 1204, when the Doge of Venice managed to divert the army of the Fourth Crusade first to Zara, a trading city off the Dalmatian coast whose trade it wished to control, and then to Constantinople, which was sacked and turned into the capital of a short-lived (to 1261) Latin Empire. Needless to say, Venice quickly secured highly favorable privileges from the new emperor, and received three-eighths of the empire's territory (the doge even began styling himself 'Lord of One Quarter and One Half of the Empire of Romania'[70]).

Markets, fairs, and the mechanics of trade

Such grand international enterprise rested on a base of regional and local trade. Markets, defined as places for the exchange of goods, either through barter or cash payment, never disappeared from the European scene; very active emporia sent goods across the North Sea and the English Chanel during the Carolingian period. In the eleventh century, the growth of the agricultural surplus allowed the seigneurial class of Western Europe to nurture a demand for products such as wine and woolen textiles that required a trading infrastructure. The classic expression of this infrastructure was the system of fairs that gathered buyers and sellers, first from specific regions, and then from all over Europe, most famously in Champagne.

Just as guilds emerged from religious confraternities, so fairs seem to have arisen out of religious festivals (*feria* in Latin) held at particular times of the year. They are documented in northern Italy from the ninth century on, and by the late eleventh century they had developed in parts of Germany, England, and Flanders, where traders from the growing towns could trade textiles for cheese, wine, and other agrarian products. In the late twelfth century, long-distance trade in Western Europe was dominated by the series of six fairs held in the county of Champagne, which was perfectly located to bring together merchants from Flanders, England, the North Sea trading networks, and the Italians, who began attending by the 1170s. Because the balance of trade strongly favored the Italians, it is not surprising that the heyday of the fairs came after the mining boom of the late 1160s, which gave the northern merchants the silver necessary to make up the deficit in goods. The counts of Champagne carefully nurtured the fairs and one of them shrewdly decided to grant privileges to the Italian traders in the 1170s, which was another reason for their late-century take-off.[71] The fairs show the complex interaction of various elements in the economy: the agrarian surplus created by the exploitative manorial relationship between lord and peasant was distributed to lords and to towns, both of which had a demand for products from afar. In the late thirteenth century, advances in naval technology allowed the Italians to sail directly to northern points, which sent the fairs into steep decline and then obsolescence in the later Middle Ages.

Merchants at the fairs came up with ways of streamlining trade by limiting the number of actual transactions, including rudimentary credit instruments called fair letters. The merchant making a purchase would issue a promissory note to the seller, who would then hold it until the last fair of the year, when accounts payable came due. Although these letters do not seem to have been interest bearing, they did allow for smooth paper-transfers of money rather than ungainly exchanges of large amounts of silver. The Italian merchants of the early thirteenth century, however, would begin to engage in business practices that anticipate modern arrangements. Here, however, they had to work with, or around, an existing cultural impediment: canon law had strict prohibitions on usury, defined as any interest on a loan, which most Christians followed, save for a few well-documented exceptions.[72] According to the prevailing interpretation, Jesus had effectively outlawed the collection of interest on loans in Luke 6:35: 'Do good, and lend, hoping for nothing thereby'. As the economic life picked up in the twelfth century, the Church became increasingly emphatic that usury was a serious crime against one's fellow man, bringing certain damnation.[73] The laws against usury served a humane purpose in the predominantly agrarian early Middle Ages, when desperate farmers or laborers could find themselves forced to take out 'consumption loans' in order to feed themselves during difficult times.[74] Since the money acquired thereby was consumed rather than invested, it was nearly impossible to repay and tended to reduce the debtor to even more dire straits. Long distance trade and economic expansion, however, depended on making lending attractive through the promise of a return, and canon law did not make exceptions at the time for business loans.

Before the general acceptance of interest-earning loans as elements in business ventures (which was achieved long after our period), businessmen, as well as secular rulers in need of funds, tried a number of alternatives. First, there was a group of people within Christian Europe that did not fall under the ban on usury, namely Jews. By unhappy coincidence the surge in anti-Jewish fervor that accompanied the First Crusade coincided with increased involvement of Jews in the medieval economy. Christians had mostly tolerated their Jewish neighbors, who were relatively common in southern Europe throughout the early medieval period but established communities in France, Germany, and then England by the late eleventh centuries. They might have been involved in agriculture, but increasingly migrated to the towns; since they were emphatically excluded from the agrarian aristocracy, but typically literate, urban life and urban professions clearly suited them. Over the course of the twelfth century they became associated, above all, with the business of moneylending, and thus with the practice of usury. As alien communities who seemed to benefit from this unsavory byproduct of economic growth, Jews found themselves in an increasingly vulnerable position in European towns. The problems stemming from this will be discussed in greater detail in Chapter 3, below. In many parts of Europe Jewish moneylenders indeed supplied the credit necessary for investment in trade, but by the mid-thirteenth century persecution and a combination of creativity and spiritual nonchalance on the part of Christian entrepreneurs made them a minority even in the banking business. The Jews of England, moreover, were marginalized as moneylenders and often rendered destitute by the repeated default of their primary debtors, the kings.[75]

The schemes through which Christian merchants avoided the ban on usury may have, on occasion, been sheer tricks of accounting. In 1182, a Genoese banker named Alcherio signed a contract of exchange that reports that he 'received from you, Martina Corrgia, a number of deniers for which I promise to pay, personally or through my messenger or to your accredited messenger, £9s.13½ Pavese [Pavian currency] before the next feast of St Andrew.' Another contract refers to a debtor having received an unspecified 'amount of exchange', while the amount to be repaid is explicitly mentioned.[76]

The first Italians to operate as bankers, in the sense of individuals who took deposits and lent them out to others, were merchants whose trade had netted them the extra cash necessary to do so. Thus, some merchants undertook their own voyages while loaning out money for others. By the twelfth century, many merchants were employing a credit instrument now referred to as the 'sea loan', which gave the borrower the money to undertake an overseas trade mission. After the successful completion of the voyage, he would pay back the loan plus the premium, a return not initially condemned as usurious because it was regarded as a compensation for risk (the sea loan would be declared usury by Pope Gregory IX in 1236). The most important innovation in trade, however, was the *commenda* contract, which seems to have antecedents in the Byzantine and Islamic worlds. Under such a contract the sleeping (non-traveling) partner would provide a set share of the capital for a commercial venture (usually two-thirds) in return for an agreed upon share of the profits (three-fourths if he invested all of the capital, half, if he invested two-thirds).[77] The traveling merchant thus provided less of the capital but stood to lose the time spent on the voyage in the event of shipwreck or another sort of loss. These contracts allowed investors to spread their risk around in exchange for excellent returns, and are regarded as an ancestor of modern joint-stock companies. The profits from these, and increasingly more complicated ventures, allowed for the rise of great banking families, especially in inland cities like Florence; it was not until well after our period that German banking families came to prominence, but towns like Lübeck were increasingly aggressive in establishing long distance trade in the eastern Baltic after 1200.[78] Lübeck's expansion, linked as it was to the crusading movement, shows how elite policy, population growth, migration, and religious fervor intertwined as Europeans adapted to twelfth-century material conditions. These factors also helped condition a complex set of cultural responses which are the subject of the next chapter.

Chapter 3: *Spirituality and Its Discontents*

In 1226, a ten-year-old Flemish girl named Margaret noticed a crucifix hanging in a church and realized that she had not done enough to repay the sacrifice Jesus made for her on the cross. She then 'wept most bitterly and at once went alone into the forest and, stripping naked, wounded herself with thorns even to the shedding of blood'.[1] Margaret would continue to scourge her body, observe absolute poverty, and receive visits from Jesus—he showed her a vision of her heart as an immaculate chapel at one point—until her death at age 21. She never joined an organized religious foundation, but shared her spirituality with the lay world. While her stories seem extraordinary, they were not unheard of, and reflect a general proliferation of dynamic and emotional piety in the High Middle Ages. In some respects, Margaret (known by the toponym 'of Ypres') experienced something similar to what the monk Anselm of Canterbury had pleaded for in the 1090s when he begged Christ: 'will you not make it up to me for not [...] having kissed the place of the wounds where the nails pierced, for not having sprinkled with tears of joy the scars that prove the truth of your body?'[2] The monk and the girl each revered the body of Christ and celebrated the humanity they shared with him; Anselm expounded on these ideas in explicitly theological tracts, but the experience of women like Margaret shows that they were diffused throughout the wider culture. In and out of religious institutions, Europeans explored new ways of channeling their spiritual energies, while ecclesiastical leadership adapted itself when it was possible, and developed means of oppression when it was not.

Margaret neatly embodies several important currents in twelfth-century religious life, including women's piety and a fascination with the physical sufferings of Christ. One should approach her story with a certain degree of caution, since it comes to us in a hagiography by a man, Thomas of Cantimpré, who projected his own ideals on his subjects, many of whom were women to whom he attributed extraordinary deeds.[3] But the mere fact that Thomas saw fit to disseminate her example meant that her devotion, if not all of her actions, resonated with mainstream trends in lay piety. In general, literate clerical authors tell us little about the religious experience of the most ordinary Europeans, and in the case of heretics we encounter them almost entirely in unremittingly hostile sources. What is clear is that both in and outside of monasteries, people were making a number of choices about their spirituality, and those choices reflected and encouraged major shifts in religious attitudes.

Although eleventh-century movements such as ecclesiastical reform and the Peace of God certainly radiated spiritual energy, scholars have long identified the twelfth century as a period of spiritual awakening and renewal.[4] This awakening manifested itself through a surge in the creation of new religious orders, including some that were especially suited to changed demographic and economic conditions; increasing evidence of lay piety outside the cloistered monasteries, some of which came in the form of heretical movements (one historian remarked that 'reform and heresy were twins'[5]); and increased concern with identifying and practicing the key components of a shared Christian life. In the last 30 years, scholars have more carefully studied the darker side of these changes: many of the same figures who inspired their coreligionists with pious zeal also encouraged the repression of the non-orthodox or otherwise deviant. Jewish communities experienced large-scale pogroms for the first time in 1095, and suffered a decline in their fortunes in the Latin West that would last up to and well beyond the Black Death of 1348. At the same time, secular and ecclesiastical authorities alike increased their efforts at repressing religious dissent, culminating in the so-called Albigensian Crusade against heretics in southern France during the early thirteenth century. Whether this repression was an unfortunate aberration from the reform movement, or its logical culmination, is perhaps a matter of opinion. What is certain is that options for religious expression, and the vitality with which it was conveyed, intensified after the middle of the eleventh century, and authorities and individuals responded in novel and sometimes unexpected ways. In 1215, the Fourth Lateran Council attempted to come to terms with the spiritual dynamism of the previous century and laid down directives for the Christian life that held sway until the Counter-Reformation.

Even the most orthodox of sources often betray more than a little tension between individual spirituality and the expectations of authorities, for existing structures were being adapted to a changed religious landscape.

Patterns of Religious Experience

Since the second half of the twentieth century, scholars have puzzled over the nature of everyday Christian devotion in medieval and early modern Europe. Since most Christians could not read or write, but our sources for the material are almost entirely written, it has been very difficult to determine how they followed their religion, or, more controversially, precisely what religion they followed. In a particularly radical formulation, the Reformation scholar Jean Delumeau argued that the European countryside was only marginally Christianized and populated by 'pseudo-pagans' until after the Council of Trent (1545–1563).[6] Although most scholars allow that residual pagan elements influenced religious practice throughout the Middle Ages, few go as far as Delumeau. Most accept that people in towns and villages alike were recognizably Christian insofar as they believed in a creator God who intervened in the natural world and whose son Jesus had died for the redemption of mankind.[7] Instances of popular enthusiasm, such as the lay response to the First Crusade, indicate that people from all classes had at least some shared Christian identity—the devotional similarity between Anselm of Canterbury and Margaret of Ypres reflects more than just the clerical prejudices of Thomas de Cantimpré's hagiography.

It is impossible to generalize about the nature of Christian practice throughout twelfth-century Europe, but a great deal of evidence suggests that Europeans practiced a vigorous faith that assimilated diverse Christian, classical, and (in the north) Germanic elements. An oft-cited example of this syncretism comes from a late eleventh-century manuscript from England that includes a series of charms intended to heal sickness, ensure safe childbirth, and bring about good harvests. One promises a cure for diarrhea, if one will only wreath the patient's neck with a parchment bearing an inscription that is obvious gibberish (meant to sound like Latin), with some Anglo-Saxon words added. The illiterate laymen and women who formed the likely audience for the charm must have had some understanding of the sacral quality of Latin scripture, even though the precise words meant essentially nothing. An earlier, far more elaborate charm instructs farmers how to improve their fields' fertility. It instructs them to take sods of earth from the afflicted land, along with some agricultural produce and trees, sprinkle holy water on them, then subject them to an elaborate ritual in a church. The charm continues with an incantation to 'Erce, Erce, mother of Earth', as well as 'the almighty Eternal Lord', mixed with Latin scriptural passages ('be fruitful and multiply'). This kind of blending of 'white magic' with Christian practice certainly attracted the suspicion of some Church authorities, but it does speak to a sincere and practical piety, and to a rich and sometimes contradictory set of religious influences.[8] The twelfth-century Church, in response to some of these idiosyncrasies, made a concerted effort to define and standardize the Christian life throughout Europe in traditionally Christian regions as well as the recently converted lands of the north and east. The vehicle for this effort was the ordained clergy, who had the responsibility of interpreting and disseminating knowledge of the scriptures, and of administering the sacraments of the Catholic faith.

The literate clergy and its organization

By the end of the twelfth century, most Europeans lived reasonably close to a parish church, where they directly encountered the Christianity theoretically overseen by the papacy. In principle, an ordained priest would preside over the parish, perform the necessary sacraments, and bury the dead. All these tasks required that he know at least the basics of the Latin language, though there was wide variation in the literacy levels of parish clergy. While a few trained at urban schools, many clearly struggled for the basic grammatical competence necessary to make it through the liturgy. The ordained clergy represented the universal Church as well as the Latinity that bound it together. In contemporary Latin, the terms *clericus* ('cleric', or 'clerk') and *litteratus* ('literate man', or 'man of letters') were essentially interchangeable; clergy said mass in a language foreign to themselves and utterly incomprehensible to their congregations (except in regions like Italy where the vernacular was still somewhat close to Latin). Although the liturgy was in Latin, sermons, when they were delivered at all, were in the vernacular: a French-born priest in early thirteenth-century London admitted he had stopped giving sermons because he never learned English properly.[9] There is also some evidence for vernacular translations of scripture, which were regarded as appropriate vehicles for instruction, in most parts of Europe.[10]

The male clergy, through its learning and its ordination, had a monopoly on the keys to salvation, that is, the sacraments of baptism, communion, confirmation, ordination, penance, and extreme unction (last rites), and marriage. There were some exceptions. Midwives, for instance, could be called upon to perform a baptism in an emergency, and many marriages were sanctioned by family rather than clergy. Over the course of the twelfth century, canon lawyers worked out unanswered questions, until by 1215 they had established a reasonably coherent sacramental theology that exalted the role of the clergy. As a result, the Church reform movement that had developed in the eleventh century continued to stress that the clergy were fundamentally different from laymen and held to different standards of conduct. Twelfth- and thirteenth-century councils repeatedly implored clerics not to hunt, gamble, drink excessively, keep concubines (or marry, which was common enough), or to help secular government in anything that could lead to the shedding of blood. Although the reforms never took hold everywhere, by the thirteenth century the Church had undergone a significant process of clericalization and had at least driven home the point the clergy played a special role in society.

The purity required by this special role had significant consequences for attitudes toward sexuality and gender. Clergy needed to be men, but men who renounced their male sexuality—the distinction between laymen and clerics in this respect hinged on sex. The ban on clerical marriage had seldom been enforced prior to the eleventh century, but now the Church strove to ensure, insofar as was possible, a celibate clergy. Women in turn became regarded as grave threats to the ritual purity of the Church as a whole, even as they participated in the religious life and became saints in greater numbers than in any previous period of Christian history.[11]

The clergy who presided over local parishes were tied to the larger Church through the organizational system in which bishops presided over a diocese. Dioceses varied greatly in their size and organization. In medieval Italy there were hundreds, while in England there were fewer than 20. In frontier areas, newly established bishoprics became effective agents of colonization and conversion.[12] While their size and purpose differed depending on their region, age, and relations with the secular powers, dioceses everywhere formed the primary unit of large-scale ecclesiastical organization. Bishops had jurisdictional and sacramental authority over their dioceses and periodically undertook (or delegated their archdeacons to undertake) visitations of the local clergy. As we have seen, however, bishops were also great landholders and could easily become involved in struggles with lay powers at the local and regional level.

As the bishop of Rome and hence the heir of St Peter, who was purportedly martyred there, the pope claimed authority over all Christendom. Constantly citing Jesus's declaration that 'thou art Peter and on this rock I will build my church' (Matthew 16:18), the papacy sought to standardize Christian thought and practice, and was partially successful at this between 1095 and 1229. Some of the most important popes of the Middle Ages—Paschal II (1099–1118), Alexander III (1159–1181), and Innocent III (1198–1216)—ruled during this period. They made their presence felt throughout Europe by sending legates to represent their personal authority whenever a pressing matter arose. Henry II's penance at Avranches, for example, was overseen by the legates of Alexander III. The popes of the twelfth century gained firm acceptance of their role as leaders of Latin Christendom and oversaw a gradual codification of uniform beliefs and practices. Changes in, for example, the protocol for canonization, which affected all believers, came about through papal initiative. In other ways, however, the papacy had to adapt to changes originating from among the faithful.

Devotion to the human Christ

Popes claimed that they were the true vicars of Christ through the 'Petrine Commission', whereby Jesus had given Peter power to 'bind and loose' in earth and heaven. The clergy's authority was increasingly bound to its crucial role presiding over the miracle of the Eucharist, in which the communion bread and wine was transformed, that is, transubstantiated, into the real body and blood of Christ. Both in terms of doctrine and devotional practice, the human, suffering Christ took on a central focus in the Christian experience of both clergy and laymen and laywomen. Anselm of Canterbury had laid out a coherent theological foundation for the importance of Christ's humanity in his 'Meditation on Human Redemption' (1100), describing Him as 'the good friend who redeemed you and set you free by laying down his life for you'. The sin of the first man, Adam, against God, had utterly wrecked human nature, to the point that no person tainted with that sin could possibly atone for it. On the other hand, fairness dictated that the debt incurred by sin be repaid by a human. The only one who could pay off the debt was Jesus—fully man, fully God, and born without sin: 'a man hangs from a cross and lifts the load of death from the human race', as Anselm put it.[13] So while God still appeared as the terrifying and just judge of the Old Testament, God's human-ity could mitigate the terror one felt at His certain judgment. The German abbess Hildegard of Bingen echoed the sense of wonder at Christ's sacrifice through vivid light imagery when she recounted a vision:

> And I saw a light-filled man emerge from the aforesaid dawn and pour his brightness over the aforesaid darkness; it repulsed him; he turned blood-red and pallid, but struck back against the dark-ness with such force that the man lying in the darkness became visible and resplendent through this contact, and standing up, he came forth out of the darkness. And thus the light-filled man, who had emerged from the dawn, appeared in greater splendor than any human tongue can express, and he proceeded to the utmost heights of glory, where he shone out wondrously in the fullness of great fragrance and fruitfulness.[14]

Because the man lying in the darkness (Adam or humanity as a whole) shared a common humanity with Christ, he could share in His glory.

Artists and sculptors emphasized this human element when they depicted Christ, especially in death. Crucifixes became common in the churches of the Latin West by the early eighth century, but manuscripts still tended to portray him as a king in majesty, enthroned in the manner of Old Testament and contemporary monarchs alike. Early medieval painters and sculptors tended to pic-ture the crucified Christ as a calm, almost passive victor over death, still alive and stoically enduring the torture of the cross. Although there is significant dispute over the date of the shift, it seems that starting perhaps in the tenth century, and with increasing frequency in the eleventh and twelfth, artists showed Christ as dead and bro-ken (but generally without the liberal spatterings of blood that would appear in later medieval art). Similarly, visual representations of the Passion underscored the grief of mourners, like the Virgin Mary as well.[15] Contemporaries were exhorted to be mourners themselves, to share in the grief, as when Gerhoh of Reichersberg asked them to see in a crucifix Christ 'naked and lacerated by blows [...] pouring forth copious streams of blood from the five wounds in His hands, feet, and side'.[16]

As Anselm's reference to Jesus as a 'friend' suggests, Christ's humanity entailed more than just suffering. His willingness to endure pain was a sign of his love which, when internalized and then shared, could bind the Christian community together. According to the English monk Aelred of Rievaulx (1110–1167),

> and so in friendship are joined honor and charm, truth and joy, sweetness and good-will, affection and action. And all these take their beginning from Christ, advance through Christ, and are perfected in Christ. Therefore, not too steep or unnatural does the ascent appear from Christ, as the inspiration of the love by which we love our friend, to Christ giving himself to us as our Friend for us to love, so that charm may follow upon charm, sweetness upon sweetness, and affection upon affection.[17]

Because of Christ's humanity, he could be a friend and a model for friendship in a way that the majestic king of heaven perhaps could not.

In some contexts, Christ took on the human qualities of not only a friend but of a mother; he transcended his gender, at least metaphorically, when Anselm of Canterbury called him 'the mother who, like a hen, gathers her chicken under her wings'.[18] Subsequent writers like Aelred continued this theme with striking imagery of the female body: 'On your altar let it be enough for you to have a representation of our Savior hanging on the cross', because 'his naked breasts will feed you with the milk of sweetness to console you'.[19] Christ's human body not only suffered, it nurtured and continues to nurture. According to the historian Caroline Walker Bynum, this imagery developed not only as an expression of devotion to the human Christ, but as a means of portraying authority as nurturing rather than intimidating—abbots were referred to as mothers as well.[20]

Finally, Christ's humanity and his earthly ministry provided a model for human behavior in the world: the *imitatio Christi*, or imitation of Christ. One could imitate Christ in several ways. Monastic authors tended to argue that one followed in the footsteps of Christ through humility, love, and willingness to suffer, but there were also more literal ways of following him. A French bishop rode a donkey, while some abbots took to washing the feet of their monks in the spirit of the Gospel of John (13:5–17). Hugh of St Victor turned Christ into an example for nearly everyone, referring to him as a pastor, guard, merchant, soldier, exile pilgrim, traveler, and pauper.[21] But it was probably Francis of Assisi who followed the *imitatio Christi* most spectacularly. He not only ministered to the poor and to lepers and healed the blind and sick, but he physically took on the wounds of Christ, usually known as stigmata. On Mt. Alverno in 1224, he had a vision of a man 'like a seraph with six wings'. Afterward, '[H]is hands and feet seemed to be pierced through the middle by nails, with the heads of the nails appearing in the inner side of the hands and on the upper sides of the feet and their pointed ends on the opposite sides'.[22] Many people had expressed the desire to share the pain of the crucifixion in one way or another before Francis, and the notion of wanting to be 'crucified with Christ' was commonly expressed throughout the twelfth century, as was the metaphorical language of taking on the stigmata. The French mystic Marie d'Oingies (1177–1213) even seems to have inflicted the wounds on herself.[23] So although Francis was the first to receive the actual wounds of Christ through purportedly supernatural means, his stigmata operated in a broader universe of piety based on Christ's body.

Even after Francis, relatively few people received, or claimed to receive, the stigmata, but Christ's body and His passion were accessible (in theory) to the entire Church in the form of the Eucharistic sacrament. This had firm scriptural grounding, for Christ had presented bread and wine to his disciples at the Last Supper, called it his body and blood, and urged them to partake. With regard to the wine, He said, 'drink ye all from this, for this is my blood [...] which is to be shed for many unto the remission of sins' (Matt. 26:27–28). Although in the early Church the Eucharist took on the form of a communal meeting, by the twelfth century it had become thoroughly clericalized, a mysterious rite in which consecration by a priest transformed bread and wine into real flesh and blood. Moreover, the rhetoric of the body and blood of Christ began to suffuse all areas of ecclesiastical life. Two developments in the theory and practice of the Eucharist are particularly important for our understanding of the twelfth-century Church. First, theologians and canon lawyers insisted on the absolute necessity of the doctrine of transubstantiation, according to which the bread and wine did not merely symbolize Christ, but in fact became him in substance. In the late eleventh century scholars like Berengar of Tours were proposing alternative explanations of what occurred in the Eucharist's elements, but they were all rejected and the orthodox doctrine was confirmed emphatically in 1215 at the Fourth Lateran Council. Second, as scholars came to exalt the importance of the sacrament and devotion to it was expressed in increasingly emphatic ways, the institutional Church began both to require and regulate it. It is thought that before and even during the twelfth century most Christians took communion only rarely if at all. The Fourth Lateran Council, however, would require all the faithful to do so a minimum of once a year. It had effectively become a requirement for Church membership, then, to accept the doctrine of transubstantiation and to experience it ritually, and the Church was beginning to realize even grander implications. Christ's body became understood as the Church itself. In the 1090s, Anselm of Canterbury had suggested this in a prayer directed to Christ before receiving communion: 'May I be worthy to be incorporated into your body, which is the Church, so that I may be your member and you may be my head, and that I may remain in you and you in me'.[24] References to Christ's body pervade the decrees of the Fourth Lateran Council, which quote St Paul's declaration that all of us are 'one body in Christ' (Romans 12:5).[25] The devotion to the human Christ formed an element in popular piety while it also underscored the rising power of an increasingly clericalized Church.

Saints, relics, and pilgrimage

Despite the comfort that Christ's humanity and friendship offered, the sacrament of his body and blood inspired awe and occasionally fear in laity and clerics alike. Peter of Blois told a friend that he had put off full ordination to the priesthood for so long because of his fear that he was inadequate to handle Christ's body.[26] And as the ultimate judge of the universe, Christ judged the souls of everyone. As a result, it was essential to be favored by him, and Christians sought intercessors among the saints they venerated in all parts of Europe. Anselm of Canterbury (once again) was utterly convinced that a saint, such as the famously repentant sinner Mary Magdalene, could prevail upon Christ to save him when his own poor efforts could not. 'Recall in loving kindness what you used to be, how much you needed mercy, and seek for me that same forgiving love that you received when you were wanting it'.[27]

Some saints were venerated throughout Christendom, above all the Virgin Mary and the Apostles, and are generally referred to as 'universal' to distinguish them from those with a more local appeal, like Adalbert of Prague, whose cult flourished primarily in Bohemia, Hungary, and Poland. For a variety of reasons, the universal saints, especially Mary, came to predominate all over Europe during the twelfth century. Although Mary had always held a special place in the community of saints, Marian devotion expanded greatly after the middle of the eleventh century, as the proliferation of French churches dedicated to Our Lady, *Notre Dame*, demonstrates. Her popularity stemmed from many of the same factors that drove the devotion to the human Christ. On the one hand, she played a role in the theology of redemption by being the vessel that brought the Redeemer into the world to reverse the sin of Eve (the Latin *ave*, the first word of the ubiquitous prayer 'Hail Mary', is the reverse of *Eva*, the Latin version of Eve); on the other hand, because of her maternal and nurturing qualities she could be the focus of a highly affective and individualized piety. Several collections of miracle stories sprang up around her in the twelfth and thirteenth centuries, and it is especially noteworthy that in several of them she forgave nuns for sexual sins, on one occasion ordering angels to steal away an abbess's illegitimate child.[28]

No one disputed the sanctity of Mary, the Apostles, or those who had died martyrs for Christ. Over the course of the twelfth century, however, the authorities became concerned with the unregulated proliferation of local cults. Guibert of Nogent, who approached the faith of his social inferiors with a certain degree of snobbery, complained that 'if all the church is in agreement about [Saint] Martin, [Saint] Rémy, and similarly well-known figures, what can I say about others whom commoners—envious of these saints just mentioned—create every day in every village and in every town?'[29] Informal, local canonization directly contradicted the centralizing and codifying impulses of the contemporary papacy, so the pope and the College of Cardinals gradually took a greater role in the process of identifying and beatifying candidates for sainthood according to standard criteria. For example, popes came to expect a proper hagiography that recorded a saint's manner of life and miracles (including those performed after his or her death). Papal decrees in 1179 and 1200 set forth additional guidelines, and in 1229 canonization became the exclusive prerogative of the papacy.[30] There were, of course, some cases in which individuals were more or less sainted by acclamation—Bernard of Clairvaux's hagiography was underway a few years before his death.[31]

Popes and bishops looked after the cults of the saints because saints not only interceded on behalf of the faithful, but helped symbolically mediate between heaven and earth. The temporal and the eternal worlds met in the saints' bodily relics, which were venerated for their holiness and valued for the miracles they were thought to perform. A relic could be any object associated with a saint's life, but ideally it was the body or some portion thereof. Hair, fingernails, and clothing all circulated widely and became parts of sometimes vast collections. Relics associated with Christ's passion were especially prized, and included the Crown of Thorns, the Holy Lance that pierced his side, and fragments of the True Cross itself. Since Christ's body ascended to heaven, he left no bodily relics, though a few monasteries claimed to possess his milk teeth or the foreskin from his circumcision.

Local saints could perform miracles through their relics, and thus the bodies of especially holy men and women were carefully guarded when they died. In 1198, the bones of the Icelandic Bishop Jón of Hólar were exhumed and washed, and his skull given special treatment. Shortly thereafter the water used to wash the skull was reported to heal a girl of an eye ailment as well as insomnia.[32] But the value of relics went far beyond miracles. To see or even to touch a relic was to experience perfection, and the stories of the opening of saints' tombs testify to sweet smells, perfectly intact bodies, and other signs of absolute holiness, even in seemingly small details. After Jocelin of Brokeland, monk at the English monastery of Bury-St Edmund's, witnessed the opening of his patron saint's tomb, he observed that the body fit so flawlessly in the casket that 'it was hardly possible for a needle to be placed between the head and the wood'.[33] Saints represented what could be achieved on earth through divine influence, and their remains were eagerly sought, fought over, and even stolen.[34] Churches and monasteries tried to obtain relics of their founding saints, as well as of great universal saints. The chronicler of Abingdon Abbey in England provided a list of relics of nearly a hundred saints from all over Europe going back to the time of Christ, including fragments from some of the Virgin's clothes, parts of a nail from Christ's crucifixion, bits of St Peter's beard, one of the stones that killed St Stephen, wood shavings that had been used to stuff the pillow of Saint Edmund, and the shoulder blade of St Aethelwold.[35]

Many contemporaries were suspicious of stories of relics and miracles, not because they rejected them *per se* or denied the possibility of divine intervention, but because the unscrupulous could clearly take advantage of the gullible. Furthermore, rival claims about relics could be embarrassing. Around 1120, Guibert of Nogent complained that two different monasteries claimed to have the head of John the Baptist: 'Could there be anything more ridiculous preached about such a man, other than both groups saying he was two-headed?'[36] What Guibert sought, then, was for the Church to more carefully regulate the system of relic veneration, which perfectly matched the centralizing endeavors of the contemporary papacy. Sometimes the authenticity of a particular relic was disputed, but twelfth-century Christians in principle accepted that many, if not most, relics were what they were claimed to be.

Since not everyone had access to the remains of the greatest or most powerful saints, people went on pilgrimages to visit their shrines. While some pilgrims travelled in the hopes of miraculous cures, and some presumably out of sheer curiosity, most journeys were penitential acts undertaken to help earn forgiveness of sins, and the theology of penance increasingly defined the Crusades over the course of the twelfth century. As we have seen, chroniclers and polemicists tended to call the military journeys to the east *peregrinationes*—'pilgrimages'—though scholars debate precisely how military and non-military pilgrimages related to each other.[37] Church courts routinely imposed pilgrimages as punishment for grievous sins such as heresy, and some commentators were more comfortable with required than voluntary journeys.

By the twelfth century, every corner of Europe boasted a shrine of some significance, and the increased traffic in relics meant that the great universal saints could be venerated almost everywhere. Rome and the Holy Land retained their positions as leading pilgrimage sites, while the shrines of St James at Santiago de Compostela in far north-western Spain, the Three Kings at Cologne, and Thomas Becket at Canterbury emerged as major destinations during this period. Each of these shrines grew in popularity in part because of other political, economic, or cultural phenomena: the *Reconquista* in Spain, the rise of commerce along the Rhine, and the struggle between Church and state in England, respectively. Still, no purely material or political factor can explain medieval pilgrimage.

Pilgrims recounted their journeys through detailed travel records, and their narratives form a sub-genre of medieval writing. Less than a decade after the capture of Jerusalem in 1099, an English monk named Saewulf toured the Holy Land and wrote a detailed guide to the major sites there, as did the German John of Würzburg in the 1160s.[38] An unknown author in the mid-twelfth century produced a guide to Santiago de Compostela that described the four routes through France to northern Spain and described the church and shrine in great detail. Although it is not clear that the guide was widely used, if at all, it bears witness to the excitement that such shrines generated among the population.[39]

At the same time that pilgrimage shrines were being established or becoming more popular on the fringes of Europe—as at St David's in Wales, Trondheim in Norway, and Prague in Bohemia—travelers from the farthest reaches of Christendom trekked to the major shrines. An abbot of the Greek Church in Russia named Daniel reached Jerusalem shortly after Saewulf, and several Icelandic pilgrims to Rome and Palestine documented their journeys or were mentioned in the sagas.[40] It has been argued that this network of pilgrimage sites helped expand the idea of a unified Christendom to formerly peripheral areas.[41] Pilgrims also affected the material culture of medieval Europe (and its extant sources): they collected souvenirs from their travels, especially pilgrim's badges (a conch shell for Santiago and a palm frond for Jerusalem, among others), and forced the expansion or reconstruction of several major churches to accommodate their numbers. Abbot Suger of St Denis, on the outskirts of Paris, complained that because of a lack of space the pilgrims who came to venerate his church's relics could not do 'anything but stand like a marble statue, stay benumbed or, as a last resort, scream'.[42]

Like relic veneration, pilgrimage had its critics. Hildebert of Lavardin, then bishop of Le Mans, warned the count of Anjou in 1128 that the journey to Santiago de Compostela would take him close to his political enemies and could compromise his ability to rule well. To take such a journey would be disobedient, as it would neglect his duty: 'Consider therefore whether the fruits of the journey are such that they can make up for the loss incurred by the failed obedience'. Half a century later, Christ appeared in a vision to the well-travelled Raimond Palmario and told him that 'I do not wish you henceforward to wander around the world, but to return to your own land of Piacenza; where so many poor, so many abandoned widows [...] demand my mercy, and there is none to help them'.[43] In a similar vein, Ralph Niger cautioned against performing a pilgrimage in the form of the Third Crusade, arguing that France had its own problems with sinfulness and heresy and that 'the value of that mystical pilgrimage, which one can always and everywhere undertake, is to be preferred to the laborious [i.e., worldly] pilgrimage'.[44] The debates about pilgrimage confronted the basic problem of how one could best be a pious Christian in the temporal world.

The Church and Its Religious Orders

Pilgrim journeys show how penitential theology operated in the lay world, and how high theological concepts could influence ordinary behavior. The fundamental struggle of the Christian soul for salvation had long been playing out in ways that were reflected in the social order. Since the days of the early Church, Christians had closed themselves off from the world to live lives of penitential self-denial, either as solitary hermits or as monks in communities (such monks are referred to as coenobitical). The first hermits, 'athletes of Christ', fled to the deserts of Egypt and Syria to gain control over their flesh and thus purify their spirits. During late antiquity, Greek saints like Pachomius and Basil drew up 'rules' according to which ascetic communities would adhere to vows of poverty, chastity, and obedience. By the ninth century, monks in the Latin West almost universally followed the monastic rule written by St Benedict of Nursia (480–547) and lived in communities rather than in solitude. They served as the designated penitents for medieval society, praying for forgiveness for the sins of the warrior aristocracy, whose job descriptions required sinning (generally by killing as a matter of routine). William the Conqueror famously founded Battle Abbey on the site where his army had killed Harold Godwinson, an anointed king of England. Because of original sin, however, everyone benefitted from having monastic intercessors to pray on their behalf. In his founding charter for the famous monastery of Cluny (909), Duke William I of Aquitaine carefully catalogued the relatives whose souls stood to benefit from the foundation.[45] Although monks never formed more than a tiny minority of the population, they had an influence on society out of all proportion to their numbers because they were a social, collective endeavor that benefitted all the faithful. After the Investiture Controversy, new options for living the religious life exploded onto the European scene and challenged traditional Benedictine monasticism. Christians sought to share the energy of the spiritual awakening in ways that took into account the changed social circumstances of the twelfth century.

The Benedictine tradition

Anselm of Canterbury wrote his remarkable series of prayers and theological treatises while serving as one of society's professional penitents at the Benedictine abbey of Bec in Normandy. He dedicated one of his prayers to St Benedict of Nursia, the founder of Western monasticism, whom he calls 'peerless leader among the great leaders of the army of Christ, [who has] pledged me to serve under your leadership, however feeble a soldier'.[46] Even though his political career took him far outside the cloister, he always identified as a Benedictine monk dedicated to atoning for original sin. Essentially all organized Latin monasticism prior to the late eleventh century is called Benedictine because Benedict's Rule, variously interpreted, informed most communal monastic practice. When new religious orders emerged, they were challenging an old and established tradition, but one that called forth inspiring displays of devotion. Many of the orders established after the 1090s regarded themselves as Benedictine even as they claimed to interpret the Rule more literally than the traditional houses did. Such claims would give rise to intense polemical wars. Despite pronounced regional variation, monastic practice in the Latin West evolved in the twelfth century according to a yearning for an idealized primitive Church, a push for greater austerity, and increasingly emotional, affective devotion.

Under ideal circumstances, monks lived strictly ordered lives according to the Rule of Saint Benedict, which allowed for some flexibility of interpretation. Above all, they practiced obedience (to the abbot), remained chaste, and worked in silence. Life in a monastery was frequently described as a battle, or as an imitation of the suffering of Christ. Abbot Peter of Celle (d. 1183) wrote that 'a genuine claustral [i.e., a monk] must crucify his whole self with his vices and lusts', and that leaving the monastery was akin to 'coming down from the cross'.[47] They did not just resist vices, but fought with the weapon of liturgical prayer according to a strict schedule. Typically, monks would perform around eight liturgical services a day, from Nocturnes between 2:00 and 3:00 am to Compline shortly after nightfall, with additional time devoted to a morning and a high mass, a chapter meeting, and group readings. Benedict's rule also prescribed manual labor, but in many religious houses its place was gradually taken by an ever-expanding liturgical round.

Because of the centrality of the monastery to social life, it makes perfect sense that many monastic personnel came from the higher rungs of society. Although canon lawyers eventually seemed to agree that serfs were eligible for the monastic life, in practice most choir monks came from aristocratic, or at least prominent, families. Their great prestige made monasteries an acceptable, even desirable, social space for the European nobility, and later, for the urban rich, and most of the great Benedictine houses were communities of the elite. Hildegard of Bingen, the theologian and abbess of Disibodenberg in the Rhineland was proud of her nuns' high social status to the point of excluding women of less-than-exalted rank.[48] Prior to the twelfth century, families would routinely make some of their children 'child oblates', literally 'offerings to God' who would be cloistered for the rest of their lives. Some of the most famous writers of the Middle Ages, including the great historians Bede (673–735) and Orderic Vitalis (1075–1142), were oblates, and they demonstrate the educational opportunity and spiritual vigor that could arise from an unintended lifetime commitment to God in the cloister. On other hand, the presence of monks who had entered the monastery without a personal calling could weigh on community discipline. Particularly in the early Middle Ages, even non-oblates, whose vocation had more to do with the social cachet of a great house, could be less-than-ardent members of the 'militia of Christ'.

Political difficulties also militated against the higher ideals of cloistered life. When the Carolingian world fragmented in the ninth century, many monasteries came under the control of local, secular rulers, who often regarded them as a kind of family property. They were institutions that oversaw large estates (and their incomes), and secular lords made sure that they appointed abbots who would make friendly administrators for them. Under these conditions, the spiritual mission of monasteries could suffer and adherence to the Benedictine Rule could become lax. When popes, bishops, and especially pious laymen had the resources and political opportunity, they attempted monastic reform, which generally entailed first the re-establishment of observance of the Rule, and second the disentanglement of the monastery from local secular, and occasionally even from episcopal, interference. In 909, Duke William of Aquitaine founded the Burgundian abbey of Cluny, and in his foundation charter he guaranteed that the monks would always be subject to the Rule of Benedict, freely elect their abbot without outside interference, and enjoy direct protection of the pope. He then neatly summarized the main political goals of monastic reform:

It has pleased us also to insert in this document that, from this day, those same monks there congregated shall be subject neither to our yoke, nor to that of our relatives, nor to the sway of the royal might, nor to that of any earthly power. And, through God and all his saints, and by the awful day of judgment, I warn and abjure that no one of the secular princes, no count, no bishop whatever, not the pontiff of the aforesaid Roman see, shall invade the property of these servants of God, or alienate it, or diminish it, or exchange it, or give it as a benefice to any one, or constitute any prelate over them against their will.[49]

Freed from outside influence, the monks at Cluny could theoretically perform their proper social role in the purest possible fashion. In time, Cluny's reforms spread to other monastic houses until the Cluniacs represented a distinct subdivision within Benedictine monasticism, often allied with the papacy.[50] Over the course of the eleventh and early twelfth centuries, Cluny came to preside over a loosely organized, sometimes ill-defined empire of monasteries and priories (houses without their own abbot) that sprawled throughout Europe. A similar reform movement, whose influence has perhaps wrongly been ignored in favor of that of Cluny, centered around the German monastery of Gorze. Reform could also re-emphasize the social role of the monasteries, for aristocrats who made gifts to Cluny became the 'neighbors of Saint Peter' and thus beneficiaries of saintly intercession. The economic transactions surrounding the monastery were thus intimately related to the monastery's role as an aide to winning heaven for the larger society.[51]

Benedictine foundations not only received benefits from the surpluses of others, but they actively joined in the economic activity that attended the commercial revolution and the geographical expansion of Europe. In the High Middle Ages, scores of new monasteries appeared in Germany beyond the Elbe, Hungary, Scandinavia, and Northern Spain. Their economic role in the towns became more pronounced in some cases. In 1201, the monks of Bury-St Edmunds defended their town's market (which they ran) against the threat of a rival market that the monks of Ely wished to found a few miles away. In order to avert the possible loss of revenues, Abbot Samson 'ordered his bailiffs to gather together the men of St Edmund, with their horses and arms, and destroy the market, binding and bringing back with them any persons found buying and selling'.[52] Revenues from commercial activity, along with traditional rents from agricultural holdings and gifts from elite families, combined to make the abbeys spectacularly wealthy. While individual monks lived relatively simple lives, their churches displayed an opulence that reached its highpoint in the spectacular third abbey church of Cluny, consecrated in 1130. Decorated with ornate sculptures and known for its magnificent candelabra, Cluny III remained the largest building in Western Europe until the construction of St Peter's, Rome, in the sixteenth century. Traditional monasticism thus combined the spiritual vitality, economic progress, and artistic passion of the twelfth century, but as it did so it invited both criticism and the suggestion of alternatives.

The new orders

Even in the early Middle Ages, there were some alternatives to the usual Benedictine form of monastic practice. Groups of hermits inhabited the woods of Cluny itself, for example. Eremitical, or anchoritic, monasticism had a stronger tradition in the Greek East, but periodically some Latin religious strove for a more solitary life, particularly in areas like Italy that were subject to Byzantine influence. Romuald of Ravenna in 1022 had founded a monastery at Camaldoli in the hills of Tuscany, where a group of hermits lived in private huts high above the main church. Removed from the usual monastic routine, their private devotions included absolute silence and self flagellation. At Vallambrosa, near Florence, John Gualberto established an abbey in 1038 which, though communal in form, sought to isolate the community from society more thoroughly than was the case with most Benedictine houses. They also claimed to follow a more literal interpretation of Benedict's Rule than was customary. Both Camaldoli and Vallambrosa gave rise to small orders of monks with their own organization and came to be regarded as distinct models for monastic practice. They sought reform through appeal to ideals of the primitive Church and to a more austere reading of the Rule, and implicitly rejected the social role of traditional monasticism.

Reformed Cluniacs and many other Benedictines were far from dissolute and they included many happy monks with happy benefactors. Still, observers in the burgeoning population were anxious about the new wealth that surrounded them, and sought more emphatic ways of rejecting it. While some of the reformers explicitly criticized the excesses of Cluny, others simply offered forms of the religious life that seemed to embody more completely the original monastic ideal of retreat to the desert. It is striking that many of the foundation stories of new religious orders involve a specific rejection of the profit economy. In the 1080s Bruno, the chancellor of the cathedral of Reims, was so mortified by the avarice of the local archbishop, Manasses, that he fled to the Alps and 'chose to live on a steep and rather forbidding promontory, attainable only by a difficult and rarely traveled path (there was a gaping, cragged valley below it)'.[53] Eventually, Bruno established a religious house high in the mountains, at a site called Grand Chartreuse, where a small group (which, according to Guibert of Nogent quoted above, was initially thirteen men) combined some communal liturgy with solitary living. Each of Bruno's monks slept in a private cell with a garden behind and performed many of the daily prayers alone. The Carthusian order, as it became known, channeled the impulses that characterized the new monastic practices of the late eleventh and twelfth centuries: a desire to recreate the desert of the monks of late antiquity by retreating away from the towns, a fervor for individual meditation and contemplation, and a press for ever-greater austerity. Throughout the twelfth century, observers almost universally praised the Carthusians for their devotion to the ideals of the primitive Church.

While the Carthusians fled the world and saw solitude and austerity as the chief components of primitive monastic observance, others were convinced that a life that truly followed the example of the earliest apostles, the *vita apostolica*, could be practiced by working priests who preached, taught pupils, and ministered in the world to the poor and sick. The pastoral work of most great churches had traditionally been undertaken by secular clergy called canons; over the course of the twelfth century, many such churches turned their groups of canons into canons regular, that is, canons who followed a rule (*regula* in Latin), usually the one referred to as the Rule of St Augustine, and lived as a monastic community. Some of the greatest scholars of the period, including Hugh of St Victor (discussed in Chapter 4, below), lived in such communities, demonstrating how this form of the religious life was tied into the role of towns as educational centers.

The Cistercians

Some of the reformers tried several times to find a place whose monastic routine was sufficiently severe. Robert, the abbot of an important monastery in Burgundy, resigned his position and started a community of hermits which eventually became a religious house at Molesme (and thus he is generally known as Robert of Molesme). When new recruits seemed to some to soften the austerity there, Robert set off with a group of monks to find somewhere where they could practice the Benedictine Rule as they interpreted it, favoring a less elaborate liturgy and greater emphasis on manual labor. Eventually they established a new monastery at Cîteaux in the Burgundian wilderness, 'where men rarely penetrated and none but wild things lived, so densely covered was it then with woodland and thorn bush'.[54] With the support of the local bishop and the Duke of Burgundy, they attempted to curb what they saw as excesses in contemporary monastic life:

> [M]indful of their solemn promise, [the brethren] took the unanimous decision to institute and keep in that locality the Rule of blessed Benedict, rejecting whatever contravened it: namely, long-sleeved tunics and furs, fine linen shirts, caps and breeches, combs, quilts and coverlets, and a variety of courses in the refectory, as well as lard and everything else that militates against the purity of the Rule.[55]

The Cistericans, whose name derives from the Latin version of 'Cîteaux', considered themselves fundamentally conservative, but they provided an institutional example of major innovations in contemporary religious life. They aimed for almost complete austerity to the point of wearing habits of undyed white wool, earning themselves the nickname of the 'White Monks' (traditional Benedictines wore dyed black habits, and were called 'Black Monks'). In addition, they sought to re-introduce manual labor into the daily routine, at the expense of some elements of the old liturgy.

The new abbey scraped by for over a decade. It attracted some new recruits, but Cistercian writers made clear that relatively few young men were initially drawn to such a difficult life. Then, in 1112 or 1113, the young aristocrat Bernard, having struggled with extreme anxiety over the fate of his soul, arrived at Cîteaux with some thirty followers, many of them relatives whom he had convinced to join him in the monastic life. Clearly Bernard had incredible charisma and powers of persuasion; according to his primary biographer, Bernard instilled such passion for conversion among his brothers that only the youngest was 'left to be a comfort to his ageing father'.[56] After that, he turned his attention to cousins and other kinsman, and eventually brought with him to Cîteaux a veritable army for Christ. This sudden influx of monks, combined with increased recruitment, allowed Cîteaux to found 'daughter houses' throughout the region including Clairvaux (in 1115), over which Bernard himself became abbot. Within 50 years, there were over 300 Cistercian monasteries all over Europe, fairly tightly organized into a single order that held a yearly general chapter to ensure uniform observance of the Rule.

It is a great paradox of Cistercian history that a group of monks explicitly rejecting the world became a major force in European society and politics by the second third of the twelfth century. They attempted physically to remove themselves far from any possible worldly influence. As the account of Cistercian origins known as the 'Little Exord' puts it, 'and knowing that blessed Benedict had built his monasteries not in cities, towns, or villages, but in places unfrequented and remote, they vowed to imitate him'.[57] The names of many of the abbeys—Bonnevalles, Clairvaux, Fountains—refer to natural features, and embody the Cistercians' goal of colonizing marginal areas. Tintern Abbey in Wales, the focus of Wordsworth's meditation on escaping city life during the Romantic period, was a twelfth-century foundation of White Monks and part of an expansion of monasticism into frontier regions. On the other side of Latin Christendom, Cistercians helped clear previously pagan-held land as part of the German *Ostsiedlung*, and by the later Middle Ages they had established abbeys on the frontiers of Russia and at Tuterø, well up the coast of what is now Norway.[58]

The new order was not shy about distinguishing itself from its rivals, and Bernard of Clairvaux unleashed masterfully savage rhetoric against the Cluniacs in particular. Cluny, he argued, had gone soft and neglected the true spirit of Benedict's Rule. In his *Apologia for Abbot William*, Bernard ridiculed the excess of its clothing, sleeping habits, food, and drink. 'Who could describe all the ways in which eggs are tampered with and tortured', he fumed, 'or the care that goes to turning them one way and then turning them back? They might be cooked soft, hard, or scrambled [...]. What reason can there be for all this variation except the gratification of a jaded appetite?'[59]

Despite their attempts at seclusion, and their rejection of some of the social roles of the monastery (demonstrated by their refusal of child oblation, for instance), Cistercians could not leave behind all the trappings of society, including class distinction. In order to allow the monks adequate time to perform the liturgy they did retain, they employed large numbers of *conversi*, lay brothers recruited from the peasantry, to work the land and undertake domestic chores. The Little Exord confirms that

> they decided to take in bearded day-laborers and to accept lay-brothers [...] whom they would treat as themselves in life and death—the status of monk apart—and also hired men, because without such backing they did not see how they could fully observe, day and night, the precepts of the Rule.[60]

In some cases, these peasants outnumbered the choir monks by more than three-to-one. Life as a lay brother clearly appealed to the growing peasant population, who did not seem to object to the 'social apartheid' that the Cistercian monasteries maintained through architectural schemes that separated them from the choir monks.[61]

Nor could Bernard of Clairvaux and his followers avoid being swept into contemporary politics. Bernard himself played pivotal roles in disputes at the papal curia, and his support proved invaluable to several popes in their quarrels with rivals and anti-popes. In 1145, a protégé of Bernard's became Pope Eugenius III, inspiring Bernard to reflect on the dilemmas of a monk called to work outside of the cloister, ripped from 'the pleasant delights of solitude', in his great work *On Consideration*.[62] Moreover, despite their efforts to reject wealth and practice austerity, the Cistercians played a major role in the agrarian economy, opening up new areas and cultivating, with the help of *conversi*, previously unused land. They sometimes even appeared as a threat to the traditional order, as was strikingly illustrated when villagers in Gascony murdered a monk who was helping to establish a Cistercian agricultural estate nearby.[63] Some saw them as complicit in the new economic order, and their corporate wealth made them targets for satire before the century was done. Walter Map (c. 1140–c.1210) portrayed the White Monks as spectacularly avaricious, finding in their ranks 'such [men] as find and follow every path to gain with all their might, such as open and enter in at every gate of avarice, such as never think out any cruel way of profit without putting it in practice'.[64] Elsewhere, Walter compared Cistercians unfavorably to Jews.[65]

Within the monastery, Cistercians developed a profound, mystical piety that they fashioned into literature by means of some of the most beautiful devotional Latin of the Middle Ages. Bernard of Clairvaux provided the finest example of this in his exquisite series of sermons on the Song of Songs, the Old Testament work of often erotic love poetry. In the passionate language of the Song, Bernard found a compelling metaphor for the monastic life. Contemporaries would have seen nothing untoward about Bernard devoting several sermons to the single verse 'let him kiss me with the kiss of his mouth' (Song of Songs 1:1). The kiss symbolized the way that monks experienced the love of Christ that they entered the cloister to enjoy:

> A fertile kiss therefore, a marvel of stupendous self-abasement that is not a mere pressing of mouth upon mouth; it is the uniting of God with man. Normally the touch of lip on lip is the sign of the loving embrace of hearts, but this conjoining of natures brings together the human and divine, shows God 'reconciling himself to all things, whether on earth or in heaven'.
>
> (Col. 1:20)[66]

The Song of Songs provided a model for contemplation in the cloister and a complement to the Rule of St Benedict; according to one commentator, it was the 'rule of love'.[67] Cistercian monks found in scriptures like this, and in the daily liturgical routine, a means of experiencing not simply a retreat from the world but a return to God. That they simultaneously transformed parts of the European landscape outside the cloister was not a paradox but rather a reflection of their spiritual program.

The military orders

Despite rejecting the world in principle, most of the religious orders responded and adapted to it in highly idiosyncratic ways. Perhaps the

best example of a compromise between traditional monastic observance and twelfth-century novelties is provided by the military orders,
comprised of monks who fought for Christ in the Holy Land, Iberia,
and the Baltic frontier. There may in fact be no better example of
the way that twelfth-century people reconciled contradictory cultural
elements, since knights and monks represented opposite poles of
contemporary society. The belligerent way of life of these warrior-
monks seems utterly incompatible with the principles of ecclesiastical
reform, which prohibited regular and secular clergy from bearing
arms, but their rise and acceptance can be understood in the context of a number of traditions and trends. Monks, after all, had long
used military imagery to describe what went on in the cloister. Since
late antiquity monks had been 'soldiers of Christ', it may not have
been so difficult to translate the metaphor into reality. In addition,
the First Crusade had introduced the previously unknown ideal of
armed penitential pilgrimage to the Latin West. Crusading warfare
had itself become a penitential space just as the cloister had always
been. Finally, if warfare and its attendant killing had always been
regarded (in clerical circles) as an unfortunate and deeply regret-
table element in the life of an aristocrat, the crusades had endowed
it with a decidedly positive value. As Bernard of Clairvaux put it,
'at the death of the pagan, the Christian exults because Christ is
exalted'.[68]

In 1119, King Baldwin II of Jerusalem granted a group of knights
from Champagne a residence adjacent to the 'Temple of Solomon'
(the Crusaders' name for the al-Aqsa mosque). They had come
together to live a monastic life while also vowing to protect pilgrims
in the Holy Land. Eventually they constructed a rule based on that of
St Benedict and received formal papal recognition as a new order,
the 'Knights of the Order of the Temple', now known simply as
'Templars', in 1139. Their rule ignored some traditional monastic
practices, like private reading, and emphasized others, like poverty,
chastity, and obedience. Later statutes included directives for striking
campsites and forming battle lines. From the early 1130s, Bernard
of Clairvaux preached and wrote enthusiastically on their behalf,
apparently seeing in them a chance to bring the Cistercians' spiritual tenacity to the fight for the land where Christ walked. Templars,
he argued, were good and gentle monks, following the precepts of
the Benedictine Rule, but 'once in the thick of battle they set aside
this earlier gentleness'.[69] The Templars became one of the largest and
wealthiest orders in Latin Christendom, and served as seasoned advisers to the hordes of untrained pilgrims who thronged to Palestine on

the major expeditions.[70] On the Second Crusade, Louis VII implored his knights to let the Templars lead them.[71]

The Knights of the Hospital of St John, or Hospitallers emerged as the other leading military order in the Holy Land. Originally they served as the administrators of a hostel for sick pilgrims that had been founded by Italian merchants in the eleventh century. After 1099, they catered to the great influx of armed and unarmed pilgrims and transformed the hostel into a huge hospital that was quite unique in Latin Christendom. It has been argued that most of its patients would have slept in their own bed for the first time there, and that it provided a nearly unheard of standard of care.[72] Over time, the Hospitallers also took on a military function, and were put in charge of some of the most important castles in the crusader states. Along with the Templars, they provided the model for additional orders such as those of Calatrava and of Santiago in Iberia, and the Teutonic Knights in the Baltic. The Muslim leader Saladin acknowledged their significance when, after his defeat of the Christian army at Hattin in 1187, he ordered his troops to decapitate any captured Templars and Hospitallers.

Women in the new orders

The experience of Margaret of Ypres, with which this chapter began, demonstrates that women partook in the spiritual currents of the long twelfth century, but clerical anxiety about sexuality along with traditional misogynistic attitudes ensured that their place in formal religious life would be highly ambiguous. Women had participated in Benedictine monasticism almost since its inception, and queens who retired into monasteries late in life are the subject of many early medieval hagiographies.[73] In some areas, including England, 'double monasteries' of men and women living in separate but adjacent accommodation, sometimes ruled by a women, were not uncommon. There is no reason to suspect that women had radically different reasons for entering the religious life than men had, but certainly their different social and sexual roles on occasion influenced their choice of vocation. Life as a nun provided an alternative to marriage for those who, through choice or necessity, were not marriageable; nuns brought dowries to their abbeys just as wives brought them to their husband's families. Some women took monastic vows after a marriage had failed, been annulled, or ended with the death of a husband, and there is anecdotal evidence that some who fled abusive marriages found safe haven in the cloister; the reformer Robert of

Arbrissel apparently accepted such women into his double monastery of Fontevrault and rebuffed the requests of angry husbands that he forcibly return their wives.[74]

Hildegard of Bingen, whose parents gave her to God when she was eight, became the most important female theologian of the twelfth century as a member of an elite and rather conservative Benedictine foundation in the Rhineland, but even she found it necessary to employ traditional misogynist tropes in her rhetoric. In her great visionary work *Scivias* she acknowledged that she was 'remaining in the fragility of the weaker rib, but filled with mystical inspiration'.[75] Hildegard corresponded with another important Benedictine mystic, Elisabeth of Schönau (1129–1165), who spent her career in a double monastery but could not herself write Latin (she dictated her works in German to a priest, who translated and wrote them down). Female monasticism not only produced these luminaries, but also continued to grow. In Germany, for example, the number of houses for religious women more than tripled from between the period of 150–500 to the period of 1100–1250.[76] Monastic reformers, however, often treated women cautiously, and women remained a small minority of Christians in religious orders. Moreover, with a few significant exceptions, the main reformers saw female houses as only tangentially important. Cluny established a handful of convents for women, starting with Marcigny in France in 1056, but subjected them quite strictly to male control. The Cistercians initially wanted little to do with nuns, and declared in 1134 that they would not admit female houses, but some nunneries began following Cistercian practices independently and referred to themselves by the name of the order. In 1228, the order confirmed its official refusal to accept women, but that does not seem to have stopped some nobles from founding nunneries that they deemed 'Cistercian' and receiving papal approval for them.[77] In early thirteenth-century Champagne, nuns in a number of Cistercian foundations seem to have lived the monastic life in order to share the sufferings of their fathers and brothers crusading in the East.[78] That some nunneries followed Cistercian customs without being formally incorporated into the order suggests that the structures for expressing female piety could be ill-defined and fluid, and this is borne out by the experience of several prominent women.

Ironically, one of the most famous and respected nuns of the twelfth century, Heloise, abbess of the monastery of the Paraclete, had little initial interest in being one. As will be discussed in the next chapter, she entered the religious life under duress after her teacher-turned-lover-turned-husband Abelard had been disgraced and mutilated by her uncle. Despite her misgivings about the manner of her conversion and her conviction that 'it was not any sense of vocation which brought me as a young girl to accept the austerities of the cloister, but [Abelard's] bidding alone', she fashioned herself into a very good leader of the Paraclete, which Abelard had originally founded as a simple oratory in the wilderness. As he set about establishing the monastic practice there, she sought Abelard's help, and recognized in strikingly frank terms that the Rule of St Benedict would need to be modified. What use had women for the Rule's concern with male clothing, or 'with tunics or woolen garments worn next to the skin, when the monthly purging of their superfluous humors must avoid such things?' More significant perhaps were the Rule's requirements for manual labor, since it was not customary for women to work in the fields.[79] Abelard responded with a lengthy and rambling set of prescriptions that he intended as a kind of rule for nuns. Although it does not seem to have been taken up as a model for the female monastic life, it addressed Heloise's anxieties adequately, providing instructions for elements of the daily round, procedures for dealing with death and burial, clothing, and the administration of the sacraments.[80] Several other writers, including Aelred of Rievaulx in a letter to his sister, and the anonymous authors of a dialogue called the *Speculum Virginum* ('Mirror for Virgins') in the 1140s and *Ancrene Riwle* ('Rule for Anchoresses') in the 1220s, attempted to codify the proper religious life for women. Interestingly, many of these tracts seem to have circulated primarily among male monasteries.[81]

Hard evidence for the form of life actually practiced in nunneries is relatively scarce, but the documented examples are highly illuminating. Two male monastic reformers, Robert of Arbrissel (*c.* 1045–1116) in France and Gilbert of Sempringham (*c.* 1090–1190) in England, established foundations with women's spirituality especially in mind. Robert founded a double monastery at Fontevrault (in the county of Anjou) in 1101 after a career as a wandering preacher. His message had long resonated with women; in 1098 Bishop Marbode of Rennes had warned Robert about the gossip his preaching mission had generated:

> They say that women follow you on your wanderings and are constantly by your side when you preach. They assert also that you keep not a small number of women in different places and regions, in hospices and lodgings, women intermingled with men (not with impunity), on the pretext that you have assigned them to the care of the poor and pilgrims. How dangerous is this practice the wailing of babies, not to put too fine a point on it, has betrayed.[82]

We cannot verify Marbode's insinuations, which were repeated by others, but it is clear that anxiety about sex was never far from contemporary discourse about religious women. Robert's foundation at Fontevrault, however, flourished. Although begun as a double monastery, women were always more important, and an abbess rather than an abbot presided over it. The male members served primarily as priests, fulfilling sacramental roles that women were canonically prohibited from performing. Across the English Channel, Gilbert, a secular cleric rather than a monk himself, founded a double monastery of nuns and regular canons at Sempringham, primarily to meet the needs of women in the north of England. Sempringham gave rise to several daughter houses, for which Gilbert wrote customs after the Cistercians refused to incorporate them into their order. The Gilbertines, as they became known, would be one of England's most original and enduring contributions to the medieval religious life.[83]

Because so many monks and secular clergy resisted the institution-alization of female religious life in new orders, women sought other alternatives. Since late antiquity, some pious women chose to live a chaste, eremitical life outside an organized cloister, often attached to a church or monastery. Generally referred to as 'recluses' or 'anchoresses', these women often became famous and inspired both reverence and extreme suspicion in clerical authorities. Their numbers seem to have increased dramatically in the twelfth century, and they appeared all over Europe, including England, Germany, Spain, and Italy. Although men had long lived as hermits or anchorites throughout Latin Christendom, female recluses seem to have outnumbered them in the twelfth century both in England and the Continent.[84] Nuns might choose an anchoritic life after determining that the communal monastic routine was not sufficiently religious, but laywomen (initially mostly nobles but increasingly the daughters of burgesses) also chose enclosure. Often a recluse would be symbol-ically 'buried' in a cell built along the wall of a church or monastery, where she would continually reject the worldly life even as travelers came to learn from her example.

The Englishwoman Christina of Markyate (c. 1096–c. 1155) shows how one woman could navigate several options for the religious life while constantly facing the often violent resistance of family as well as certain elements of the male ecclesiastical establishment. On a visit to the great abbey of St Albans when she was still a young girl, she marveled at the piety of the monks there and, in order to emulate them, pledged her chastity to God. When she was a teenager one of the most powerful men in England, the bishop of Durham Ranulf

Flambard, sought to marry her, and when she refused he attempted to rape her. Sexual violence thus followed an act of resistance to male clerical authority: according to her biographer, 'the only way in which he could conceivably gain his revenge was by depriving Christina of her virginity'.[85] He then colluded with her parents to arrange a marriage to a man named Burthred, whom she fled by jumping a high fence. Having freed herself in turns from a lascivious bishop, a pining husband, and a controlling family, Christina escaped with the help of a local hermit, first hiding in a tiny cell under the care of a recluse named Alfwyn. The conditions were miserable, and on one occasion a swarm of toads squirmed into the cell and took up residence on her psalter.[86] She moved several times and for a time lived with an unnamed cleric, with whom she fell passionately in love. Her biographer assures us the feeling was mutual when he related that this man sometimes 'came before her without any clothes on and behaved in so scandalous a manner that I cannot make it known, lest I pollute the wax by writing it, or the air by saying it'.[87] Despite such temptation she remained chaste. All the while she had the protection of prominent men, including the archbishop of York and the abbot of St Alban's. She made her formal religious profession as a recluse attached to St Albans only late in life. Christina's experience illustrates the extent to which religious women depended on male authority and the highly sexualized terms in which their careers could be described.

If Christina of Markyate's life reveals the institutional instability that surrounded women's spiritual choices, an attempt to deal with such instability in urban environments points to a possible solution. By the year 1200, women in the towns of northern Europe had begun to form loosely organized communities and became known, for reasons that are not entirely clear, as 'Beguines'. While not organized according to any formal rule, the Beguinages (as their communities are known) provided non-noble urban women with an opportunity for the communal life, which was combined with ministry to the poor. They bound themselves with a pledge to remain celibate and observe personal poverty, but did not enclose themselves are take any monastic vows. While some lived in communities, others continued to live at home. The lives of Beguines (written by men) confirm that these women were deeply pious and orthodox, although hostile commentators feared their independence, and their precise position in the Church was never truly established. And even the most sympathetic biographers emphasized that women were almost always at the mercy of their emotions. Jacques de Vitry observed that Marie d'Oignies, about whom he wrote a glowing hagiography, 'clearly did not have power over her own body'.[88] Although authorities continually tried to subject them to tight clerical control, the Beguines provide an important exception to the general rule of religious women being increasingly placed in foundations sharply distinguished from the lay rule. In an ironic twist, Clare of Assisi (1194–1253), the spiritual sister of Francis and thus the female representative of the religious order that most emphatically advocated for the religious life in the world (see below), was herself willingly enclosed as a recluse late in life.

The increasing rate at which women who lived after 1100 were canonized (they represented 45 per cent of the lay saints in the twelfth century[89]), as well as their repeated attempts to find appropriate institutions for their piety, testifies to their importance to the contemporary spiritual awakening, but in every example above the women in question depended at least some of the time on sympathetic male clerics. They circumvented the authority of male, Latin-speaking clerics primarily through mystical experience and, more and more during the thirteenth century, by writing in the vernacular.[90] The encounter with Christ occasionally took on an erotic character, as with Beguine Lutgard of Aywières (1182–1264), who would swoon into ecstatic trances in which she would see Christ as a lamb 'positioning himself on her breast so that one foot was on her right shoulder and the other on her left. He would place His mouth on her mouth, and by this sucking, would draw out from her breast a wondrous mellowness'.[91] The imagery of her biographer, Thomas of Cantimpré, is typical in being direct and sensory. Thomas offered an even more striking exemplar of female spiritual charisma in his *Life of Christina the Astonishing*, which recounted the death and life of a Flemish girl who was resurrected at her funeral; her body shot up to the rafters of the church. She then embarked on a career of penitential exhortation and self-denial marked by bizarre supernatural feats. She walked on water, survived throwing herself into blazing bread ovens, lactated oil, and felt such guilt when she ate that 'she would cry out as if in childbirth'.[92] In such cases, women were portrayed as vessels of divine power rather than examples of piety to be followed. When men praised female piety, they often reinforced prevailing constructions of gender.

Heretics and Friars in the Urban Context

The new religious orders and the trials of devout women show how the effervescent spirituality of the twelfth century challenged the traditional boundaries of institutional religious practice, but some individuals challenged the ecclesiastical establishment even more directly and developed forms of piety that could not be contained within it. The New Testament had itself warned of heresy. The Second Epistle of Peter claimed that 'there were also false prophets among the people, even as there shall be among you lying teachers, who shall bring in sects [ultimately from Greek *hairesis*] of perdition, and deny the Lord who bought them: bringing upon themselves swift destruction' (2 Peter 2:1). Many of the earliest heresies were sophisticated intellectual movements that focused on highly technical, but doctrinally fundamental points of theology such as the nature of Christ and the relationship of the three persons of the Trinity. Church councils, most famously those at Nicaea in 325 and Chalcedon in 451, established orthodox doctrine on these topics. After the controversies of the late antique period, however, heresies appeared only rarely in the Latin West. Since the details of orthodox thought may not have penetrated too deeply into popular religious life, this should not be especially surprising. In the early eleventh century, a group of people at Orléans denied that Christ was fully human and that a human could be saved through the Church's sacraments. They were accused of heresy, as well as partaking in nocturnal orgies, and sentenced to death by burning.[93] It was only in the twelfth century that what had previously been isolated incidents became regarded as an epidemic. Most heretics thought of themselves as pious Christians, and they shared many ideas with the orthodox reformers of the day. As a result, some of the new religious orders that emerged from the travails of the twelfth century ought to be considered alongside heterodox movements.

Waldensians, Humiliati, and Cathars

In 1173, a rich merchant of Lyon named Valdès (though often referred to as 'Peter Waldo'), after hearing a wandering poet sing about St Alexius's renunciation of his wealth, began to fear for his soul. When a local master of theology told him that the balm for his anxieties lay in the Gospel passage in which Christ said 'If thou wilt be perfect, go sell what thou hast and give to the poor and thou shalt have treasure in heaven', Valdès, who had apparently made much of his money through usury, took it literally. Allowing his wife to keep his real estate, he liquidated his moveable wealth, some of which he used to endow his daughters in a convent, and the rest he gave to the poor. But rather than join a monastery himself, he embarked on a ministry to the poor of Lyon, feeding them and preaching about the need for penance. Valdès then began to commission translations of scripture so as to learn the Bible for himself and instruct others in its message.

Through his embrace of poverty, Valdès certainly participated in the spiritual movement that inspired the new orders, and also sought to address the urban conditions that were a by-product of the period's economic growth, but in his desire to preach and to read and interpret scripture he implicitly attacked the Latin clergy's monopoly on the keys to salvation. His preaching, the theology of which seems to have been entirely orthodox, struck a chord with laymen and he began to gain followers, who pursued the *vita apostolica*, travelling about barefoot in pairs, holding what goods they had in common. When he came before the Third Lateran Council in 1179, Pope Alexander III 'embraced Valdès, and applauded the vows of poverty he had taken, but forbade him and his companions to assume the office of preaching except at the request of priests. They obeyed this instruction for a time, but later they disobeyed, and affronted many, bringing ruin on themselves'.[94] The pope, then, tried to encourage Valdès's piety while resisting his anti-clericalism. When some of his followers, known as Waldensians, flouted the injunction against preaching, they effectively lapsed into heresy.

Valdès was not the first heretic of the twelfth century, but his example is one of the most instructive, for it shows how heresy could spring from genuinely pious energy that reacted to material conditions, and that the ecclesiastical authorities tried to adapt as subtly as their theological certitude allowed. Because antagonistic clerical writers tended to ignore the precise views of heretics, or conflate them with those of other people they did not like, it is hard to know exactly what medieval heretics believed. What most heresies have in common, however, is a discomfort with the role of the clergy in contemporary religious life. The account of the preaching of Henry of Lausanne at Le Mans in 1116 gets bogged down in clichéd accusations of sexual impropriety, but leaves no doubt that 'his heresy turned the people against the clergy with such fury that they refused to sell them anything or buy anything from them and treated them like gentiles or publicans'.[95] The Church needed to tread carefully, for outright oppression could have the effect of radicalizing heretics further, as with certain Waldensians who adopted heterodox theological stances in the face of persecution.

A similar group of pious laymen sprang up in northern Italy, especially around Milan, in the 1170s. Known as the Humiliati, they rejected wealth and wore simple clothing and avoided oath-taking (reflecting a literal interpretation of Christ's admonition to 'swear not at all' [Matt 5:34]). Like the Waldensians, they went out into the urban streets to preach the Gospel, and also like the Waldensians, they were admonished at the Third Lateran Council in 1179 to refrain from preaching. When they continued to preach, they were declared heretics by Pope Lucius III in 1184. But in 1198, they brought their case, including a detailed plan for their way of life, to Pope Innocent III, who treated them with remarkable perspicacity. He consulted with several prelates, and reached a decision that was rather complicated, but the essence of which was that as long as the Humiliati were truly humble, they could be established as a proper order, and even the laymen among them could preach. Their preaching, however, was to be strictly exhortatory, urging the faithful to penance and high morals—the clergy retained exclusive rights to preach on the meaning of scripture.[96]

Not all groups of suspect orthodoxy could be approached with such a spirit of compromise. By the early 1150s, clerical observers in several parts of Europe had noticed and preached against deviants expounding dualist theology. Dualists held that all matter was fundamentally evil, and thus that goodness only existed in the world of the spirit. The most famous dualists of antiquity had been the Manichees, whom the Church father Augustine had joined as a youth, and as a result twelfth-century writers may have been quick to level accusations of Manicheism at any proponents of dissident views. Still, the available sources offer consistent evidence for a vaguely coherent set of dualist beliefs in southern France and Italy.[97] An early anti-heretical tract attributes the following belies to a group of heretics in Lombardy:

> [They] believe and preach that there are two gods or lords, without beginning or end, one good and the other evil. They saw that each of these has created angels, the good god good angels, and the evil god evil ones, and that the good god is almighty in Heaven, while the evil god controls the mechanisms of this world.[98]

The view that matter is the inherently evil creation of an evil god runs into obvious problems with orthodox Christianity for myriad reasons, including orthodoxy's insistence that a loving God made the created order; that God became man; and that the consecrated host of the Eucharist physically became flesh and blood. The twelfth-century dualists became known, eventually, as 'Cathars', from the Greek *katharos* meaning 'pure'; through rigorously ascetic practices they tried to conquer, and so purify, their evil, earthly bodies. Because we have no extant accounts written by Cathars themselves about what they believed, they must be approached with great caution by modern readers. While it has recently been argued that the notion of Catharism as a heresy was itself a fabrication of hostile clerical witnesses and gullible modern historians, there is still a certain scholarly consensus that it did represent a threatening, though always relatively small strand of dissident belief in several parts of twelfth-century Europe that was based on dualist notions from Eastern Europe.[99] The term Catharism, though in some cases anachronistic, serves as a reasonable catch-all for such beliefs. Although Church authorities tended to paint all heresies with a broad brush, several accounts indicate that they recognized some distinctions between groups of heretics, even if the nuances were lost on the observers. At any rate, authorities became increasingly anxious at the emergence of heretical groups throughout Europe, but especially in the Low Countries, the Rhineland, Southern France and Northern Italy. They certainly did not coalesce into a coherent sect, but they shared a few key beliefs: discomfort with urban wealth and often an embrace of poverty, a rejection of sacraments themselves and of the sacramental authority of the clergy, and an emphasis on wandering preaching.

The Friars

The Waldensians and Humiliati showed that the institutional Church did not always effectively cater to devout, orthodox-leaning individuals. The Cathars, however, presented theological challenges that needed to be refuted point by point by competent intellectuals, and fought by example through a firm rejection of wealth and ostentation that obviously appealed to many in the towns of Christendom. These two threats were effectively countered by the creation of religious orders that provided an outlet for the spiritual energy of the sort of people who found heresy attractive, and created an orthodox alternative for them. In the origin stories and early histories of the mendicants, that is, the Franciscan and Dominican orders, can be found explicit responses to the threat of the heresies that sprang up in the decades before their founders Saint Francis of Assisi (c. 1182–1226) and Saint Dominic (1172–1221) lived and worked.

Giovanno di Bermardone, later nicknamed Francesco (i.e. 'Francis', probably because of his affinity for French literature), was the son of a French cloth merchant of Assisi in central Italy, which was not a major urban center but did play a role in the regional economy. After an enjoyable but not dissolute youth, Francis in his early twenties had a profound conversion experience when the image of Christ on a crucifix in a dilapidated country church moved its lips and told him to 'go, repair my house, which, as you see, is falling completely to ruin'.[100] After this vision he sold the shipment of his father's wool he was transporting and, returning to the church, gave the proceeds to the resident priest. His father, concerned that his fortune might be further dissipated by Francis's newfound piety, first imprisoned him, and then brought him before the bishop of Assisi. At that point, Francis stripped naked and threw himself at the mercy of the bishop. After this spectacular display, Francis gradually gathered followers while he ministered to the poor and to lepers, presenting himself as a bit of a social outcast. In 1209 he and his companions (adding up to the apostolic number of twelve) appeared before Pope Innocent III, who, almost certainly aware of the great similarities between Francis and Valdès, approached Francis with his usual circumspection, approving his proposed way of life but not formally establishing a new order. It was only in 1223 that Pope Honorius III approved a rule for the Order of Friars Minor (literally, 'little brothers' or 'lesser brothers'). The rule, written by Francis on at least his second attempt, initially consisted of scriptural passages strung together, reflecting Francis's commitment to a direct imitation of Christ. Francis had also joined up with the Fifth Crusade in Egypt, where he unsuccessfully tried to convert the sultan of Egypt to Christianity. In ever failing health—severe fasting may have ruined his digestive system—he returned to Italy, where he received the stigmata, the wounds of Christ (see above), two years before his death in 1226.

Whereas the monastic reformers of the early twelfth century consistently appealed to the Benedictine Rule as the impetus for the changes they sought, Francis was in a very real sense an innovator. Traditional monasticism sought to embrace God by doing penance for society's sins, contemplating God in the cloister, and joining with him. Francis sought God in the world and served him by serving those left behind by economic growth and urbanization. He certainly claimed to return to the earliest known apostolic practice, but in the context of medieval religious institutions he was a revolutionary. His followers did not bring endowments from their families' landed holdings into a foundation. Instead, they went out into the world and lived by begging, that is, by scrounging for the economic surplus of the towns (hence the moniker 'mendicant', from the Latin *mendicare*, 'to beg'). They rejected money to the point of insisting on absolute corporate poverty, meaning that the Franciscan order would not flirt with the dangers of amassing wealth from donations that way that Cluniacs and even Cistercians had.

Francis rejected wealth, but not the created order, which he celebrated in stark contrast to the Cathars who thought it evil. The imagery surrounding his life, conversion, and mission is concrete and striking: talking crucifixes, dilapidated churches in need of repair, leprous bodies with festering sores in need of healing. Even through his famous love of animals he showed that the world was not a problem to be shunned but an arena for doing the work of Christ. Moreover, in his great poem 'Canticle of Brother Sun' (or 'Canticle of the Creatures'), written in the Italian vernacular rather than Latin (which he never mastered as Bernard of Clairvaux did), he praised the sun, the moon, the stars, and the rest of the cosmos. To a humble man, creation was beautiful.[101]

Francis saw himself as a layman who ministered not through the sacraments or the interpretation of scripture but through word and deed. He fought heresy by example rather than through meticulous argument. The other great mendicant order of the early thirteenth century, that of the Dominicans, was explicitly clerical, as emphasized by its official title, the Order of Friars Preacher. If the Franciscans represented the institutionalization of the affective piety of the twelfth century, the Dominicans embodied its intellectual vigor (discussed in the next chapter). Their founder, the Castilian Dominic of Guzmán, began his career as a regular canon in the town of Osma, one of the learned elite who also followed a monastic rule. While traveling through the Cathar-infected south of France in 1206, he and his bishop noticed that the lavish clothing and entourages of the Cistercians delegated to combat heresy there drew an awkward, and unfortunate, contrast with the austere asceticism of the heretical evangelists they strove to discredit. They urged the Cistercians to defeat the heretics with a true show of humility, to 'use a nail to drive out a nail'.[102] And so they sent away all their worldly possessions, except, significantly, their books, which they would use to prepare for debates.

Dominic proved the most competent debater of the group, and immediately began to disrupt the activities of the heretics. He established a monastery 'to receive certain noble women whose parents had been forced by poverty to entrust them to the heretics to be educated and brought up', and preached the 'true Gospel' to the countryside. Dominic's efforts, however, were not effective enough to forestall a military solution to the perceived problem of heretics, and the Albigensian Crusade began soon thereafter. In the midst of the military conflict, he continued his preaching, mostly on his own, though he had a few associates. By 1215, he had assembled what was essentially a small order, which, after initially being received tepidly by the papacy, was authorized to preach and to live a regular life according to the Rule of St Augustine. In 1217, he sent the brothers out into the world to preach, explicitly rejecting the idea of keeping them living together in a community. These earliest Dominicans travelled to the university towns of Paris and Bologna, indicating that theirs was an intellectual mission to bring the learning of the schools to fight heresy and to disseminate a uniform understanding of the faith. In 1220, the now official Order of Friars Preacher wedded their bookish approach to the affective piety of voluntary poverty, as they renounced all individual and corporate poverty. They quickly colonized the universities of Europe, and at mid-century one of their number, Thomas Aquinas (1225–1274), would become the most important philosopher of the Middle Ages.

Order, Exclusion, and the Fourth Lateran Council

When the Church managed to integrate the Franciscans, Dominicans, and others into its institutional structure, it demonstrated that it could alter its structure when necessary, but it also drew sharp and non-negotiable boundaries. Canon lawyers and theologians had been trying for decades to synthesize their understanding of the meaning of the faith into a coherent whole, while working out potential contradictions. Some ideas, and some people, however, were left out of this synthesis. According to the historian R. I. Moore and others, the creation of orthodoxy essentially required the invention of heresy; the persecution of heretics in the twelfth century sprang not so much from the nature of their beliefs as from changes in the Church's understanding of what it was.[103] In 1215, the Fourth Lateran Council of 1215 laid out a definition for the Christian community that depended in part on exclusion, and clearly identified who was to be excluded.

Islam and the Latin West

Aside from those who went on crusade, few Europeans in the twelfth century, outside of Spain or Southern Italy, had ever met a Muslim, and there were few who had any detailed or even general knowledge about Muslim beliefs. Scholars often point to the *Song of Roland*, written around 1100, to represent the Western view of Islam around the time of the First Crusade. In its verses, the Muslims who attacked Charlemagne's rearguard at Roncevalles are idolatrous polytheists who worship an unholy trinity of Mahomet, Apollo, and Tergavent, which of course betrays colossal ignorance of even the most basic tenets of Islam (as well as of the fact that at the actual historical event the belligerents were Basques rather than Moors). In the chronicles of the First Crusade, the Muslims are similarly described as pagans worshipping an inconsistently reported catalogue of deities. An epic devoted to the legend of Aymeri of Narbonne, written around 1200, still portrayed Muslims as polytheists, but added a fourth deity, Cahu, to their pantheon.[104] Among early twelfth-century chroniclers, only Guibert of Nogent correctly noted that Muslims (who were generally called 'Saracens') worshipped only one god, and that their faith was in fact called Islam.[105] Christians turned Muslims into pagans not only out of ignorance, but for rhetorical effect. Those who died on Crusade were regarded as martyrs and the best literary accounts of martyrdom involved heroic Christians killed in brutal fashion by Roman pagans; if someone was martyred, there presumably had to have been a pagan there to martyr him.[106] Even contemporary scholars who understood the rudiments of Islam treated the faith with relentless hostility and frequently tried to conflate it with various Christian heresies. Guibert of Nogent, even as he assured his readers that the rumors about Muslims worshipping Mohammed as a god were not true, wrote a slanderous biography of the prophet in which he ended up being consumed by pigs. Before embarking on this character assassination, he admitted to his readers that 'one may safely speak ill of a man whose malignity transcends and surpasses whatever evil can be said about him'.[107]

Abbot Peter the Venerable of Cluny, recognizing that the lack of good information about the Muslim 'enemy' made it difficult to confront Islam rhetorically and theologically, had the Qur'an translated from Arabic into Latin in the 1140s. This does not seem to have inspired greater understanding of Islam in the West, for Peter's intentions were more polemical than theological. He presented the Qur'an to the Christian faithful so they 'may know how detestable both [Mohammed's] life and his doctrine appear'.[108] His introduction further argued that Mohammed himself was some kind of hybrid between the worst of heretics, Arius, and the Antichrist. Peter's translation and his letters about it, however, were largely academic exercises, born more out of hostility than curiosity. Most Europeans had no real experience of Islam, but those who had heard about it still regarded it as an existential threat.

In the areas of southern Italy and northern Spain that had been returned to Christendom, however, Christians and Muslims did live alongside one another—in Sicily Muslims still probably made up the majority in the early thirteenth century. Relations in these areas were always tense but the tension only rarely flared up into anti-Muslim riots and massacres like those which spread across Sicily in the 1160s (although these had as much to do with Muslims' role in an unpopular government than with strictly religious antipathy).[109] The Castilian epic *Poem of the Cid* conveys no special contempt for the Muslims of Iberia, but their status did decline when their territories fell the one or another of the Christian kings. Moreover, as the *Reconquista* increasingly took on the ideological character of a Crusade, the religious polemic became sharper. Apparently unaware of Peter the Venerable's efforts, a man named Mark, deacon of Toledo translated the Qur'an into Latin, and preceded it with an odd fantasy of a biography of Mohammed (here presented as a conniving magician). Mark and the bishop of Toledo, Rodrigo Jiménez de Rada, saw the *Reconquista* as the purification of Spain from Muslim pollution, a purification that would be made manifest in the conversion of mosques to churches and the substitution of the *Te Deum* for the call of the muezzin.[110]

Jewish communities

Christians in Western Europe may have approached Islam as an unknown, alien, and threatening faith from a distant land, but they experienced Jewish communities more directly, especially in urban settings. Still, they understood their Jewish neighbors largely through traditional stereotypes, including the one that considered them guilty of crucifying Jesus Christ. Such stereotypes could be especially toxic in the north, where Jewish communities were newer. We get a sustained view of traditional Judaism in the south from a remarkable travel narrative by Benjamin of Tudela, a Jew from Christian Navarre whose hometown had switched from Muslim to Christian control in 1119. In the late 1160s he set out eastward toward Jerusalem, and described the Jewish inhabitants of several southern French and Italian cities. About Rome he wrote:

> Rome is the head of the kingdoms of Christendom, and contains about 200 Jews, who occupy an honourable position and pay no tribute, and amongst them are officials of the Pope Alexander, the spiritual head of all Christendom. Great scholars reside there, at

the head of them being R. Daniel, the chief rabbi, and R. Jechiel, an official of the pope.[111]

Benjamin found established Jewish communities whose members played significant roles in their towns. The size of these communities varied widely, from two in Genoa to 2000 in Constantinople (apparently sequestered in a Jewish quarter). Although relations could be tense, Jews seem to have been tolerated, and occasionally valuable citizens of most major towns through which Benjamin passed.

Although there is some evidence for walled ghettos in late eleventh-century Germany, European Jews participated in the life of their towns and cities throughout the eleventh and twelfth centuries. The small numbers of Jews in northern Europe prior to the eleventh century seem to have included peasants and rural landholders, but by 1100 they were moving into a greater number of towns, and by 1200 they were nearly universally associated with moneylending.[112] Many Jews spoke Latin, and, as Benjamin of Tudela's description of Rome shows, helped the great and powerful as advisers, and in some cases, like in England, as personal bankers to the kings. Their culture flourished and Jewish writers and theologians certainly kept up with the so-called 'Renaissance of the Twelfth Century'.[113]

On the other hand, it has been argued that same impulse toward fear and intolerance that led to the persecution of heretics spilled over onto Jewish communities. Especially in the north, to which they had immigrated relatively recently, Jews there were a conspicuously alien presence. The dangers of the consequent resentment were vividly demonstrated by the massacres of Jews in the Rhineland after Urban II called the First Crusade in 1095 (there had been smaller-scale pogroms in 1009 when news of a Muslim ruler's destruction of the church of the Holy Sepulchre in Jerusalem reached France). A contemporary Hebrew writer found the murderers' motivation to be quite straightforward when he reported that they exclaimed, '[B]ehold, we journey a long way [...] to take vengeance on the Muslims. But here are the Jews dwelling among us, whose ancestors killed [Jesus] and crucified him groundlessly. Let us take vengeance first upon them'.[114] At the time of the Second Crusade, St Bernard intervened to prevent a repeat of the slaughter. Even Bernard, however, and others who offered Jews protection, betrayed plenty of ambivalence. Jews ought not to be killed, he argued. Rather, God wished them to live 'to remind us of what our Lord suffered'.[115] Bernard's Cluniac rival Peter the Venerable echoed the sentiment: 'God does not at all wish for [the Jews] to be killed, nor for them to be altogether wiped out, but that, like the fratricide Cain, they be preserved, for their greater suffering and shame, in a life worse than death'.[116]

In the English town of Norwich in 1144, townsmen discovered the body of a young boy, William, and blamed his death on the Jews. When Thomas of Monmouth wrote down the story in 1173 he described it as a ritual murder—a crucifixion no less—orchestrated by the Jews after a conspiratorial meeting of their elders in Narbonne. William of Norwich, it could be argued, suffered the ultimate *imitatio Christi*: 'Having shaved his head, [the Jews] stabbed it with countless thorn-points, and made the blood come horribly from the wounds they had made'.[117] Blood libels, as incidences like this are known, were repeated for the next 100 years and beyond, especially in England, France, and the Rhineland.[118] Once such libel led in 1171 to Count Theobald approving the massacre of the Jewish community in Blois, and inspired an organized period of mourning for Jews on both sides of the English Channel. 'Woe to us, for we have been plundered, and the tender beauty, the lovely community of Blois, known abundantly for both Torah and law went up in fire', wrote the poet Ephraim of Bonn.[119] Similar libels, often resulting in riots or executions, occurred at Würzburg in 1147, Saragossa in 1182, and Gloucester in 1186. Throughout the language of the blood libel we find unmistakable echoes of the contemporary devotion to Christ's body.

By the early thirteenth century, then, Jews, who 200 years earlier had been at worst an unpopular minority, had become threats to the pure body of Christ that was Latin Christendom. Lester K. Little, building on earlier work, has convincingly argued that twelfth-century Christians turned Jews into scapegoats for their anxiety about the profit economy.[120] At any given moment, particularly later in our period, there were as many if not more Christian moneylenders as Jewish ones, but Jews took a disproportionate share of the blame. Others have argued that there was more than simple psychological projection at work. In the case of the blood libel at Blois, the local count allegedly had a Jewish mistress, and Jews were often caught up in the sometimes unpopular policies of their secular protectors. In England, an anti-Jewish riot erupted at Richard I's coronation in 1189.[121] Kings, moreover, could be fickle protectors; Philip Augustus expelled the Jews from France's royal demesne in 1182. Philip's official biographer Rigord claimed that the expulsion was in part a response to the Parisian Jews' practice of meeting annually to 'slit the throat of one Christian in the hidden underground caverns on Maundy Thursday or during the Holy Week of penitence, as a kind of sacrifice in contempt of the Christian religion'.[122] They were re-admitted in 1198, but their position continued to deteriorate and they were definitively evicted from France in 1306, sixteen years after England had taken the same step. Anti-Jewish violence thus featured prominently at the highest levels of power. Although pogroms were not a universal fact of Jewish life in the twelfth century in all parts of Christendom, the trend toward greater hostility in both popular culture and secular and ecclesiastical legislation is unmistakable.

The Fourth Lateran Council

Elected to the papacy at the young age of only thirty-seven or thirty-eight, Pope Innocent III managed to combine severity, legalism, and great political acumen with great religious enthusiasm. When he dealt with matters of canon law or religious enthusiasts both orthodox and heretical, he showed that he understood the possibility and danger all around him. Throughout the twelfth century, boundaries had been challenged, cultural streams combined and transformed each other. Now Innocent seems to have sensed a need to come to terms with all of this change, to fix the new religious sensibility into something both comprehensible and prescriptive. While he may not have seen himself as channeling a century's worth of novel spiritual developments, he encountered evidence of them every day. In 1215, Innocent III called for a general council of the Church to be held at the church of St John Lateran at Rome, site of his papal palace. The call itself may not have implied anything out of the ordinary, since a general council had been held there by Alexander III in 1179, and Innocent clearly intended to reaffirm much of what was declared there. In the event some 1200 clerics of all ranks, including 19 cardinals and 361 bishops, travelled to the Lateran, making it the best attended council of the High Middle Ages. They came from western Ireland, Poland, the Holy Land, Scandinavia, and the Mediterranean regions and deliberated throughout the month of November, 1215. Innocent explicitly dedicated the council to two major problems: the reform of the Church and the recovery of the Holy Land, which he clearly saw as intertwined. Like Urban II at Clermont, Innocent III saw that only a pure, unified Church dedicated to reform could bring the land where Christ laid down footprints back under its tutelage. The council worked with remarkable speed, and on 30 November it promulgated 70 decrees, or canons, that would inform Church policy and governance until the sixteenth century. But it would be a mistake to see the council strictly in terms of ecclesiastical legislation;

it offered a comprehensive vision for the Christian world and the place of individual souls in it. At the earliest sessions Innocent confronted problems arising from secular politics. He nullified Magna Carta, accepted Frederick II as king of the Germans, and deposed Count Raymond of Toulouse, before moving on to matters related more strictly to the faith.[123]

More than any other council since Nicaea in 325, the Fourth Lateran Council (or 'Lateran IV' as it became known) provided a path forward that responded directly to recent developments and laid the groundwork for the Christian life in a universal Church. The opening canon proceeds methodically, beginning with a confession of faith in the one God and the Trinity, and implicitly targets the Cathars and other heretics. God is 'the one principle of all things, creator of all things invisible and visible, spiritual and corporeal'.[124] It proceeds to clarify Trinitarian theology and the nature of Christ before defining the Church as the 'one universal Church of the faithful', and immediately affirms the doctrine of transubstantiation, belief in which, in the following century, would become perhaps the most important test of orthodoxy for anyone accused of heresy. By extension it underscored the special status of the clergy who presided over the miracle of the mass. The attachment to Christ's suffering body that motivated so much contemporary piety here found institutional sanction. The comprehensive reach of the canons make them rather difficult to summarize without thoroughly paraphrasing them, but a few key themes can be identified in light of the preceding discussion of twelfth-century religious life.

Lateran IV acknowledged and enhanced the clericalization of the Church through a series of canons that insisted on the personal reform of the clergy and its radical distinctness from the laity. Canons 14, 15, and 16 reaffirmed old prohibitions on clerics marrying, getting drunk, or wearing ostentatious clothing, and sometimes went into great detail. 'Let them not indulge in red or green cloths, long sleeves or shoes with embroidery or pointed toes, or in bridles, saddles, breast-plates and spurs that are gilded or have other superfluous ornamentation'.[125] These were to remain the accoutrements of the laity, of knights. But more than appearances were at stake. Canon 18 declared that clerics could not 'decree or pronounce a sentence involving the shedding of blood', which, given the prevalence of clergy on the royal benches of England, for example, would have immediate practical consequences. Moreover, clergy were forbidden to 'extend [their] jurisdiction, under pretext of ecclesiastical freedom, to the prejudice of secular justice'.[126] Other canons dealt with reforming the clergy in more indirect ways, such as Canon 11, which required cathedrals and other sufficiently wealthy churches to appoint a schoolmaster to teach the clerics grammar and other disciplines.[127]

Lateran IV thus provided for a pure and learned clergy to lead the rest of the faithful to salvation. It also made demands on ordinary Christians, namely that all members of the Church, 'once they have reached the age of discernment', should confess their sins once a year, and to receive communion at least every Easter.[128] If nothing else, this helped provide a working definition of what it meant to be a Christian that would be universally applicable. Individual piety was regulated in other ways. We have seen that some critics like Guibert of Nogent had scorned certain peasants who revered suspicious relics, and Lateran IV addressed this by mandating the relics be venerated only in proper reliquaries, and only if they 'have previously been approved by the authority of the Roman pontiff'.[129]

The council preoccupied itself with purity, and not just that of the clergy. The Church was the body of Christ, which was in danger of pollution. Thus, Canon 20 urged that the chrism and the Eucharist be locked away 'so that no audacious hand can reach them to do anything horrible or impious'.[130] Similarly, the final four canons sought to avoid the contamination threatened by the existence of Jewish communities within Christendom. Jews who charged extortionate interest were to be 'removed from contact with Christians'.[131] Anxiety about sexual contamination motivates canon 68, which stipulated that Jews and Muslims should wear distinctive clothing because 'it sometimes happens that by mistake Christians join with Jewish or Saracen women, and Jews or Saracens with Christian women'.[132] In practice this could entail badges on one's clothing, such as a yellow star of David.

Although to some modern readers these final canons seem to take off in a new direction from the sometimes mundane regulation of episcopal elections and minutiae about ecclesiastical court cases, they are in fact implicit in the Council's opening statement, the product of the same zeal that inspired the prohibitions on clerical drinking.

Chapter 4: Intellectual Syntheses

Over the course of the eleventh, twelfth, and thirteenth centuries, Icelanders circulated stories, in both oral and written form, about the Vikings who had sailed to North America, to a place they called Vinland, around the year 1000. In the early or mid-thirteenth century, an anonymous scribe drew on this tradition and wrote it down in Old Norse prose; it was re-written later as *Eirik's Saga*, which included the following story of an unfortunate cultural encounter across the Atlantic Ridge:

> One morning Karlsefni's men saw something shiny above a clearing in the trees, and they called out. It moved and proved to be a one-legged creature which darted down to where [their] ship lay tied. Thorvald, Eirik the Red's son, was at the helm, and the one-legged man shot an arrow into his intestine.[1]

The experience of Vikings in Newfoundland has been corroborated by archaeological evidence, but the monstrous 'one-legged creature', also known as a uniped, that here accompanies a band of Native American warriors certainly strains one's credulity. What was a uniped doing in North America, or in the saga tradition for that matter? It seems likely that its presence has something to do with the near universal popularity in Latin Christendom of Isidore of Seville's (*c.* 530–634) encyclopedic *Etymologies*, which included unipeds in a catalogue of monsters. Isidore himself transmitted them from classical antiquity, in this case probably from Pliny the Elder (23 AD–79 AD). At any rate, unipeds were popular monsters who appear beyond the bounds of civilizations in contemporary maps, where they usually appeared in Africa. Since monsters were to be expected in the peripheral spaces of the earth, it may have been perfectly natural for an educated author to place one in Vinland. Thus, a short passage captured from an oral tradition but written down in the Norse vernacular, set beyond the edge of Christendom, shows an encounter between the Christian author's pagan ancestors and a monster from the Latin Classical tradition. In its cultural richness, this passage neatly illustrates a collision of diverse cultural streams that characterized written culture in the long twelfth century. One of the characters from *Eirik's Saga*, a woman named Gudrid, is said to have taken a pilgrimage to Rome before becoming a nun, further tying the periphery of Latin Christianity to its center.[2]

While the term 'renaissance', so often applied to the twelfth century, suggests a rediscovery and appreciation of a classical past, the above example demonstrates that something far more complex animated the cultural flowering of the period. Contemporary thinkers never fully accepted the pagan past, even as they bragged about how many Classical authors they had read.[3] To call the intellectual change of the period a re-birth of classical learning is to miss its great novelty as well as the uneasiness of its appropriation of ancient sources. Without question urbanization played a role, for schools located in towns produced the most important advances in speculative thought and theology beginning shortly after 1100. The development of lordship and government also proved a boon to intellectual production, since the courts of counts, kings, and bishops patronized the arts and sciences, and employed the men produced by the schools; twelfth-century thought emerged from a more thoroughly literate culture than Europe had seen since late antiquity. The proliferation of letter collections, which contained the (sometimes fictive) correspondence between literate elites, vividly demonstrates the creation of a transnational intellectual tradition in the common language of Latin. But literature proliferated in other languages as well, which brought alternative streams of culture into the contemporary thought world. Writers, readers, and listeners unpredictably synthesized a great variety of sources, and in the process created some new cultural possibilities.

The Intellectual World: Contexts, Institutions, and Personnel

Anselm of Canterbury appeared in the previous chapter to illustrate the emotional fervor of twelfth-century religious life as well as its devotion to saints. His piety also motivated him to embrace speculative thought, and he stands, in many surveys, as the first great philosopher in the Western tradition since Augustine. Anselm, who adopted the phrase 'I believe that I might understand' as a kind of motto, saw faith as fundamental for any real knowledge. When he proved the existence of God by means of the so-called 'ontological argument' in an extended prayer called *Proslogion*, he used a logical proof to explain what he already knew to be true. Subordinating reason to faith, however, did not necessarily denude his thought of intellectual vigor and originality. His proof has been called 'the only general, non-technical argument discovered in the Middle Ages which has survived to excite the interest of philosophers who have no other interest in the period'.[4] Starting with the definition of God as 'that than which nothing greater can be thought', Anselm argued that if such a being only existed in the mind, it would not be the greatest thing one could think of. The argument, which is not uncontroversial, proceeds as follows: God is that than which nothing greater can be thought; anything than which nothing greater can be thought exists in reality as well as in the mind; therefore God exists in reality as well as in the mind.[5] The proof is elegant and simple. It is at heart a grammatical argument, for God's existence is required by the definition of God as the greatest possible thing that exists. To say 'God is nonexistent' is to make a grammatical error, for the predicate 'nonexistent' is incompatible with the subject God, which, if it did not exist, would not be that than which a greater cannot be thought.[6]

Anslem's proof was challenged in its own day and eventually rejected by Thomas Aquinas in the thirteenth century, but it provides an ideal introduction to the twelfth-century intellectual milieu. Anselm himself found the proof fundamentally inadequate, for he represented a monastic tradition that sought to experience God mystically rather than understand him analytically. In a later chapter of *Proslogion* he asked 'but if I have found [God], why have I not experienced what I have found?'[7] A powerful current of affective spirituality accompanied much of the speculative thought of the twelfth century. As a monk, Anselm represented traditional intellectual culture, for in the early Middle Ages, the monasteries were the primary intellectual centers. In a prelude of things to come, Anselm bitterly debated the theology of the Eucharist with Berengar of Tours (*c.* 1000–1088), who worked in a cathedral school in an important urban center. He also displayed the occasionally grandiose ambition of twelfth-century thought, which sought to synthesize knowledge into a comprehensible unity. Anselm did not write systematic theology, and he used rather traditional methods. Over the next century the institutional settings, intellectual tools, and the uses to which learning was put would all change radically.

Translation and cultural interaction in the twelfth-century Mediterranean

Whereas Anselm helped inaugurate a period of vitality in speculative thought for the Latin West, the Arabic world had been steadily advancing in that field, as well as in science and mathematics, since the ninth century. Such thinkers as al-Farabi (*c.* 870–950), al-Kwarizmi (*c.* 780–*c.* 850), and Avicenna (980–1037) all made original contributions while preserving the intellectual heritage of ancient Greece. The Arabs in the Near East, Sicily, and Spain had access to Greek texts that had been unknown in the Latin West since antiquity. That Anselm gave Greek-derived names (*Proslogion* and *Monologion*) to two of his works, even though he personally could not read the language himself, shows that the idea of Greek antiquity still had some resonance in the Latin West.

Already in the later tenth century Western scholars had tried to reacquaint themselves with Arabic science and philosophy, and with the Greek part of the Classical tradition. Gerbert of Aurillac (*c.* 946–1003) had crossed the Pyrenees to the Christian kingdoms of northern Spain and acquired a working knowledge of mathematics then unparalleled in Western Europe, along with the ability to use the abacus and astrolabe. This prodigious learning helped lead to his election as Pope Sylvester II in 999. In the twelfth century the pace of such transmission quickened thanks to a number of individuals who travelled to the Muslim world in search of scientific knowledge, as well as to changed political circumstances: the fall of Toledo to Christian armies in 1085 and the continuing growth of Norman power in southern Italy helped make Greek and Arabic texts more accessible to Latin Christians. In the mid-to-late eleventh century a native North African, Constantine 'the African', became a Benedictine monk in the monastery of Monte Casino and translated the Arabic versions of some of the ancient Greek medical treatises by Hippocrates and Galen. In part because of its proximity to Greco-Arabic learning, Salerno developed the most important medical school of the period. Under King Roger II of Sicily, Palermo became a site of intense interaction between the three great traditions of the Mediterranean. Although not known particularly for speculative thought, his court shimmered with the artistic representation of this cultural blending. The royal chapel, the Capella Palatina, featured a Byzantine-style domed sanctuary, a vaulted ceiling in an Islamic style, and brilliant mosaics with Latin inscriptions.[8]

The emphasis of some translators on medical and scientific texts makes clear that this was not an antiquarian movement. Scholars were attracted from diverse parts of Europe to places where they could find ancient learning they could put to use. Adelard of Bath (*c.* 1080–1152) left his home in England, studied first at the cathedral school of Tours in France's Loire region, but then struck off for the Mediterranean world. He may have learned his Arabic in southern Italy, for he wrote of a stint in Salerno. He then went to the crusader states and learned directly from Arabic scholars. Upon his return to England he produced a series of translations of Greco-Arabic scientific works, as well as some original writings. Among the translations were the astrological tables of Al-Khwarizmi and Euclid's *Elements*, an introduction to mathematics especially important for its treatment of geometry. In his original dialogue *Questions on Natural Science*, he vigorously defends Arabic learning against his skeptical nephew, who complains that 'you both extol the Arabs shamelessly and invidiously accuse our people of ignorance in a disparaging way'. Adelard responds that 'I know what those who profess the truth suffer at the hands of the vulgar crowd. Therefore, I shall defend the cause of the Arabs'.[9] Adelard then ranges widely over a vast terrain of scientific knowledge, though he is perhaps at his most interesting discussing astronomy. He may have been aided in his translation efforts by Peter Alfonsi, a converted Spanish Jew who collected a set of fables from the Islamic world and rendered them into Latin as the *Clerical Discipline*.[10]

In Spain, especially after 1150, a circle of Latin-speaking scholars converged on Toledo to generate translations of crucial Arabic works. A representative figure here is Gerard of Cremona (*c.* 1114–1187), who,

> out of love of the *Almagest* [Ptolemey's (*c.* 90 AD–*c.* 168 AD) work on the mathematics behind astronomy], which he could not find at all among the Latins, went to Toledo; there, seeing the abundance of books in Arabic on every subject, and regretting the poverty of the Latins in these things, he learned the Arabic language, in order to be able to translate.[11]

In the end, Gerard translated nearly 50 scientific works from the Muslim and Greek traditions, the latter of which were all found in Arabic versions. In Sicily, which had been home to Greek-speakers consistently since antiquity, translators were more likely to translate directly from Greek—at least they did so whenever possible. It is worth knowing that Latin scholars often knew precisely what they were looking for, as was the case with Gerard and the *Almagest*. Although the discovery of Greco-Arabic texts opened myriad new possibilities to Western scholars, those texts helped satisfy an impulse that had its roots within Europe.

Schools and their curricula

That impulse came from a flowering in organized teaching and learning that had deep roots in the previous century. The Benedictine monasteries retained their roles as intellectual centers and continued to produce great devotional writers and historians right through and beyond the great historian Matthew Paris, who died in 1259, but the intellectual landscape shifted profoundly around them. In towns like Cologne and Würzburg in Germany, and Chartres and Laon in France, eleventh-century clerics assembled groups of students around them to study the liberal arts and so prepare them for careers in the Church or in the courts of great men.[12] By 1100 there were identifiable schools in several major towns throughout Europe; within 130 years, in Paris, Cologne, Bologna, Oxford, and elsewhere, these schools would coalesce into the first European universities.

Medieval students, whatever their aspirations, pursued the seven liberal arts: grammar, rhetoric, dialectic (logic), arithmetic, geometry, astronomy, and music. The first three of these formed the *trivium*, the latter four the *quadrivium*. According to John of Salisbury (*c.* 1115–1180),

> those to whom the system of the *trivium* has disclosed the significance of all words, or to whom the rules of the *quadrivium* have unveiled the secrets of all nature, do not need the help of a teacher in order to understand the meanings of books and to find the solutions of questions.[13]

The Bible and the writings of the Church fathers, like Augustine, were the most valued texts in the curriculum, but from their earliest education most students learned the liberal arts through classical authors. From the hoary old textbooks of Donatus (mid-fourth century) and Priscian (sixth century) they learned grammar; Cicero provided them with the rudiments of rhetoric, and they gleaned dialectic from such parts of Aristotle as were available in Latin translation. Essentially all intellectuals depended on the classical tradition, but this was not new. They treated the pagan classics with the same combination of reverence and suspicion that had characterized Christian thought since its beginnings. The classics could teach one to read, and carried a degree of timeless authority. John of Salisbury, in his handbook for princes called *Policraticus*, showed an odd combination of deference to classical authority and lack of interest in its actual content when he claimed to transmit the wisdom of the ancient historian Plutarch. Rather than claiming his ideas were original, John argued he had found his political thought in Plutarch's *Institutes of Trajan*, an advice book to the great Roman emperor. No such work ever existed. While twelfth-century writers certainly benefitted from increased exposure to examples of classical style, the cultural flowering was, again, not a 'renaissance' in the sense of an awestruck return to the ideals of antiquity.

Using the classical and patristic traditions as their building blocks, twelfth-century scholars began to move the old areas of studies in new directions. At Laon, a master named Anselm (not to be confused with Anselm of Canterbury) attracted students to his lectures on the various books of the Bible and began the systematic collection of scriptural glosses that would become the *Glossa ordinaria*, one of the most important and little known (outside of academic circles) texts of the Middle Ages. The *Glossa* gave the aspiring exegete all the tools he needed to delve into the study of holy scripture, and testifies to the systematizing tendencies of the age. Although Anslem of Laon's works seem dry to the modern reader (and indeed have not been translated into English), to his students they represented, essentially and perhaps even enthrallingly, pathways to the discovery of the truths of scripture.[14] Although most schools practiced exegesis, other specialties emerged. Tours and Orléans became known for the study of rhetoric and Chartres for philosophy.

The increased pace of learning, the discovery of new texts, and the rivalry between masters opened explosive possibilities that were realized when Peter Abelard arrived at Paris for the second time in 1108. Though Abelard was an unusual, even an extraordinary case, his career nicely encapsulates this early period in the history of twelfth-century schools. In the self-serving autobiography known as *The History of My Calamaties*, Abelard reports that he made a habit of besting his teacher William of Champeaux in classroom arguments, driving the latter to intense jealousy. Abelard then went off to start his own school in Melun, suggesting that the schools had little institutional continuity that did not depend on having charismatic masters. He returned to Paris, where he acquired pupils, including a young woman named Heloise whom he later seduced in a scandal that led to his castration (thanks to Heloise's angry uncle). He resumed his career, having already begun working as a theologian rather than a dialectician.[15] He wrote on a variety of controversial topics, which we cannot discuss in detail here, but what is important is that, in a way, controversy was the point for Abelard. In his work *Sic et Non* ('Yes and No'), Abelard sought to reconcile passages from scripture and other authoritative writers that seemed to contradict each other. The only way out of the apparent impasse was vigorous questioning. Indeed, 'consistent or frequent questioning is defined as the first key to wisdom'. This was not only intellectually, but completely pious, 'for by doubting we come to enquiry, and by enquiry we perceive the truth'. After all, as a boy, Jesus sat among the teachers of the temple and questioned them repeatedly.[16] Abelard took the application of dialectic to scripture further than most were comfortable with, attempting to use it to explain the mystery of the Trinity. This most complicated of Christian doctrines resisted his attempts to describe it in terms of human logic, and he was forced to retract and burn his book *Theologia* (which had argued, among other things, that the pagan philosophers had anticipated the doctrine of the Trinity) at the Council of Soisson in 1121.[17] Toward the end of his life his views on ethics, including the idea that the intention of an act, rather than the act itself, determined whether it was sinful, as well as further arguments on the Trinity, were branded heretical at the Council of Sens through the efforts of Bernard of Clairvaux.[18] Abelard was condemned to perpetual silence as a heretic, but it is clear that many observers thought Bernard had gone too far. A contemporary poem celebrated Abelard as a brilliant scholar whose prowess equaled that of the ancients, but who was 'silenced by the hatred of monks'.[19]

Even scholars who rejected Abelard's theology followed his method of marshalling contradictory authorities. While teaching at the cathedral school of Notre Dame in Paris between 1142 and 1159, Peter Lombard set out to lay out a comprehensive collection of statements about Christian doctrine in what became known as the *Four Books of Sentences*, or simply the *Sentences*. Although somewhat dry stylistically (the *Sentences*, too, have never been translated into English in their entirety), they represent one of the most conceptually enthralling projects of the twelfth century, an attempt to bring the whole of the Christian life into a knowable, systematic unity. Lombard ranged over every possible point of sacred doctrine, beginning with the nature of God Himself and proceeding to the creation, the fall, and eventually the sacraments and the last things. Its topics follow upon one another with elegant inevitability.[20] Despite its use of Abelard's message, moreover, the effect of the *Sentences* is of certainty in the truth of the faith. Because it answered so many questions so effectively, the *Sentences* became the most important textbook of the medieval university, and every aspiring theologian was expected to write a commentary on it. When Martin Luther wrote his commentary in the fifteenth century, the book's importance had started to wane, but commentaries were produced into the nineteenth century.

The weighing of authorities that informed Peter Lombard's writing reflected what went on in the medieval classroom. Typically, the master would lecture on a specified text in the morning (this was called the *lectio*), and then he would discuss a set of points of argument (*quaestiones*) later in the day, in what was called the *disputatio*. It would not be inappropriate to liken this to a modern course, in which a morning lecture is followed by an afternoon discussion section. In Paris, especially, what began as a loosely (if at all) organized collection of masters slowly gained a degree of institutional coherence. Originally, the local bishop would grant a license to teach to prospective masters, but gradually masters began to organize themselves as a kind of guild devoted to learning. There are references to groups of masters working together as early as mid-century, but the first documents referring to anything that could properly be called a university date to the first decade after 1200. In 1215, a papal legate issued rules for the schools' governance and curriculum. He stipulated minimum ages for lecturers (35 for theology, for instance), noted holidays that had to be observed, tried to regulate students' drinking, and required that half the members of a faculty attend the funeral of one of their number.[21]

The new schools provided options to scholars that did not always fit with received ideas about the proper education. Scholars argued endlessly over where to send students and what subjects to start them with. Some monks, like Bernard of Clairvaux, were convinced that the schools of Paris were a hell on earth designed to distract young men from more noble pursuits, such as the cloister. A rich tradition of satire developed, in which scholars were lampooned as career-obsessed pedants in search of elusive rewards. In Nigel of Longchamps's *Mirror for Fools*, a young ass named Burnellus sought to make up for his grotesquely long ears by advancing through the schools. His travels took him to Salerno and the schools of Paris, but ultimately, the poet assures us, his true condition was that of a monk.[22] On the other hand, the regular canon Philip of Harvengt argued that 'the school ought to be called another cloister'.[23]

The critics could not push back the march toward institutionalization, however, and universities sprang up throughout Western Europe. In France, Montpellier established itself as a leader in medical training, while in England, Oxford and Cambridge both emerged by the early thirteenth century. Bologna, whose origins go back much further, was an identifiable university by 1200. While Paris and Bologna had decidedly international outlooks, and Paris especially had international personnel, when Emperor Frederick II founded a new university at Naples, it was explicitly to provide competent administrators for his Sicilian court. He presented it as a place where students could study rather than study in other lands, presumably France.[24]

Scholars in courts and administration

Frederick II's remarks on founding his university remind us that relatively few of the students who completed courses of study in the schools stayed on as teachers or scholars. Most needed to secure employment, usually in ecclesiastical or secular administration. A study of scholars at Paris in the late twelfth and early thirteenth century suggests that English kings were especially keen to employ school-trained clerics in positions of administrative responsibility.[25] There was a constant stream of clerics between Paris, the administration of the archbishops of Rouen, and various parts of England as well.[26] The courts of kings, bishops, and lesser nobles became magnets for educated intellectuals, who formed a kind of trans-national elite throughout Europe. We find Englishmen and Frenchmen working in the Sicilian court in the 1160s, and the letters of some well-travelled clerics allow us to re-create an intellectual world stretching from the Holy Land to Ireland.[27] Some sources, including the poems known as the *Carmina Burana*, suggest the emergence of a kind of educated underclass, comprised of clerics who regarded themselves as under-employed. 'I am a leaf in the wind', wrote the so-called Archpoet of Cologne in one of the *Carmina* before launching into a raucous celebration of wine, women, and song that also betrays a detailed knowledge of the Bible (if only to satirize it relentlessly). His poem pleads with Frederick Barbarossa's chancellor to provide him with some kind of generosity, or, barring that, forgiveness.[28] Others attacked the court as a den of iniquity where good clerics lost their souls because of ambition or avarice. While monastic critics could smugly criticize court life from the spiritual safety of their monasteries, some of the most evocative and brutal assessments of the court came from those with experience.[29] In old age, Gerald of Wales, who had trained at the cathedral school of Lincoln and spent time at Paris as well, claimed to repent of his earlier careerism:

But now that others run and follow the court [. . .] let [Gerald] take his rest and in his humble habitation indulge his love of books and in the corners of churches weep for his sins and wail for his offences, and for the welfare of his soul with penance wash them away and wipe them out.[30]

What is clear is that by the early thirteenth century a new kind of administrator with newfound importance was reading and writing the documents that made European governments work.

In addition to being administrative centers, these same courts patronized writers. Count Henry the Liberal (1127–1181) of Champagne created a vital literary atmosphere in his court that drew on writers in Latin as well as the vernacular, monks as well as secular clerks. Peter of Celle, the Benedictine abbot and writer of highly emotive spiritual treatises (who was discussed in the previous chapter), figured prominently in this circle, as did one of the clerks who ridiculed Saint Bernard for his attacks on Abelard. Though he probably did not attend Henry's court, the great writer of Arthurian romance Chétien de Troyes mentions the Countess Marie in the introduction to *Lancelot*. The literary production of the court similarly showed the collision of sacred and secular and Latin and vernacular— especially important in this regard is a lengthy verse translation of Genesis written by the otherwise unknown Evrat. The combination of diverse figures with court patronage and power led to a strikingly diverse assortment of texts.[31] We have seen that Sicily under the Norman kings as well as Frederick II had a thriving court culture that, at least initially, took great advantage of the island's multicultural influences. Frederick attracted Michael Scot, a renowned mathematician who had worked in Toledo, to southern Italy where he translated some works of Aristotle and Avicenna.[32]

All the while, these literate clerics of the Latin West adopted received literary forms and took some of them in entirely new directions. In particular they ushered in golden ages of two genres with long traditions: letter-writing and historiography. Their letters helped them form political networks, advise their friends, and comment on politics and theology as they reported current events, while their chronicles placed those events into the context of a divine plan for their kingdom, the Church, or even the whole universe. Letter collections and histories discussed the Becket Controversy in England and the debates between various religious orders. From the Norman Conquest until Magna Carta, historical writing in England exploded to the point that modern historians of the reigns of Henry II and

Richard have several good sources to choose from.[33] 'Nothing', wrote the historian Henry of Huntington, 'is more excellent in this life than to investigate and become familiar with the course of worldly events'. Well-written history, after all, has profound benefits to the soul, for 'it is quite common for the path of history to lead us straight back to moral purity'.[34]

Monks and clerics in every other part of Europe devoted themselves to history writing with similar zeal, employing different genres depending on their situation and often reflecting a conscientious concern with accuracy (even if they made no attempt to meet modern standards of 'objectivity'). In Bohemia, Cosmas of Prague prefaced his history of the Czechs by noting that he had included things gleaned from 'the fabulous stories of old men' so that the tales would not be forgotten.[35] Like many other historians, Cosmas followed a long tradition by beginning his history with the incarnation of Christ (although many others did begin with creation) in order to place his story into a divine trend. Otto von Freising's chronicle of *The Two Cities* took the story from the Garden of Eden to 1146 CE, but included a final book on the eternal disposition of the City of Christ after the resurrection of the dead. For Otto was writing about the German Empire, heir to the Roman Empire: 'I have shown how kingdom was supplanted by kingdom up to the end of the empire of the Romans, believing that the fulfillment of what is said of that empire—that it must be utterly destroyed by a stone cut out from a mountain—must be awaited until the end of the ages[...]'[36] A concern with accuracy did not need to conflict with prophesy or eschatology.

Others adopted a somewhat more mundane framework. An Icelander named Ari compiled *Islendingabók* in the 1130s to provide a systematic history of the founding of Iceland and of its earliest inhabitants. Scholars in Normandy, the Celtic-speaking regions, France, Sicily, all showed a pronounced interest in origins narratives, but national and family histories began to show signs of adapting to contemporary political concerns. In one case, the French noble family of Amboise changed its family history, *The Deeds of the Lords of Amboise*, which recounted the deeds of its members who had gone on crusade after 1095, to 'rehabilitate their crusading ancestors' in the face of pressing political challenges.[37] On a more exalted political level, Saxo Grammaticus re-worked earlier Latin histories to reflect the coming of age of the Danish monarchy at the end of the twelfth century. Finally, to return to England, William of Malmesbury, writing in elegant and learned Latin, confidently recounted the history of the English kings from before the Norman Conquest to their twelfth-century period of dominance. In recounting the expansion of the Anglo-Norman kings into Wales and Ireland, he struck (according to John Gillingham) a 'condescending new note' against England's barbarian neighbors, making them out to be less cultured, even less human.[38] The art of history, perhaps unwittingly, became an instrument of Latin triumphalism at that very moment that some vernacular languages were entering the literary mainstream.

Women as patrons and scholars

The world of schools and scholars was a male world. Students at the proto-universities were ordained in at least minor clerical orders, which effectively prohibited women from enrolling in courses. Under appropriately controlled conditions, such as under the tutelage of a chaplain, women of the higher social ranks were encouraged to read and appreciate books, but school-learning was out of the question.[39] There are some tantalizing intrusions of women into the scholarly world, however, such as a song in the *Carmina Burana*, written in the voice of a young woman who was seduced and made pregnant by a dashing young clerk, presumably one of the male literate elite. One of the greatest literary talents of the twelfth century, Abelard's paramour Heloise, entered the historical record largely because she became the object of a master's sexual advances. Heloise herself shows that women did participate in the cultural effervescence that animated Paris, Bologna, and cathedral schools across Europe. Their lives and writings always point to the determining role of gender in intellectual life, and the anxiety with which men greeted women who engaged with the world through their wits.

Some scholars in the past viewed Heloise as a mere ornament to Abelard's illustrious career, a helpless, if precocious, teen-aged girl, and her place in his work that of a distraction. It was even suggested that the letters attributed to her, in a gorgeous Latin style replete with classical references, were fictions created by Abelard. And yet everything we know about her autobiography makes her emergence as a major writer entirely believable. Her uncle, Fulbert, served as a canon in the cathedral of Notre Dame, and had charged Abelard with her education. Abelard, though he clearly appreciated her mind, seems to offer support to the notion of a weak and vulnerable Heloise when he states that 'if [Fulbert] had entrusted a tender lamb to a ravening wolf it would not have surprised me more'.[40] Michael

Clanchy, Abelard's most recent biographer, has argued that Heloise may have been as many as ten years older than traditional scholarship has allowed, which would put her in her mid-twenties when she met her alleged seducer.[41] This is entirely plausible and consistent with Abelard's avowal that all of France admired her for her great learning. In both his autobiography and the letters he exchanged with her, Heloise appears as his intellectual match, engaging in *disputatio*-style debates with him over such topics as whether they ought to get married after the birth of their son Astrolabe. They were indeed married, but when Abelard sent her away to stay in a convent (without taking vows), a heartbroken Fulbert had him castrated, possibly emasculated. As Abelard put it, 'they cut off the parts of my body whereby I had committed the wrong of which they complained'.[42] Heloise would end up the respected abbess of the convent of Argenteuil, for which Abelard dutifully wrote a kind of rule. She made a good nun, but her letters suggest she hated being one.

As a writer, Heloise matched her Latin style to the immense power of her feelings for Abelard. More than a decade after the end of their affair she could launch devastating broadsides against Abelard. After expressing her sorrow that he had not written her recently, she reminded him that 'when in the past you sought me out for sinful pleasures your letters came to me thick and fast'.[43] His replies seem evasive and feeble, and she continued to bury him with emotionally devastating rhetoric: 'even during the celebration of the Mass, when our prayers should be pure, lewd visions of [our former] pleasures take such a hold on my unhappy soul that my thoughts are on their wantonness instead of on prayers'.[44] In all, Heloise wrote three letters to Abelard that are now regarded as unquestionably authentic, along with a brief missive to Peter the Venerable of Cluny after Abelard's death. Despite their emotional weight, they proceed methodically and betray great learning. She may even have changed the trajectory of Abelard's thought. Early in his career, Abelard was a grim dialectician obsessing over arguments, while Heloise had a humanist's love of the Latin classics, which she could well have imparted to Abelard. Her letters ring with allusions to Seneca, Cicero, and Lucan, while Abelard seems more comfortable quoting scripture. The later Abelard, as we have seen, tried to impute to pagan philosophers an understanding of the Trinity. Clanchy has even argued that her background in moral philosophy informed Abelard's intentionalist ethics.[45] A contemporary witness, Peter the Venerable, told her that he had heard of her great learning as a young man, and that when it came to the knowledge of letters, 'you have surpassed all women in carrying out your purpose, and have gone further than almost every man'.[46]

While Heloise diligently served out her career as a nun in France, Hildegard of Bingen (1098–1179) produced some of the most original and wide-ranging theology of the period. Hildegard had entered the religious life at the age of eight when her parents entrusted her to the tutelage of a teenaged recluse, Jutta of Spanheim. Jutta and Hildegard then joined the double monastic foundation (consisting of two segregated houses for men and women) at Disibodenberg on the Rhine. Afflicted all her life with spectacular waking visions, in 1141 she began to write down and interpret what she learned from the 'Voice of the Living Light', as she called it. Over the next 30 years Hildegard wrote prolifically and corresponded with the great men of the Church, including Popes Eugenius III and Hadrian IV, and Bernard of Clairvaux, all of whom encouraged, even ordered her to write down the contents of her visions. One of these visions was discussed in the previous chapter. In her visionary writings, the most striking of which is *Scivias* ('Know the Ways'), she tended to proceed by offering a vivid description of what she saw, and then to explicate its theological meaning. As a woman she did not have the authority to interpret scripture; instead, she practiced a highly original kind of exegesis on her visions. Her visions, that is, granted her a way of subverting the monopoly on scriptural interpretation claimed by the male Latin clergy, and she suggested this in a letter to Pope Eugenius III in which she humbly acknowledged that she was 'formed in the weaker rib and not taught by the philosophers'.[47] A lengthy quotation, this one from her account of seeing a blazing image of a man surrounded by fire, can give some sense of how she practiced her method:

> Therefore, you see 'an extremely bright light', which signifies the Father, who is without the stains of illusion, failure or deceit. And in the light is 'the figure of a man the colour of sapphire', which represents the Son, who is without the stain of hard-heartedness, envy or evil, and who before all time, according to his divinity, was begotten of the Father, but afterwards, in time, according to his humanity, became incarnate in the world. And 'it was all burning in a delightful red fire'; this is the fire without the stains of aridity, mortality or darkness, which represents the Holy Spirit, by whom the Only Begotten of the Father was conceived in the flesh, born in the time of the Virgin and poured out his light, truth and brightness all over the world.[48]

Thus Hildegard explains the doctrine of the Trinity through an arresting, but entirely orthodox natural metaphor, only decades after Abelard had come to grief attempting to present the same doctrine with logical terminology.

Like many other writers of the twelfth century, Hildegard celebrated the natural order, and saw creation as fertile, vital, and dynamic. She praised God's creation throughout her works, and saw humanity as bound to it. In *Scivias* she wrote that 'All the elements are present in human beings and each human being is able through the elements, which are fire, air, water and earth'.[49] In addition to writing visionary works, Hildegard channeled her view of the world order into songs (for some of which the musical notation is extant), a medical work called *Causes and Cures*, homilies, and hundreds of letters. She also illustrated her books, offering brilliantly colored renditions of her visions. According to one scholar, despite her orthodoxy (which was occasionally questioned, but not seriously), Hildegard developed a distinct 'theology of the feminine' that deployed women's symbols to construct an original system of thought outside the male clerical tradition.[50] Although Hildegard engaged in conventional, gendered self-deprecation—in a letter to Eugenius III she calls herself 'a poor female figure who was formed in the rib and not taught by philosophers'—she wrote confidently and repeatedly praised the Virgin Mary, for 'the highest blessing in all of creation lies in the form of a woman'.[51]

Hildegard's orthodox theology impressed many of her male correspondents with its interpretive power. Still, her visionary works sit somewhat outside of the mainstream of twelfth-century thought; she cites few contemporaries and builds her theology on its own foundations. Around the time of her death, another nun living in the German Empire produced another masterpiece that managed to synthesize much of the clerical culture of the age. Herrad, abbess of the reformed Augustinian monastery at Hohenbourg, put together an extraordinary illustrated compilation of learning known as the *Garden of Delights*. It is not an original work of theology, but a compendium of contemporary learning that seems to owe some of its organization to Peter Lombard's influence. Over 300 folios bring the world of the schools to Herrad's nuns. Herrad included prose and poetry on a variety of themes and topics including sacred history, canon law, the sacraments, and the nature of God. She also had it lavishly illustrated with allegorical depictions of the seven liberal arts, a vision of hell, and the story of Ulysses and the sirens. At the same time that Herrad compiled the *Garden of Delights*, she founded a house of male regular canons nearby, so that her nuns would have the required sacramental supervision. She thus called in male collaborators to ensure the spiritual welfare of her nuns.[52]

Hildegard effectively circumvented male clerical authority by speaking of her direct visionary experience of the divine. Herrad, on the other hand, positioned herself and her nuns firmly within the male literate culture of recent decades. While Heloise, Hildegard, and Herrad wrote in Latin, in the later Middle Ages more women religious would use the vernaculars for their writings. But the three of them demonstrate how women could take advantage of a highly fluid point in European intellectual history to create intellectual monuments, even though they were quite explicitly circumscribed by male clerical authority.

Varieties of Latin Culture

The twelfth century inherited a number of genres for intellectual expression, including scriptural commentary, formal letters, prayers, and chronicles, though most of them changed somewhat in response to the new intellectual conditions. John of Salisbury left a large body of work in genres both traditional and novel, including letters both personal and professional, a hagiography, an eyewitness history of the papal court, and two works that he titled, perhaps a bit pretentiously, with pseudo-Greek terms: a defense of the liberal arts called *Metalogicon*, and an odd work than can reasonably be considered political theory, *Policraticus*. John's work built on classical and patristic foundations but struck out in new directions that responded to his learning in the new scholastic environment as well as the political realities he faced. He famously reported that his teacher Bernard of Chartres had said that he and his students were 'like dwarves sitting on the shoulders of giants', and therefore 'we see farther than they'.[53] Although the comparison between dwarves and giants seems a bit self-deprecatory, Bernard and John were certain that they, as moderns (*moderni*, as they called themselves in Latin), could take advantage of traditions to create something new. There was a decidedly conservative strain in twelfth-century thought that looked suspiciously at the learning of the schools, but even critics like Bernard of Clairvaux were themselves innovators: Bernard's *Sermons on the Song of Songs* contain some of the most elegant Latin of the century, and unlocked the potential of symbolic scriptural interpretation in a manner never before seen in the Latin West. It would be impossible to provide a comprehensive survey of twelfth-century Latin culture in the space allotted, but a few exemplary figures can illustrate the key trends.

Paths to theological truth

John of Salisbury corresponded with hundreds of other clerics all over Christendom and shared books, insights, and jokes in hundreds of letters that he later collected and circulated. One of his correspondents, Peter of Celle, abbot of an important Benedictine monastery, sent him a book titled *De Panibus* ('On Bread'), which compiled and interpreted as many scriptural references to bread as he could find. John then thanked Peter for the gift, and turned the bread of Peter's work into a metaphor for the spiritual and intellectual nourishment that Peter's writing provided. He went on to liken the book to the tasty cakes and waffles referred to in an old poem by Horace, and then asked for another literary gift, which would play the role of wine to wash down the 'bread'.[54] John and Peter here demonstrate what has been called 'the symbolist mentality', an intellectual approach that explores the different symbolic meanings of a particular text or object. We have already seen an example of this in Bernard of Clairvaux's mystical interpretation of the Song of Songs, in which a kiss could refer to the joining of a soul with God. Rupert of Deutz (*c.* 1075–1129), another Benedictine, explored the deeper meaning of each element in the liturgical ritual of the monastic day, and so implicitly argued that the understanding of divine truth came from the experience of worship. Over the course of the twelfth century, thinkers like Hugh of St Victor (*c.* 1096–1141), Peter Lombard (*c.* 1100–1160), and Peter the Chanter (d. 1197) gave their writings a more systematic approach. While some monastic commentators viewed the methods coming out of the schools suspiciously, the scholastic and monastic milieus shared many common assumptions, and the fact that monks like Peter of Celle and clerical scholars like John of Salisbury were frequently on the same page (literally) shows that both methods fed into a common theological current.

On Paris's left bank, somewhat southeast of the cathedral of Notre Dame where Abelard had briefly taught and where Peter Lombard would later work, the church of St Victor was home to regular canons who took theology in important new directions. The leading figure of this new Victorine school was Hugh of St Victor, whose work combines his reverence for Church fathers, especially Augustine of Hippo, with a veneration for the liberal arts and a belief that to learn was to reform the soul. Despite original sin and man's fallen nature,

Hugh saw something in the human intellect that could, if properly trained, bring man closer to his pure state.[55] Moreover, knowledge was essentially self-knowledge, an understanding of man's rational nature. At the beginning of his work on the liberal arts, *Didascalicon*, Hugh outlines the goal of any educational program:

> Of all things to be sought, the first is that Wisdom in which the Form of the Perfect Good stands fixed. Wisdom illuminated man so that he may recognize himself; for man was like all the other animals when he did not understand that he had been created of a higher order than they. But his immoral mind, illuminated by Wisdom, beholds its own principle and recognizes how unfitting it is for it to seek anything outside itself when what is in itself can be enough for it. It is written on the tripod of Apollo: γνοθι σεαυτον, that is 'Know thyself', for surely, if man had not forgotten his origin, he would recognize that everything subject to change is nothing.[56]

The human mind, then, proceeds from an understanding of things outside itself to meditation on the God that created them. Abelard had also quoted the expression 'know thyself', and even used it for the title of his book on ethics. Historians who see the twelfth century as an important stage in the development of Western individuality have focused on this widespread concern with self-knowledge. For Hugh, everything starts with reading, and thus *Didascalicon* moves methodically through all the things that can be known, continually dividing every problem into smaller components. Philosophy, for example, is divided into theoretical, practical, mechanical, and logical. The mechanical arts are those relating to human labor, and thus he discusses food at one point: 'Food is of two kinds—bread and side dishes[...]. there are many kinds of bread—unleavened, leavened, that baked under ashes, brown bread, sponge-cake, cake, pan-baked, and so on'.[57] The point is to place the highest knowledge in its human context, and Hugh makes clear that the point of all knowledge is to lead the mind on to deeper meanings.

In his most ambitious work, *On the Sacraments*, Hugh synthesized his knowledge of the faith into a sprawling but meticulously organized whole stretching from the creation to the 'End Times'. Its organization into two huge books reflects salvation history, again emphasizing Hugh's belief that the processes of learning and redemption are linked: Book I begins with God creating heaven and earth, Book II begins with Christ's incarnation. Parsing problems into digestible subdivisions just as he did in *Didascalicon*, Hugh shows how man moves through history, by means of the sacraments of the faith, to his proper end. Although Hugh's concerns were ultimately mystical, focused on the soul's eternal union with God for all eternity, he gave knowledge of the world an important role in reforming mankind.[58] In the schools of Paris and elsewhere, the systematic element in Hugh's *De Sacramentis* reverberated in the works of the schoolmen, who, following in the footsteps of Peter Lombard, gradually created the genre of the *summa* (literally 'highest' in Latin): a work that tried to encompass the totality of knowledge by gathering together authorities and organizing them by topic.

An intensely practical approach to the systematization of knowledge motivated the work of Peter the Chanter, who stood at the center of a group of intellectuals associated with the Parisian schools as they continued to coalesce into a university. They brought systematic theology to bear on pressing contemporary issues like the Crusades, the proper role of clerics in government, and usury.[59] The *Verbum Adbreviatum* calls itself 'the *summa* of Peter the Chanter of Paris taken from authorities to condemn the vices and commend the virtues'.[60] Among its chapter headings are 'against usurers', 'against Lawyers', and 'against those who exempt themselves from the jurisdiction of their superiors'. Peter's method was to introduce a problem and then bury the reader in authoritative quotations from the scriptures and other writings. The chapter 'against lawyers' thus refers to thirteen books of the bible as well as Augustine, John Chrysostom, Sidonius Apolinaris, Seneca, and others.[61] Several of the Chanter's students went on to active careers in the Church, including Stephen Langton, an adept theologian who became the Archbishop of Canterbury and nemesis of England's King John.

Peter the Chanter's circle is one of many intellectual networks that contemporary sources and admirers documented. That these networks overlapped is amply demonstrated by Otto of Sankt Blasien, who, some two decades after Peter's death, listed him as one of the leading lights of the earlier generation at Paris, along with Alan of Lille (*c.* 1128-*c.* 1202). While Peter and his circle discussed the implications of the social order, Alan contemplated the natural order in a series of works that combined a solid background in the liberal arts with an imaginative appreciation of the cosmos. In *Anticlaudianus*, Alan envisions the perfect man as the union of a God-given soul with a body crafted by nature. The work takes the form of an adventure story populated with personifications of the liberal arts and of classical virtues. After being advised by Reason, Prudence mounts a chariot constructed by the liberal arts and drawn by the five senses and journeys through the cosmos until she has a direct encounter with God. Along the way she learns about the planets and the zodiac, and about the properties of the four basic elements of air, earth, fire, and water. As she reaches the limits of the known universe, she also reaches the limits of human understanding, Reason gives way to Faith, and true Joy is experienced: 'This extramundane world and blessed part of the universe is clearer than clear, purer than pure, brighter than bright, more glittering than gold'.[62] Echoing Anselm of Canterbury, Alain writes, 'let Faith, then, suffice'.[63] Toward the end of the journey, Prudence discovers truths about the Virgin Mary and the Incarnation. The *Anticlaudianus* places man in a broad natural and metaphysical landscape that is unified by a divine plan, and thus it perfectly embodies a large twelfth-century concern with extolling the value of the created order.

Law and political thought

Peter Lombard's *Sentences*, and the systematic theology that followed it, had a kind of analogue in the field of canon law, the *Harmony of Discordant Canons* attributed to Gratian (a medieval myth even claimed that Gratian and Lombard were twins). Now generally referred to as the *Decretum*, this work attempted to resolve the apparent contradictions that had over the centuries accumulated in the conciliar decrees, papal letters, and patristic writings that made up the canon law tradition. It has now been persuasively argued that the *Decretum* was originally written in 1139, at which time it entered the curriculum at Gratian's law school in Bologna, and was re-issued with substantial additions by an unknown second writer around 1158. That it is thought to have been a work in progress reinforces the notion that contemporary learning could be a collaborative exercise that kept up with developments in the various disciplines.[64] Still, the *Decretum* as we have it boldly cuts through ambiguities in the tradition to show canon lawyers a path forward. Messy disputes like the Investiture Controversy had made such a collection essential. Moreover, the *Decretum* made clear that the papacy had significant power to legislate, meaning that in the future it would have wide latitude to settle disputed issues. Although its organization is not quite as obvious as that of Peter Lombard's *Sentences*, perhaps due to the nature of its composition, the *Decretum* impressively surveys the field of canon law, ranging over problems relating to marriage, the sacraments, and most aspects of clerical life.

Scholars in Gratian's Bologna had rediscovered Justinian's *Digest* of Roman law in the 1070s, and many secular rulers, especially the German emperors with their significant claims in Italy, eagerly tried to apply what they could. The practical impact of the academic revival of Roman civil law, however, was relatively meager. Frederick Barbarossa appealed to it at the Diet of Roncaglia in 1158, but it did not make his position vis-à-vis the Italian city-states appreciably stronger. Indirectly, however, the renewed interest in Roman law seems to have motivated efforts at systemization and codification in other regions like Iberia and England. The ruling bodies of the Italian communes also seem to have used Roman law to some effect, since the towns also claimed some of the aspects of sovereignty exercised by Roman emperors; it seems that Roman precedents influenced Milanese statutes relating to guilds in 1216.[65]

John of Salisbury also immersed himself in Roman law while a student in Paris, but he remained more concerned with the practical matters of Church governance as a member of the archbishop of Canterbury's inner circle. He did manage to combine his learning and experience in politics to the twelfth-century's most enduring work of political theory (though he would not have recognized it as such), the previously mentioned *Policraticus* (*c.* 1159). John subtitled this the 'Frivolities of Courtiers and the Footprints of Philosophers', as if to call attention that he was immediately concerned with life at court and the proper use of one's learning. In his preface, John lamented that he had squandered 12 years in public life, but he had observed shrewdly while there. Interspersed between his moralizing and pontificating about flattery, John sketches the properly ordered commonwealth, likening it to a body whose parts act in perfect harmony. His model is a strange amalgam of the Roman and the feudal, so the prince is the head, the senate the heart, the eyes, ears, and tongues are provincial government, while the feet are 'those who exercise the humbler duties', including peasants and artisans. Although the sensibility of *Policraticus* is far from egalitarian, he does provide a basis for a community that depends on mutual obligation in ways that seem to transcend the feudal order:

> The health of the whole republic will only be secure and splendid if the superior members devote themselves to the inferior members and if the inferiors respond likewise to the legal rights of their superiors, so that each individual may be likened to a part of the others reciprocally and each believes what is to his own advantage

to be determined by that which he recognizes to be most useful for others.[66]

John also holds princes of the world to standards of justice, though he is not entirely consistent on this. On the basis of Book III, Chapter 15, it is often supposed that John advocates the slaying of unjust rulers, that is, tyrants: '[I]t is not only permitted, but it is also equitable and just to slay tyrants. For he who receives the sword deserves to perish by the sword'.[67] Elsewhere, however, he claims that vicious rulers ought to be endured. In fact, both ideas were current in contemporary thought. Feudal tradition held that kings had obligations to their vassals that could not be abrogated, while prevailing ideas about divinely ordained kingship argued that kings were the source of, and hence above, law. In this respect *Policraticus* merely embodies the contradictions of its age. In John's homeland of England, these contradictions caused considerable political turmoil a half-century later in the period leading up to Magna Carta (see above, Chapter 1).

The Uses of Vernacular Literature

In the late 1130s, the English cleric Geoffrey of Monmouth presented his patron with a fanciful *History of the Kings of Britain,* including stories of Brutus (here appearing as an early settler of the island), King Lear, and King Arthur and his knights. He insisted that the work was not original, for a friend of his had given him 'a certain very old book in the British [i.e., Celtic] language', which Geoffrey then proceeded to translate. While it is singularly unlikely that Geoffrey told the truth, the stories of Arthur and his knights indeed came to him from Celtic traditions. Arthur had been the ancient hero of the Celtic-speaking Britons who resisted the Anglo-Saxon invasions in the fifth and sixth centuries, and Geoffrey helped re-introduce him into the mainstream of literary culture. Geoffrey wrote his *History* in Latin (the language in which William of Malmesbury wrote a significantly less fanciful, even accurate historical work for the same patron), but the future of the Arthur stories lay in the vernaculars of Western Europe. Geoffrey's position as a literate Latin clerk passing originally oral tales from Celtic to Romance vernaculars demonstrates how these various traditions were closely blended. In the early Middle Ages, England had the most highly developed vernacular tradition of Western Europe in the form of Anglo-Saxon literature. After the Norman Conquest, Anglo-Saxon essentially went underground as Norman French became the language of the aristocracy. Similarly, Old Norse had been written down in the Latin in the eleventh century, and during the twelfth the materials for the great sagas of the late thirteenth century were being gradually assembled. The various forms of northern Old French found written expression by the year 1100, as did the southern French language of Occitan, sometimes referred to as Provençal. Several varieties of German emerged over the course of the twelfth century, and by 1200 Middle High German was one of the most important languages of romance literature. In the south, partially because of their similarity to Latin, Spanish and Italian arose relatively late, surviving in examples from the late twelfth century but found in earnest only in the thirteenth. Hebrew, which functioned as a kind of vernacular in Iberia and elsewhere, also found expression in several forms of poetry.

Courtly society, love, and vernacular romance

Vernacular poets wrote for an aristocratic audience, many of whose members must have been illiterate and thus heard their stories in oral performances at the courts of the great, where the written and oral, the lay and clerical, the secular and Christian collided in a setting that can usefully be termed 'courtly culture'. The ideological world of this literature is as turbulent as court life, full of contradictions, and thus it is very difficult to extract a particular ethos regarding love or war, but scholars have certainly tried. The business of the aristocracy was mounted combat, governed by a code of conduct that long predated Christianity; the term 'chivalry' generally refers to the attempt to express warfare and the other duties of a knight in positive terms consistent with Christianity. Initially the French term *chevalerie* simply referred to the behavior expected of a mounted knight (*cheval*), but in the hands of poets in the self-contradictory world of the twelfth-century court, it acquired considerable baggage related to honor, heroism, and love. That is, the expectations of a mounted warrior became combined and perhaps confused with those of a noble in a more genteel setting (sometimes called courtliness or *cortoisie*). In the vernacular genre known as romance, this complicated mix of competing cultural imperatives found its greatest expression.

The French poet Jean Bodel (1165–1210) referred to the cycle of stories introduced to the Latin world by Geoffrey and now grouped under the heading of 'Arthuriana' as the 'matter of Britain', distinguishing them from two other topics of French narrative: the 'matter of Rome' (stories of classical provenance, including those about Alexander the Great, heroes from the known epics, or characters from Greco-Roman myths) and the 'matter of France' (covering the legends that had cropped up around the historical figure of Charlemagne). Bodel's taxonomy only gives the slightest indication of the diversity of twelfth-century literature in Old French, and comparatively little of the second two categories is extant today. On both sides of the English Channel, as well as in Germany and even Iceland, stories about Arthur and his knights, the Crusades, as well as more mundane topics, found enthusiastic audiences and patrons.

The most important writer of Old French romance, Chrétien de Troyes (*fl.* 1160–1190), laid out the fundamental dilemmas of knighthood in stark terms, but rarely resolved them. In *Erec and Enide*, the problem seems straightforward. Erec, the greatest knight of Arthur's court, first demonstrates his knightly prowess by protecting Queen Guenivere from an evil knight and foul-tempered dwarf. He then weds the beautiful but impoverished noble girl Enide and takes her back to court. There, distracted by Enide into incessant lovemaking, he starts sleeping in and missing tournaments, leading to rumors at the court that he has gone soft: 'Erec left her with such true love that now, the God of War bored him'.[68] When Enide tells him about the whispering campaign against him, he saddles up their horses and sets out to find adventures that will allow him to salvage his reputation. On their journey, however, he brusquely demands that she stay silent, as if he has brought her along simply so he can reject her and what she represents. Enide, for her part, sees danger coming and must decide between obeying her husband's command not to speak, and potentially saving his life. She speaks up, and though he is initially furious, Erec is eventually grateful, and several dead opponents later, the story ends happily while leaving the reader several unanswered questions about what the right thing to do was at several points in the poem.

Erec and Enide is relatively straightforward insofar as the main characters are clearly meant for each other and enjoy a pure, if passionate, relationship. In *Lancelot: The Knight of the Cart*, Chrétien confronted the problem of adulterous love. Here the tension between love and honor is presented through a concrete, and impossible, choice. Guinevere has been abducted, and Lancelot can apparently only keep up with her if he accepts a ride in a cart, which, Chrétien assures us, would mean looking like a criminal who had lost all respect. Seeing no good way out of the situation, Lancelot hesitates and takes two steps before mounting the cart, a choice that he never fully lives down:

> Reason, which warred
> with Love, told him to take care[...].
> Reason's rules come from the mouth, not the heart.
> But Love, speaking from deep
> In the heart, hurriedly ordered him
> Into the cart. He listened
> To Love, and quickly jumped in,
> Putting all sense of shame
> Aside, as Love commanded.[69]

After a series of complicated plot developments, Lancelot and Guinevere have an adulterous tryst. Although the author does not condemn them for it, Lancelot's troubles continue. When he fights in a tournament in disguise and threatens to give himself away through his valor, Guinevere orders him to fight badly, and he becomes the joke of the tournament. It has been suggested that Chrétien left the work unfinished because the subject of infidelity troubled him, but the story is so riven with ambiguity that it is difficult to read it as a celebration of adulterous love.

Wolfram von Eschenbach's Middle High German romance *Parzival* is somewhat more successful in reconciling conflicting ideals. The eponymous hero undertakes a series of adventures, both romantic and martial, culminating in his marriage on the one hand and his quest for the Holy Grail on the other. His amorous and military energies are both thus appropriately channeled. At times Wolfram seems to ridicule the courtly love tradition, as when he writes, 'Lady Love, it ought to grieve you that you teach the body lustful habits, for which the soul suffers'. He later concludes that 'if a man endures hardship for a lady's sake, it brings him joy, although sometimes sorrow weighs heavier in the balance. Such is the reward that Love offers'.[70]

Gottfried von Strassburg took an even more complex view of love in his *Tristan and Isolde*, which chronicles a destructive adulterous affair between a young knight and the wife of his lord, King Mark, who did nothing to deserve his betrayal. Love sends the lovers into a confusing and tortuous set of conflicts, as they try to pursue their affection for each other while seeming to be honorable. At one point, Gottfried stops to analyze their condition:

> Thus in one way or another these two were both mournful and happy. Nor did it fail to happen that there was anger between

them—anger without malice, I mean. And if anyone were to say that anger is out of place between such perfect lovers, I am absolutely certain that he was never really in love, for such is Love's way.[71]

Again and again, Gottfried explores the emotional toll of the affair on the two lovers and on Mark, who always tries to take the high road. Tristan and Isolde are wracked with doubt at nearly every turn, despite their overwhelming love. Mark never finds happiness in love or honor, and his courtiers rebuke him for it: 'you hate your honor and your wife, but most of all yourself!'[72]

Scholars have long debated the extent to which romance literature either reflected or prescribed social reality. The dilemmas that come up repeatedly in the texts suggest that these were things that people thought about, but it is hard to detect a single code of conduct for chivalry or love. Even Andreas Capellanus's *Art of Courtly Love*, which is supposedly a lovers' how-to manual, is not necessarily to be taken seriously as a guide to what people actually did or thought they should do. Throughout the work he offers suggestions for wooing women, including happily married ones. He offers sly suggestions for getting a lady into bed by promising nothing untoward would happen, and then repeatedly upping the ante. Elsewhere, however, he argues that one would best just refrain from loving. It has been suggested that the *Art of Courtly Love* takes on the nature of a scholastic *disputatio* that is never quite resolved, and that Andreas simply reported on the irreconcilable tensions he saw in contemporary love.[73]

The Crusades and the vernacular imagination

When Urban II exhorted the knights of Christendom to take their armed pilgrimage to the East, he preached in Latin, and most of the earliest crusader historians wrote in that language. But the crusaders themselves were aristocrats who spoke about and presumably thought about fighting in their vernacular languages. Gerald of Wales travelled around Wales with the archbishop of Canterbury recruiting for the Third Crusade, and boasted that he preached so eloquently in French and Latin that even the Welsh-speakers in the audience were moved to tears, so it is clear that the crusading preachers used the vernacular.[74] The French, Castilian, and German vernaculars all developed around the same time, and all engaged with the ideology of the Crusades in one way or another.

The French written vernacular was coming into its own just as the crusading era began at the end of the eleventh century, and the

Crusades figured prominently its earliest literary expression. Emerging from a much earlier oral tradition, the *chanson de geste*, known as the *Song of Roland* (*c.* 1100), projected the experience of crusading back to the era of Charlemagne.[75] The defeat of the Frankish emperor's rearguard at Roncevalles in 778 served as the kernel of truth for the *Song's* story of an ambush by an army of unchivalrous, idolatrous, tri-theistic Muslims. The loyal vassal Roland commands the Frankish rearguard and is overrun and killed by the Moorish army. But it was not a fair fight, for a treacherous vassal named Ganelon betrayed Roland to the enemy. Thus the poet endows the old story with prevailing 'feudal' values while giving it contemporary resonance as a call for a united Christendom to evict the Muslims from Spain. Despite its emphasis on the warrior ethos and graphically violent depictions of hewn skulls and splattered brains, the poem conveys elements of popular piety; the hilt of Roland's sword contains a tooth of St Peter and a lock of St Denis's hair. Moreover, the Franks' warfare is explicitly penitential and led by devoted if bellicose clergy. The armed, mounted, and fictional Archbishop Turpin appears as a loyal vassal who helps lead the army into battle, a detail that might have troubled certain Gregorian reformers. Shortly before slicing a Saracen in half with his sword, he exhorts the warriors to confess their sins and 'as a penance he orders them to strike'.[76] The poet of the *Song of Roland* used Old French to tell a warrior's story while incorporating the popular religious and ecclesiastical values into a rich cultural mix.

Crusading and chivalrous ideals, as they applied to the *Reconquista* in Iberia, helped condition the formation of the first major monument in a Spanish vernacular. The Castilian poem now generally referred to as the *Poem of the Cid* sticks somewhat closer than the *Song of Roland* to actual historical facts as it mingles crusading fervor with feudal and courtly sensibilities over the course of 3700 lines. Written down around 1207, it also vividly displays the complicated political relationships of contemporary Iberia. The Cid (from the Arabic *sayyid*, an honorific term signifying lordship), based on the historical Rodrigo Díaz de Vivar (*c.* 1043–1099), is the loyal vassal of the somewhat incompetent and capricious Alfonso of Castille, who initially exiles him. 'God, what a good vassal, if only he had a good lord', cry the throngs who come to see him pass through their town.[77] The Cid, however, never shirks his obligations to his lord, and sends him spoils from his military victory over Christians and Moors alike. Throughout the poem chivalry and political expedience trump religious conflict; Rodrigo occasionally takes on Muslim allies, and even entrusts his daughters to the care of a Moorish friend at one point. In this respect the poem accurately portrays the Iberian scene. The poem's Moors are gift-giving, honorable nobles, though the Cid is less than magnanimous with Jewish characters. All the while, the Cid's behavior remains almost unbelievably courteous to all despite personal crises involving the ill-fated marriages of his daughters. The hero emerges as the conqueror and defender of Valencia, but his Crusading fervor remains firmly under the control of his chivalrous instincts. After conquering the town of Alcocer, he refuses to kill or enslave the Moorish inhabitants and when he leaves they tell him that 'we're deeply satisfied, our lord, with all you've done'.[78]

Other writers employed the vernacular to present emphatically historical accounts of the Crusades. Within five years of Richard I's return from the Third Crusade, a Norman known only as Ambroise, who was probably a cleric, combined the skills of a poet, propagandist, and journalist in his *History of the Holy War*, which in 12,000 verses follows the king's exploits from Gregory VIII's calling for a crusade to his imprisonment in Germany on the way home. Despite his own clerical orders, Ambroise displays a soldier's impatience with intellectuals when he has Richard tell a fearful cleric advising retreat to 'concern yourself with your writing and come out of the fighting; leave chivalry to us, by God and Saint Mary'.[79] His treatment of Richard I is almost hagiographical, but with the political aim of supporting Richard I in his quarrels with fellow crusader Philip Augustus of France. Unlike many vernacular writers, Ambroise had no obvious model for his project. His poetry is gritty and occasionally florid but clearly intended as a contribution to ongoing political controversies.

Ambroise was not the only French-speaking crusader to explore new literary territory. The Fourth Crusade's diversion to Constantinople gave rise to what is probably the first prose history in French. Geoffrey de Villehardouin, the marshal of Champagne, wrote a vivid account of the preparations for and prosecution of the Crusade through the founding of the Latin Empire of Constantinople after its sacking of the imperial city. As was the case with the poet of the *Song of Roland*, his crusading zeal and soldier's values sometimes combine in surprising ways. Once the journey is underway, he regarded it as a holy crusade irrespective of where it went, so he expressed no qualms at all that his expedition ended up in Constantinople rather than its intended target of Egypt. The knights who plunder the Christian city are 'pilgrims', just like any other crusader. Moreover, when a group of barons complains that the army ought to hasten to Syria rather than linger in Constantinople Villehardouin dismisses the barons as 'those who wanted to see the army disband', and he approvingly notes that several knights who defected for Antioch were killed in battle there.[80] His history integrates elements of courtly literature with a detached, matter-of-fact style that illustrates the gradual disentanglement of history from earlier vernacular genres.

Lyric and fabliaux

In addition to the longer narrative forms of epic, *chanson de geste*, romance, and history, vernacular writers produced shorter works, the most accessible of which are lyric poetry and fabliaux. As a poetic genre, the lyric emerged in southern France as the songs of wandering troubadours, who worked in the Occitan language and spread northwards after 1100. Twelfth- and early thirteenth-century lyrics survive in Latin and several highly diverse languages, including Occitan, Middle High German, northern dialects of French, and the Iberian languages of Galician, Hebrew, Arabic, and Mozarabic. The earliest extant Italian lyrics are attributed to St Francis of Assisi, reminding us that the genre could be used for sacred as well as secular purposes. Poets did cross genres, and we have extant lyrics from the romance writer Wolfram von Eschenbach. Although some wandering lyric poets may have been social misfits, lyric was a genre of the court that tended to deal with aristocratic values and aristocratic problems. Richard I Lionheart of England, who, as Count of Poitou, had presided over a regional French court, himself wrote an amusing reflection on his time as a prisoner in Austria, in which he lamented that 'Over the plains I don't see a piece of mail/Although I'm still in jail!'[81] More commonly, lyrics dealt with love and nature, and they combined both of those themes in 'dawn songs', which tell of the parting of two lovers as the sun rises. A late stanza in an anonymous Occitan dawn song illustrates the genre nicely through the voice of the female lover:

> 'Down in the sweet air over the meadow hovering
> I drank a sweet draught—long, so long—
> Out of the air of my handsome, noble lover'.
> Oh God! Oh God! How swift it comes—the dawn!'[82]

At the opposite pole of these exultations of love and nature lie the Old French fabliaux, which have inspired more scholarly controversy than perhaps any other body of medieval work, for reasons both moral and academic.[83] They delight in graphic depictions of sex, profoundly crude scatological humor, and vicious social snobbery, often all at the same time. Some, like the staggeringly vulgar *Audigier*, offer up a combination of lechery, trickery, and human excrement that can turn the stomach of the most cynical undergraduate student. They also present severe problems of origin and audience. The characters tend to be peasants, and the subject matter often has much in common with folk traditions, which has led scholars to claim that they represent an authentic look at rural social history. Others hold that they simply direct typical aristocratic antipathy toward the lower classes. We know that some of the authors came from a cultured background, since Jean Bodel, author of some *chansons des gestes*, also wrote fabliaux. But the fabliaux themselves are diverse enough that they may have been intended for several different audiences. As a general rule, they seem to represent the fixing in written form of oral takes that had deep roots in the rural population, but which were augmented by the influence of ancient stories like those of Aesop. Their stock characters include gluttonous priests, peasant wives with insatiable sexual appetites, and easily duped husbands. Occasionally the characters show bursts of cleverness, as does the husband, who, when his wife claims she can live without his penis, cuts one off the body of a drowned priest and presents it as his own severed member. Some fabliaux are simply charming short stories. In *Browny, the Priest's Cow*, a peasant hears an avaricious priest impart the Christian message that those who give for God's sake will receive a reward in heaven equal to double the gift. He dutifully gives his favorite cow, Berny, to the delighted priest, who takes the cow home and has her up with his own cow Browny. In the night, a homesick Berny drags Browny back to the peasant's farm who marvels that the priest could have been so prophetic. The poet sums up the moral: 'Two for the peasant, one for the priest/And those who have the most, get least'.[84] It is a marvelous satire that exposes the avarice of the clergy while slyly vindicating its message in material terms. But many more of the fabliaux make their points with liberal doses of filth and bawdiness.

The notorious *Audigier* lampoons chivalric romance with a main character who has limited control of his bodily functions and such a slight constitution that the wind blows him off his horse. He himself originated from the union of a knight, Turgibus, and a young lady who entreats him to 'polish my ass with your shirttail, or else you shall not have the gift of my love'.[85] After passing a few anti-chivalric tests which include having feces smeared on his face by two different women, Audigier successfully woos a young maiden and receives goat droppings as a wedding present. *Audigier* seems quite neatly to satirize the aristocratic world, and as such could be the product of an elite court, but other fabliaux range more widely across the social order. It is perhaps not wise to search for too deep a meaning in this kind of material, but if taken together, the stories show the versatility of the vernacular in assimilating social issues and received stories, while showing that literary dynamism and originality can go in directions not at all obvious from labels like 'renaissance'.

Chapter 5: The Crusades and the Idea of Christendom

In the early 1150s, shortly after the Second Crusade failed, an Icelandic abbot named Nikulás of Munkathvera visited the church of the Holy Sepulchre in Jerusalem. 'The center of the earth is there', he later wrote, 'where the sun shines directly down from the sky on the feast of St. John'.[1] The contemporary artists who created the world maps known as *mappae mundi* certainly agreed, for they invariably placed Jerusalem in the precise center of the world, surrounded by the three known continents of Asia, Africa, and Europe. By the second third of the thirteenth century at the latest, people and places from the Bible and from classical literature populated these maps, while monsters, including some like the uniped that killed the Viking Karlsefni in *Eirik's Saga*, populated the fringe areas.[2] Despite its distance from Rome or London or even Iceland, Jerusalem represented that which was known absolutely; the further one travelled from Jerusalem, the less the rules of an ordered cosmos applied. Gerald of Wales (c. 1146–1223) introduced his book on the alleged wonders of Ireland by observing that 'sometimes tired, as it were, of the true and the serious, [nature] draws aside and goes away, and in these remote parts indulges herself in these secret and distant freaks'.[3] At the top of the *mappae mundi*, below the image of Christ, was the Garden of Eden, generally accompanied by a depiction of the Fall, which entangled earth in a drama of sin and redemption. Warrior-pilgrims to Jerusalem sought to make the world make sense again through a penitential act in the very place where Christ redeemed mankind; one could reach the heavenly Jerusalem by seeking out the earthly one. Against this moral and cosmological background, where the literal and the allegorical, natural and unnatural, the familiar and the freakish, were juxtaposed, European Christianity expanded its reach greatly in the long twelfth century.

During the Crusades to the eastern shore of the Mediterranean, and the related expeditions to Eastern Europe and Iberia, Europeans brought the spiritual energy and political ambitions of their home-lands into a much larger geopolitical universe. They waged war and settled under conditions shaped by material developments, such as the burgeoning trading relationships that some Italian city-states had established with the Byzantine and Islamic worlds. Even as the popes preached the Crusades as the holy duty of a unified Christendom, the kings and knights who travelled East nearly always exposed the fissures and rivalries that divided them. The Crusades were a con-stant reality in contemporary politics. A substantial number of the kings discussed in this book—including Conrad III and Fredericks I and II of Germany, Richard I of England, and Louis VII and Philip II of France—went on crusade, and many others, such as Henry II of England and Alfonso VII of León and Castile, saw the idea of holy pilgrimage impinge on their reigns in one way or another. Crusading also informed contemporary aesthetics and molded the understanding of history, as at Chartres Cathedral where the Charlemagne window depicts the emperor striking a Muslim's neck with his sword.[4]

The Crusades provide an ideal finishing point to this book in part because they display the contradictions and ambiguities of contem-porary thought and culture. It is possible that twelfth-century people did not have a clear understanding of what a crusade was. It is certain that twenty-first century historians do not.[5] In 1095 and for decades afterward, such a journey to the East was thought of as a 'holy war', an 'itinerary', a 'military exploit' (*res militaris*) or, most commonly, a 'pilgrimage'. Terms cognate with modern English 'crusade', such as the French *croisade*, were not common until the thirteenth century. The privileges granted to crusaders, most importantly the indulgence, or remission of penance for one's sins, were gradually worked out as canon lawyers worked out the theology of penance. Our under-standing of crusading is further complicated by the calling of military pilgrimages to areas that lacked the sacred geography of the Holy Land, including Iberia and the Baltic. Yet even in those cases, trends in contemporary devotion helped impart holiness to the targeted regions. At least one northern crusade propagandist used the term 'our Jerusalem' to describe the Baltic region, and Livonia became associated with the Virgin Mary to the point that it was referred to as 'Our Lady's Dowry'.[6]

Traditionally, historians saw the goal of liberating the Holy Land as the defining characteristic of the crusade, and so defined the movement in terms of geography. In the second half of the twentieth century, however, many came to view the indulgence and papal leadership as its essential features. As a result, the Wendish Crusades in the Baltic, the *Reconquista*, and the Albigensian Crusade all came to be regarded as 'true crusades'. Other schools of thought center on the cultural meaning of holy war, and see the crusades as bound up in the popular piety of the twelfth century, and expressions of apocalyptic religious excitement. It is worth noting here that professional historians have almost universally discounted the widespread belief (in popular culture) that crusaders sought primarily economic gain or political power from their adventures.[7] It is nonetheless difficult to deny that the economic development of Europe, in particular the rise of trade in the Mediterranean and the anxiety toward wealth that caused some crusaders to call attention to their poverty, greatly affected the prosecution of and attitudes toward holy wars. In addition, although the Crusades were far more than military adventures for bored glory-seekers, they did provide an arena for ideals of martial conduct, and they cannot be separated from the history of chivalry.[8] In the context of this book, the Crusades, loosely defined as religiously motivated military pilgrimages to a variety of territories, serve as a point of convergence for popular piety, economic growth, theological codification, and the military ethos of the aristocracy. They exposed Europe's religious energy, and the tension between the universalizing claims of the Church and the messy realities of contemporary politics.

The Conception and Meaning of the Crusades

Although few scholars currently see the Crusades as harbingers of European colonialism, many are willing to regard them as part of a broader process in which Latin Christendom expanded to include previously pagan or Muslim areas. Settlers, often directed by kings and inspired by bishops, brought the ideas and institutions of the twelfth century to new regions and created frontier societies where diverse cultural traditions interacted and were synthesized. In the case of Eastern Europe, especially in the Baltic areas, secular and ecclesiastical leaders explicitly tied this expansion to crusading, and almost everywhere Christianization accompanied political subjugation.

At least one Muslim observer saw the First Crusade as part of a broader assault on Islam that had begun elsewhere in the

Mediterranean. With benefit of hindsight, Ibn al-Athir (1160–1233) wrote that

> the power of the Franks [as Latin Christians in general and the crusaders in particular were called in Arabic sources] first became apparent when in the year 478/1085–86 they invaded the territories of Islam and took Toledo and other parts of Andalusia […] Then in 484/1091 they attacked and conquered the island of Sicily […][9]

By contrast, when Urban II implored the knights of France to fight for Christendom, he did not (according to the extant versions of his speech) mention Iberia or Sicily. Although the Byzantines who appealed to the pope for military assistance for their eastern frontier might have had an eye on Sicily, they certainly did not care much about al-Andalus. But Urban II saw the crusade as part of a larger plan to unite the Christian world around a liberated Jerusalem. Since 1054, when a papal legate had somewhat rashly excommunicated the patriarch of Constantinople at the altar of Hagia Sophia, the Churches of the East and West had been in schism. Subsequent popes had sought to heal the rift to no avail. Now, the military crisis in the East provided an opportunity for the two sides to reach out to one another, and for an obvious rupture in the proper world order to be repaired. Even at home in the Latin West, things were not as they were supposed to be, for a good number of important people, including the German Emperor Henry IV, did not think that Urban II was the true pope and instead acknowledged Archbishop Wibert of Ravenna as their supreme pontiff (he is now recorded as anti-pope Clement III). As a result, Urban II had spent very little of his pontificate in Rome. If he could launch a successful crusade to the center of the world, he might establish himself as the undisputed leader of a unified Christendom. Finally, two major European kings were excommunicated: Philip II of France for bigamy, and Henry IV of Germany for stridently opposing papal authority and taking sides with Wibert. A well prosecuted crusade could undermine their positions as well.

And so, while Jerusalem had little to do with the immediate military weaknesses of the Byzantine Empire, its liberation would go a long way toward making the world look more like Urban II thought it should look. The Holy City already had great contemporary resonance: there had been mass pilgrimages from France and Germany in the eleventh century, including one some 7000 strong in 1054, and 'Jerusalem' was enjoying some popularity as a first name for girls.[10]

In Robert of Rheims version of the speech, Urban II described, in stomach-turning detail, how the Muslims oppressed the land where Christ lived and died. 'They circumcise the Christians, and the blood of the circumcision they either spread upon the altars or pour into the vases of the baptismal font'.[11] There is some evidence that the conditions for Christian residents of and pilgrims to the Holy Land had deteriorated after Seljuk Turks displaced the previous Fatimid rulers of Jerusalem, but it is likely that this pollution fear reflects Western anxiety about the holy sites rather than actual Muslim atrocities.[12] By restoring Jerusalem to a state of Christian purity through a penitential war, the crusaders would implement a divine plan and purify their own souls.

Thus, Urban II told his audience at Clermont (according to the version of his speech presented by Baldric of Dol) to put aside private warfare and 'rush as quickly as you can to the defense of the Eastern Church'.[13] French chroniclers in particular seem to have been acutely aware that the proliferation of disorder in decentralized France could be mitigated by channeling its aristocracy's military energy for their Byzantine neighbors. As a motive for such a long, costly, and dangerous journey, any fraternal feelings for the Byzantines paled in comparison to the prospect of liberating Jerusalem. In Guibert of Nogent's account of Urban II's speech, Jerusalem appeared unquestionably as both the geographical and moral center of Christendom: 'If all that there is of Christian preaching has flowed from the fountain of Jerusalem, its streams, whithersoever spread out over the whole world, encircle the hearts of the Catholic multitude, that they may consider wisely what they owe to such a well-watered fountain'.[14] By all accounts, the audience at Clermont reacted enthusiastically to Urban II's speech, and local seamstresses stayed busy sewing crosses on the shoulders of those who vowed to go on pilgrimage.[15] Urban II continued to seek volunteers in a series of letters that he sent to various parts of Europe for the next few months, while others picked up his message and spread it in their own way. In France and the parts of Italy that accepted Urban II as pope, bishops preached his call to pilgrimage, while in Germany wandering preachers added layers of apocalyptic fervor to the message.

To the amazement of contemporaries and a considerable number of modern historians, Urban II's plan worked. Despite internal divisions, constant struggles with the Byzantine emperor, and long marches through hostile territory, the crusading armies ultimately captured Jerusalem on July 15, 1099. A few key elements in the preaching and prosecution of the crusade place it firmly in the spiritual developments of the period, which were discussed in Chapter 3, above.

Popular Piety and the First Crusade

Among those who preached the crusade after Urban II's speech were wandering preachers like the eccentric Peter the Hermit, a priest from Lorraine. Unlike some of his contemporaries, Peter did not look to find a new institutional outlet for his piety, but went out into the world and urged laymen to liberate Jerusalem and thus cleanse the Holy Land of impurity. He convinced thousands of commoners and knights alike to take the cross, and inspired some of them to attack their local Jewish communities. From Rouen to Prague, Christians inflamed with crusading zeal terrorized Jews, murdering some and forcibly baptizing others. In Mainz, the bishop attempted to protect them by hiding them in his palace, but they were discovered and killed. The death toll there may have been over a thousand, including a fair number of suicides by Jews who preferred death to forced conversion.[16] The people attacked Jews in part because they were stand-ins for Muslims, who lived too far away to be killed immediately, and because their extermination fit in perfectly with apocalyptic prophesies about Jerusalem.

Such popular enthusiasm actually threatened papal control over the expedition, and some commoners expressed their piety in unorthodox ways, such as those who became convinced that a goose and she-goat were 'inspired by the Holy Spirit' and followed them to Jerusalem.[17] Such examples make it very difficult to understand the true motivations of the crusaders, but historians now see religious idealism as the most important factor in inspiring the nobility to leave their fiefs behind and journey to the East. Although we cannot completely discount the possibility of material reward as a motivation, the available evidence suggests it was not especially common. Crusading was expensive and dangerous, and the relevant documents suggest that most hoped to return home rather than make their fortunes in the Holy Land. Overall it seems that nobles went on crusade for much the same reason that they endowed monasteries and performed other acts of penance.[18]

In the final stages of the campaign for Jerusalem, other elements of popular piety came into play. In the summer of 1098, just when they felt deserted by the Byzantines and threatened by an expected Muslim counterattack on Antioch, a dream inspired some of the Franks to search for a relic which would utterly transform the morale of the army. After extensive digging in the cathedral church of St Peter of Antioch, a monk named Peter Bartholomew produced a spear point, which St Andrew had assured him would be the Holy Lance that pierced the side of Christ at the time of his crucifixion. That several leaders, including the papal legate for the army, probably knew it was a fake did not matter. Here was a point (pun certainly intended) where the earthly Jerusalem met the heavenly one. The discovery was accompanied by other intrusions of the supernatural; some crusaders saw visions of the Virgin, others were visited by dead relatives who implored them to keep fighting the Turks.[19] Combining apocalyptic fervor with a clever battle plan, the Frankish army destroyed the much larger Muslim relief force and now completely controlled the most important town in northern Syria. In January 1099, after half a year's stay in Antioch, the crusaders began the march to Jerusalem. They took advantage of Muslim disunity and negotiated with local rulers as they passed; they certainly did not face monolithic opposition from the various emirs, who obviously did not regard the Franks as an existential threat to Islamic control of the region. The Egyptian Fatimids, who controlled Jerusalem, even considered handing over the Holy City in return for an alliance against their Seljuk enemies, but ultimately offered only access so that the Franks could complete their pilgrimage. This, however, was not an acceptable alternative to liberating the center of the world. Sensing their moment of opportunity, the crusaders bypassed some strategically important towns to focus their energy on the holy sites, including Bethlehem.

The 15,000 or so surviving Franks gathered outside of Jerusalem and, on July 8, they fasted before processing around the city. As the Muslim defenders yelled insults and desecrated crosses, the crusaders marched barefoot around the city to the Mount of Olives, clerics marching side-by-side with knights. Five days later they attacked the city with siege engines, ladders, and miners, and were running through its streets by July 15. An oft-quoted passage from the eyewitness Raymond d'Aguilers can serve to describe the ensuing carnage:

Now that our men had possession of the walls and towers, wonderful sights were to be seen. Some of our men (and this was more merciful) cut off the heads of their enemies; others short them with arrows, so that they fell from the towers; others tortured them longer by casting them into the flames. Piles of heads, hands and feet were to be seen in the streets of the city [...]. But these were small matters compared to what happened at the Temple of Solomon [the al-Aqsa Mosque], where religious services are normally chanted. What happened there? If I tell the truth, it will exceed your powers of belief. So let it suffice to say this much, at least, that in the Temple and porch of Solomon, men rode in blood up to their knees and bridle reins. Indeed, it was a just and splendid judgment of God that this place should be filled with the blood of the unbelievers [...][20]

Elsewhere, a synagogue was incinerated along with the sizable number of Jews who were inside. This kind of slaughter, though essentially unheard of in contemporary siege warfare (in which conquered populations tended to be enslaved rather than killed), had precedent: the book of Revelation (14:20), whose vision of the 'End Time' includes a final harvest where 'the [wine-] press was trodden without the city, and blood came out of the press, up to the horses' bridles'.[21] Scripture had become reality as the crusaders restored proper order to the world.

The Crusader States and the Crusading Movement to 1229

The Byzantine Empire, at whose behest Urban II allegedly called the Crusade, experienced these things somewhat differently. Whereas the crusaders saw the conquest of Jerusalem as a miraculous restoration of the divine order, Alexius Comnenus saw it in remarkably practical terms. He had been negotiating with Muslims, as well as the crusaders, and bought the co-operation of the latter through bribery when necessary, as part of a larger strategy both to maintain order in the Levant and to take advantage of the weakness and disunity of Franks and Arabs alike.[22] He therefore could not have foreseen the foundation of Latin polities in the Holy Land on territory that had belonged to his empire until the seventh century. The Franks who remained on the eastern shore of the Mediterranean established four new 'crusader states' that are now known collectively as the 'Latin East': from north to south, the county of Edessa, the principality of Antioch, the county of Tripoli, and the Latin Kingdom of Jerusalem. Together they nominally controlled a swath of land along from the mid-Euphrates region to the tip of the Gulf of Aqaba.

In these new polities a French-speaking aristocracy ruled over a multicultural society of Franks, Muslims, Jews, and several different types of Christians, including those of Greek, Jacobite, and Armenian as well as Latin traditions. Already in 1098, after the fall of Antioch, crusaders had complained to the pope that 'we conquered the Turks and pagans, but we could not defeat the heretics, the Greeks and Armenians, Syrians and Jacobites'.[23] Indeed, in many parts of the Holy Land such Christians outnumbered Muslims, but a recent study has shown that the Franks showed not unremitting hostility but 'rough tolerance' toward them. In many cases the ruling Latin elites were not an isolated colonial class but a somewhat integrated part of the legal and cultural landscape.[24] There was, to be sure, some legal segregation, as in the laws of the Kingdom of Jerusalem, which provided for different procedures for the various ethnicities and religions.[25]

These states were not colonies in any meaningful way, for they had no institutional ties to any states of the Latin West. There would be complex dynastic relationships between the Eastern princes and the ruling families of Anjou, Blois, and elsewhere, but as rulers they were completely independent. According to Fulcher of Chartres, the Franks adapted to local customs as necessary, but they were always a minority and no amount of immigration changed that. A frontier society of sorts did develop over time, marked by the presence of Italian traders and a nascent urban class. Finally, the rise of the military orders provided protection for pilgrims as well as a kind of standing force to resist encroachments by the many enemies of the crusader states.

These states were always vulnerable, which became obvious after the first crusaders returned home, and the remaining knights suffered a series of defeats in the first decade of the twelfth century. Reinforcements arrived periodically, and when they were organized under papal leadership with broad-based support from high nobility or even kings, they coalesced into the expeditions that historians now call the 'numbered crusades'. The Second Crusade responded to the fall of the County of Edessa to the Seljuk leader Zengi in 1144. News of the disaster reached Europe at the height of the career of Bernard of Clairvaux, and it fell to the first Cistercian pope, Eugenius III, to call the crusade with the bull *Quantum praedecessores*, which recalled the heroism of 1099. Bernard's preaching helped rally a large army lead by Louis VII of France and Conrad III of Germany, but the ensuing crusade ended ignominiously with a failed siege of Damascus (a city allied with the Kingdom of Jerusalem).

After working so hard to make the expedition possible, Bernard of Clairvaux wrote off its failure as punishment for the sins of the Christians. An anonymous chronicler of Würzburg called the whole enterprise an 'error', and questioned the motives of the crusaders in ways that anticipate modern popular criticisms of the crusading movement: 'some, indeed, lusted after novelties and went in order to learn about new lands. Others there were who were driven by poverty, who were in hard straits at home [...] Such men simulated a zeal for God and hastened chiefly to escape from such troubles and anxieties'.[26] Today most historians regard the failure of this crusade as the result of poor planning and lack of resource management rather than sheer foolishness, but point to the adventure as a major step in the development of papal ambition and the conception of a unified Latin Christendom.[27]

On July 4, 1187, the Kurdish general Saladin (al-Malik al-Nasir Salah ed-Din Yusuf) destroyed the army of the Latin Kingdom at the Battle of the Horns of Hattin, and he captured Jerusalem in October (without a reprise of the bloodbath of 1099). News of the catastrophe reached Rome later in October, and allegedly caused Pope Urban III to die of grief. The ensuing Third Crusade captured the imagination of Europe's intellectual elite, who devoted numerous letters, sermons, and preaching tours to its organization. Western Europe erupted in penitential displays, and Pope Gregory set to work getting recruits from the elites, and succeeded in convincing three monarchs—Richard I of England, Philip II Augustus of France, and the aging Frederick I Barbarossa of Germany—to commit to the crusade. In the case of the first two kings, their participation was contingent on making peace with each other, since Philip II had been constantly at war with Richard I's father Henry II for most of the 1180s. Richard I had taken the cross before Henry II's death, and the beginning of his kingship was inseparable from the ideology of crusading. This connection was confirmed outside his coronation, where some residents rioted against Jews, and in the city of York, where a crusade-inspired massacre ensued.[28] Frederick I's officials, on the other hand, seem to have effectively intervened to stop similar violence in Mainz.[29] Despite some inspiring generalship from Richard I, culminating in his capture of the crucial port of Acre, this crusade failed to take Jerusalem. Richard I approached the Holy City twice, but apparently the military commander in him felt that it was an objective that would be too difficult to defend. It has recently been argued that had Richard I possessed the apocalyptic urgency of the First Crusaders, he might have captured it just as they did.[30] In the end, he settled for a three-year truce that allowed Christian pilgrims access to the city and forced Saladin to acknowledge the existence of the crusader states. Like the previous military pilgrimages to the Holy Land, however, this one simultaneously brought Christendom together in a sincere show of religious devotion while exposing some of its most troublesome fault lines.

The Fourth Crusade, which Innocent III called in 1198 to complete the unfinished business of the Third, brought a veritable earthquake. Instead of traveling to the Holy Land, the cash-strapped crusader army helped the Venetian navy seize a Christian city on the Adriatic and then conquered and ruthlessly sacked the Byzantine capital itself, all over Innocent III's strenuous objections. It may be best to regard the Latin conquest of Constantinople as unexpected but predictable.[31] When it became clear that the crusaders could not afford the cost required to cross to the prized military target of Alexandria in Egypt, the Venetians offered to forgive the payment temporarily in return for assistance in re-conquering the Adriatic trading outpost of Zedar. This port, however, was controlled by the Christian King Emeric of Hungary, who had himself taken crusader vows. Neither the mortified Innocent III nor his legates could prevent the crusaders from agreeing to the deal. After the successful raid, the crusaders received another offer, this time from Alexius Angelos, son of the deposed Byzantine emperor Isaac II, who asked their help in reclaiming the throne in Constantinople. Innocent III again protested, but in July of 1203, the military might of the Western army allowed Alexius and Isaac II to be crowned as co-emperors. Their involvement with Western 'barbarians', however, instilled great resentment in the Greek population, and these two were deposed and murdered in early 1204. Threatened by the aggression of the new ruling party in the city, the Latins sacked it in April of 1204 and elected Count Baldwin of Flanders as Latin Emperor. Innocent III initially rebuked the crusaders, but eventually saw that good could come of their diversion. Some of the rank-and-file on the Fourth Crusade do not seem to have been troubled by any moral compunction about sacking the Byzantine capital. Geoffrey de Villehardouin, our best eyewitness source for the expedition, continued to call the crusaders 'pilgrims' even as they attacked Christian cities, and harshly reproached a group of men who left the army and traveled to the Holy Land.[32]

At the end of the Fourth Lateran Council in 1215, which called for the Fifth Crusade, Innocent III gave the benediction over a fragment of the True Cross. This fragment, however, was not the same one discovered by the First Crusade in 1099. Rather it had recently been brought to Rome from the Latin Empire of Constantinople.[33] Innocent III, in the event, died before he could lead another crusade. His successors continued to struggle to control the movement; the prize recruit for the new expedition, Emperor Frederick II, did not make the journey. This group of warrior-pilgrims from Germany, Hungary, and other non-French regions attacked Egypt and succeeded in capturing Damietta in 1219, but made no further progress, as their leadership broke down. The Egyptians offered to return Jerusalem to Christian hands in exchange for Damietta, but the papal legate refused to bargain, and eventually the Christians were evicted from their footholds near the Nile. When an excommunicated Frederick II finally landed in Egypt in 1228 on the Sixth Crusade, as papal armies attacked his Italian possessions, he quickly negotiated a truce that gave him control of Jerusalem.

The Travails of the Crusading Ideal

As we have seen, what Urban II did in 1095 was altogether unprecedented, and as a result the crusading ideal had to be invented over the course of the twelfth century. Gradually, the indulgence, or remission of penance, came to be a defining feature of the pilgrimages to the East, but not all pilgrims received it. As the military setbacks mounted, the crusading ideal began to be expanded and somewhat clarified. In 1123, the Third Lateran Council extended the crusade indulgence to pilgrims fighting in Spain as well as the Holy Land, and Bernard of Clairvaux's 1128 treatise praising the Templars gave a strong theological foundation of what it meant to be a holy warrior. Bernard and Eugenius also extended the granting of an enhanced crusader indulgence to fighters in Iberia and in the Baltic region.

Taken together, the sermons of Bernard of Clairvaux and the sheer number of recruits he attracted suggest that the enthusiasm of 1146–1147 matched that of 1095–1096. Although Bernard's exhortations to convert or kill pagans in his speeches against the Wends (see above, Chapter 1) clearly contributed to a climate of hostility to non-Christians, he tried to avoid a repetition of the anti-Jewish pogroms of 1096. When a Cistercian monk named Radulf left his monastery and wandered throughout the Rhineland preaching against Jews, Bernard ordered him to stop, arguing that Jews were part of God's plan and should not be harmed. Radulf inspired a few killings, including perhaps as many as 150 in one town, but Bernard seems to have averted a general slaughter like that which had taken place at Mainz in 1096.[34] Instances of anti-Jewish violence suggest that feeling for the Crusade was running high by 1146, and the expedition seems to have had a great deal working in its favor before its ultimate failure. It had

strong, clearly articulated papal leadership represented by two talented legates, two kings willing to prosecute it, and the enthusiastic
participation of the nobility. While the ideology of crusading was still
embryonic, the First Crusade provided a clear model, and the armies
headed to the Holy Land knew the kind of military pilgrimage they
were undertaking.

By the time Gregory VIII called the Third Crusade, theology and
canon law had been codified to the point that could provide a
clearer theoretical basis for crusading. His famous papal letter *Audita
tremendi*, which has been called 'one of the most moving documents of
crusader history', blamed the loss of Jerusalem on the Christians' lack
of penitence, and presented a new crusade as a rite of purification
for Christendom itself.[35] Using the technical language of penance
that had been established by twelfth-century canon lawyers, Gregory
VIII issued a more sweeping indulgence than that of Urban II in 1095.
He promised that

> all those, who with a contrite heart and a humble mind, will not
> fear to undertake this painful voyage, and who will be determined
> to do so by motives of a sincere faith, and with the view of obtaining
> remission of their sins, a plenary indulgence for their faults, and
> the life everlasting which will follow.[36]

Less than a year after he became pope in 1198, Innocent III called
again for the liberation of Jerusalem, which remained an urgent
priority despite the territorial gains of the Third Crusade and a subsequent expedition the previous year. He returned repeatedly to Psalm
137:5–6: 'If I forget thee, Jerusalem, let my right hand be forgotten.
Let my tongue cleave to my jaws, if I do not remember thee: If I make
not Jerusalem the beginning of my joy'. During his pontificate, Innocent III constantly urged princes to head to the East, but also called
crusades to the Baltic, the south of France, and even Sicily. But after
the diversion of the Fourth Crusade, the papacy seemed to be losing control of the crusading ideal. Innocent III himself contributed
to a shift in the understanding of the movement. In 1199 he gave
crusader privileges to the knights who helped him fight Markward
of Anweiler, a renegade imperial official operating in Sicily. We have
already seen that he authorized the crusade against the Albigensian
heretics of southern France in 1208, which did little to eradicate
heresy but much to expand the French royal domain. Here Innocent III sought to fix a tear in the sacred fabric of Christendom: a
region whose lords—especially the counts of Toulouse—did nothing

to protect the people from Cathar heretics. Their obstinance ended in them humbling themselves before the French kings in 1229 and effectively signing away their patrimony.

Perhaps the most intriguing (and difficult to understand) development in crusading and its relationship to the papacy was the so-called 'Children's Crusade' of 1212. Disenchanted by constant military failures in the Latin East, thousands of children and young adults 'suddenly ran one after the other and undertook a crusade. In groups of twenty, fifty, or a hundred, with their banners flying they began heading for Jerusalem'. They claimed direct divine inspiration and in France a shepherd boy claimed to have letters from heaven.[37] When some of these 'crusaders' approached Innocent III at Rome, he apparently tried to dispense them from their non-binding vows, but a few of them may have traveled far enough to be sold into slavery.[38]

At the Fourth Lateran Council, which did so much to prescribe acceptable outlets for Christian piety, Innocent III and the conciliar fathers tried to impose some order onto the crusading movement while also urging once again the liberation of the Holy Land. The opening of Canon 71, the longest and the last of the council's decrees (coming just after the prescriptions against Jews), declared that 'it is our ardent desire to liberate the Holy Land from infidel hands'.[39] It proceeded to lay out in careful detail the time and place of departure, and the organization of the journey. The prevailing clericalization of the Church was clearly on display, as the canon first addresses the disposition of the clergy, who were expected to lead by example (in return, their ecclesiastical incomes would be protected). It also provided for an elaborate tax on the clergy to help pay the expenses.

The crusading decree engaged with most of the pressing concerns of twelfth-century culture. It expressed anxiety about the purity of the clergy, but also about the profit economy:

> If any of those setting out are bound to pay interest, we ordain that their creditors shall be compelled by [ecclesiastical censure] to release them from their oath and to desist from extracting the interest [...]. We order that the Jews be compelled by the secular power to remit interest.[40]

Knights would also have to be less worldly and focus all of their energies on fighting infidels. In the first place, an earlier ban on tournaments was confirmed for three more years 'because the business of the crusade is much hindered by them at the present time'.[41] On a larger political scale, Innocent III declared a general peace in the Latin West 'for at least four years'. He claimed, that is, to be the peacemaker for Christendom. In the following decades Innocent III's successors would wield the secular sword in an attempt to bring Frederick II to heel, but in 1215 this project might have seemed plausible given the past century's growth of papal authority.

Christendom and the Wider World

Innocent III died before he could implement the crusading decree, and we have seen that the Fifth Crusade would ultimately fail, while the Sixth would be led by an excommunicate emperor. Events of the 1220s, moreover, would demonstrate that the Latin West was coming into contact with a much larger world order comprised of leaders and religious followers with entirely different agendas. The crusades had always hinted at this. Early Arab commenters on the First Crusade knew well that its success depended as much on geopolitical change in the Islamic world as on Frankish military prowess. Several important cities, including Jerusalem, had passed back and forth between Turkish and Arabic rulers, and several important leaders had died in the early 1090s, leaving a considerable power vacuum. When the crusader armies succeeded in taking Antioch and Jerusalem despite starvation, disease, and the apparent desertion of their Byzantine allies, it seemed to them like a sign of divine approval. The Muslim chronicler Ibn al-Athir, however, was well aware that 'it was the discord between the Muslim princes [...] that enabled the Franks to overrun the country'.[42] The Franks scored their first victory, the conquest of Nicaea (just 200 km southeast of Constantinople), in part because the Sultan of Rum, the chief Muslim ruler of Asia Minor, had committed forces to fighting a rival coreligionist some distance away.

The Muslims also incorporated Jerusalem into their sacred geography. One is struck by the powerful emotions that the recovery of Jerusalem evoked in Saladin's Arabic biographies:

And how could [God] not assist in the conquest of the mighty Jerusalem and of the Masjid al-Aqsa [al-Aqsa Mosque], founded in piety, since she is the seat of the prophets, the home of the saints, and the place where the pious adore their God, the place that the great saints of the earth and angels of heaven visit.[43]

In language that unknowingly echoed that of Latin sources about 1095, other Arab writers exulted that Jerusalem had been purified from the filth of the 'polytheists'. For their part, Christian writers gained a greater understanding of, if not appreciation for, their Muslim enemies. In the 1260s, Roger Bacon warned Pope Clement IV that crusading was becoming fruitless and would only inspire antagonism to the West in its targets.[44] In the fourteenth century, a sultan in the fanciful *Travels of Sir John Mandeville* crowed that the Christians had lost Jerusalem because they lived in 'wickedness and sin', providing a scathing critique of the West from the perspective of a hated enemy.

The rift with the Byzantine Empire, which Urban II, Innocent III, and most popes in between had wanted so desperately to heal, had become an irreparable chasm in the early thirteenth century. Despite the mutual suspicion that plagued the First Crusade (the emperor's daughter, the historian Anna Comnena, had referred to Peter the Hermit as 'Kuku Peter'[45]), the Greek emperors continued to host crusaders in Constantinople, and occasionally to coordinate militarily with the Franks. Many, however, regarded the Greeks as schismatics, and tensions surfaced frequently. One of Louis VII's key advisers on the Second Crusade, Bishop Godfrey of Langres, even suggested that the king consider attacking Constantinople itself.[46] The Byzantines, meanwhile, consistently retained a strong trading partnership with the West while shoring up their Danube frontier and occasionally making bold military moves, such as an unsuccessful attempt to recapture Sicily in the 1150s. As noted above, the animosity came to a head when at least some of the crusaders joined the Venetians in sacking Constantinople. Innocent III initially issued a letter sharply rebuking the papal legate for losing control of the crusade:

> How, indeed, is the Greek church to be brought back into ecclesiastical union and to a devotion for the Apostolic See when she has been beset with so many afflictions and persecutions that she sees in the Latins only an example of perdition and the works of darkness, so that she now, and with reason, detests the Latins more than dogs?

Soon, however, Innocent III was prepared to accept the new order and even argued that

> if the Lord had granted the desires of his humble servants sooner, and had transferred, as he has now done, the empire of

Constantinople from the Greeks to the Latins before the fall of the Holy Land, perhaps Christianity would not be weeping today over the desolation of the land of Jerusalem.[47]

Byzantine contemporaries would have had no sympathy for Innocent III's initial conundrum. The Latin Empire had no real chance of surviving, and the Greeks were restored in 1261.

In Eastern Europe, the gates of Christendom were threatened by warriors of the Mongols, who were harrying Christian princes in Russia, and about whom the crusaders at Damietta heard rumors in 1221. In 1246, their leader Guyuk Khan wrote a letter to Pope Innocent IV and told him that 'now you should say with a sincere heart, "I will submit and serve you". Thou thyself, at the head of all the Princes, come at once to serve and wait upon us!'[48] Christendom was coming into contact with a wider world, and a Franciscan missionary would meet a Parisian goldsmith at the court of Möngke Khan in Karakorum a few years later.[49] This missionary, William of Rubruck, may have been trying to effect an alliance with the Mongols against the Muslims. No alliance materialized, and Acre was lost again in 1291, this time permanently.

Conclusion

Twelfth-century *mappae mundi* offered a few certainties to their readers: Jerusalem was the center of the world, classical and scriptural knowledge could coexist in the same conceptual space, and there was much that was strange and unknown in the world. Crusaders passed through the unknown, but knew exactly where they were going. In the Holy Land they found bridle-deep torrents of blood because their apocalyptic understanding of their journey required them to find it. They acted on a world map that made perfect sense even as it allowed for the extraordinary.

Similarly, two crusades—the Sixth Crusade of Frederick II and the Albigensian Crusade of the French nobility—ended in 1229 with rituals that one might have seen 130 years earlier. Kings and emperors had been wearing their crowns in great churches since the early Middle Ages, and lords routinely accepted the submission of disobedient lords in the ninth, tenth, and eleventh centuries. But now, in the early thirteenth century, both rituals acquired different meanings. The infant Louis IX had acquired a royal domain far beyond what would have seemed possible in 1095, and would gradually build up an ideology of power to match it. His vassal from the old order, Raymond of Toulouse, whose ancestors had crusaded to the Holy Land with great princes, was unwillingly sacrificing his land for the benefit of a territory increasingly defined as France. In the case of Frederick II, his crown-wearing seemed to go off well, but the presence of papal troops in Sicily, as well as the dung with which he was pelted afterward, made it a puzzling moment for the world order as then understood. In both cases, the structure of medieval politics had shifted drastically. At the moment of Frederick II's coronation, the ideals of a Christendom united around a crusade and of a strong German emperor were weakening. Meanwhile, Louis IX and his regent embodied an alternative to the universalizing ideals of empire and papacy in the form of a unified France.

When Raymond humbled himself, he also promised to endow a new university at Toulouse, which could train scholars to fight heresy. The masters there sent a letter to prospective students, noting that the cardinal legate of France had granted a plenary indulgence to all those who would study there. Academic study in this respect had something in common with crusading. At nearly the same time, however, university scholarship was changing. The Dominicans arrived in Paris in 1217, the Franciscans 1230, and the two mendicant orders would shape intellectual life there until the end of the century. In 1231, Pope Gregory IX, in the midst of his struggle with Frederick II, issued a papal bull governing conduct of students and masters at the University of Paris, attempting to codify an order of things that would avoid the kind of crisis that had just shut down the institution for two years (apparently 'town–gown' relations had deteriorated drastically). He also prohibited scholars from speaking the vernacular and walking through town armed, both of which would compromise their status as clerical elites. Two years later he prohibited the teaching of 'books of nature', presumably Aristotelian works whose orthodoxy was still in question. Still, Christianized Aristotelianism would triumph in Europe's universities two decades later with the composition of the Dominican Thomas Aquinas's *Summa Theologiae*. Thomas tied together essentially everything that could be known about God, man, and the universe in a sprawling series of questions whose internal structure has been said to mirror that of a Gothic cathedral.[50] In intellectual life, too, then, Christians negotiated certainty. The *Summa* itself, by introducing contradictory arguments, institutionalized the questioning qualities of so much twelfth-century thought even as it confidently asserted that the truth about most things could be known with certainty.[51]

In the third decade of the thirteenth century, then, the problems of the twelfth-century were being reconfigured rather than solved. This book does not end, as some books do, in 1215 with the Fourth Lateran Council, mainly to argue implicitly that simply defining Christendom could not at all reconcile its fundamental contradictions. Some of the greatest spiritual and intellectual experiments of the twelfth century would come to grief in the thirteenth. As R. W. Southern put it somewhat pessimistically, 'all the great movements in Europe between 1050 and 1300 were part of a search for order and organization, and they all [...] failed in varying degrees to obtain their objective'.[52] The great experiment of the Franciscans, the outgrowth of fervent lay piety that was integrated in the Church, bears this out. Some of their number never reconciled themselves to the compromises with poverty that came along with becoming a great clerical organization, and they continued to resist the profit economy as absolutely as Francis had. Eventually those who would not compromise became radicalized to the point that they were targeted by an inquisition.[53] Other heresies were identified at this time, but the papacy seemed to lack the sense of nuance to handle the attendant crises.

None of this is meant to argue that things declined after 1229; such an argument is beyond the purpose of this book. The twelfth century rather created a litany of possibilities—wealth, administrative efficiency, mystical experience, social mobility—that Europeans have had to negotiate ever since.

Notes

Introduction: Approaches to the Twelfth Century and Its 'Renaissance'

1. Hildegard of Bingen, *Selected Writings*, trans. Mark Atherton (London, 2001), p. 66.
2. Cited in John D. Cotts, *The Clerical Dilemma: Peter of Blois and Literate Culture in the Twelfth Century* (Washington, DC, 2009), pp. 121–122.
3. Hugh of St Victor, *De tribus diebus*, ed. Dominque Poirel, CCCM 177 (Turnhout, 2002), p. 31.
4. Chrétien de Troyes, *Lancelot: The Knight of the Cart*, trans. Burton Raffel (New Haven, CT and London, 1997), pp. 12–13.
5. Fulcher of Chartres, *Chronicle*, in Edward Peters (ed.), *The First Crusade: The Chronicle of Fulcher of Chartres and Other Source Materials*, 2nd edn (Philadelphia, PA, 1998), pp. 281–282.
6. For an overview of the use of anxiety in historiographical discussions, see W. Bouwsma, 'Anxiety and the Formation of Early Modern Culture', in *A Usable Past: Essays in European Cultural History* (Berkeley, CA and Los Angeles, CA, 1990), pp. 157–189.
7. Charles Homer Haskins, *The Renaissance of the Twelfth Century* (Cambridge, MA, 1927); Christopher Brooke, *The Twelfth Century Renaissance* (Norwich, 1969); R. N. Swanson, *The Twelfth-Century Renaissance* (Manchester and New York, 1999); Giles Constable, *The Reformation of the Twelfth Century* (Cambridge, 1995); Robert L. Benson, Giles Constable, and Carol D. Lanham (eds.), *Renaissance and Renewal in the Twelfth Century*, reprint (Toronto, ON, 1999); Colin Morris, *The Discovery of the Individual, 1050–1300*, reprint (Toronto, ON, 1987); Tina Stiefel, *The Intellectual Revolution in Twelfth-Century Europe* (New York, 1985); R. I. Moore, *The First European Revolution, c. 970–1215* (Oxford, 2000); Robert Bartlett, *The Making of Europe: Conquest, Colonization and Cultural Change, 950–1300* (Princeton, NJ, 1993).
8. J.-J. A. Ampére, *Histoire littéraire de la France avant le douziéme siècle* (Paris, 1839–1840), vol III, p. 457. This period in twelfth-century

202

studies is discussed in Alex Novikoff, 'The Renaissance of the Twelfth Century Before Haskins', *Haskins Society Journal*, 16 (2006), pp. 104–116.

9. Haskins, *Renaissance of the Twelfth Century*, v.

10. Jacob Burckhardt, *The Civilization of the Renaissance in Italy*, trans. S. G. C. Middlemore (London, 1990), p. 98.

11. W. A. Nitze, 'The So-Called Twelfth Century Renaissance', *Speculum*, 23 (1948), pp. 464–471; E. M. Sanford, 'The Twelfth Century—Renaissance or Proto-Renaissance?', *Speculum*, 26 (1951), pp. 635–642; U. T. Holmes, 'The Idea of a Twelfth-Century Renaissance', *Speculum*, 26 (1951), pp. 643–651.

12. E. Panofsky, *Renaissance and Renascences in Western Art* (New York, 1972), p. 113.

13. R. W. Southern, *The Making of the Middle Ages* (New Haven, CT and London, 1953), p. 13.

14. Southern, 'Medieval Humanism', in his *Medieval Humanism and Other Essays* (Oxford, 1970), p. 50. Southern's notion of medieval humanism is comprehensively laid out in *Scholastic Humanism and the Unification of Europe*, 2 vols (Oxford, 1995–2001).

15. See above, note 7.

16. C. W. Bynum, 'Did the Twelfth Century Discover the Individual?', in her *Jesus as Mother: Studies in the Spirituality of the High Middle Ages* (Berkeley, CA and Los Angeles, CA, 1984), p. 85.

17. Southern, 'The Place of England in the Twelfth-Century Renaissance', in *Medieval Humanism*, pp. 158–180; Rodney Thomson, 'England and the Twelfth-Century Renaissance', *Past and Present* 101 (1983), pp. 3–21; Thomson, 'The Place of Germany in the Twelfth-Century Renaissance', in A. Beach (ed.), *Manuscripts and Monastic Culture*, Medieval Church Studies 13 (Turnhout, 2007), pp. 19–42.

18. These modifications to Haskins' argument are discussed in M. L. Colish, 'Haskins' Renaissance Seventy Years Later: Beyond Anti-Burckhardtianism', *Haskins Society Journal*, 11 (1998), pp. 1–16.

19. See esp. Rita Copeland, *Rhetoric, Hermeneutics, and Translation in the Middle Ages: Academic Traditions and Vernacular Texts* (Cambridge and New York: Cambridge University Press, 1995). For a good recent overview see Leidulf Melve, ' "The Revolt of the Medievalists". Directions in Recent Research on the Twelfth-century Renaissance', *Journal of Medieval History* 32 (2006), pp. 231–252, here at p. 246.

20. R. I. Moore, *The Formation of a Persecuting Society* (Oxford, 1987).

21. John Boswell, *Christianity, Social Tolerance and Homosexuality: Gay People in Western Europe from the Beginning of the Christian Era to the Fourteenth Century* (Chicago, 1980).

22. C. S. Jaeger, 'Pessimism and the Twelfth-Century 'Renaissance', *Speculum*, 78 (2003), pp. 1151–1183.

23. Bouwsma, 'The Renaissance and the Drama of Western History', in *A Usable Past*, 348–365.

24. William Stubbs, *The Constitutional History of England in Its Origin and Development*, vol 3 (Oxford, 1897), p. 585.

25. Robert Fawtier, *The Capetian Kings of France: Monarchy and Nation, 987–1328*, trans Lionel Butler and R. J. Adam (London, 1962), vii.

26. Alfred Haverkamp, *Medieval Germany, 1056–1273*, trans. Helga Braun and Richard Mortimer (Oxford, 1988), p. 3.

27. C. Stephen Jaeger, *The Origins of Courtliness: Civilizing Trends and the Formation of Courtly Ideals, 939–1210* (Philadelphia, PA, 1985); Joachim Bumke, *Courtly Culture*.

28. M. T. Clanchy, *From Memory to Written Record: England 1066–1307*, 2nd edn (Oxford, 1993).

29. Thomas N. Bisson, *The Crisis of the Twelfth Century: Power, Lordship, and the Origins of European Government* (Princeton, NJ, 2009).

30. Archibald Lewis, *Nomads and Crusaders, A. D. 1000–1368* (Bloomington, IN, 1988); Jerry H. Bentley, *Old World Encounters: Cross-Cultural Contacts and Exchanges in Pre-Modern Times* (New York, 1993).

31. Bentley, *Old World Encounters*, pp. 113–114.

32. Joshua Prawer, 'The Roots of Medieval Colonialism', in *The Meeting of Two Worlds: Cultural Exchange between East and West during the Period of the Crusades* (Kalamazoo, MI, 1986), pp. 23–38; Jonathan Riley-Smith, 'Islam and the Crusades in History and Imagination, 8 November 1898–1811 September 2001', *Crusades*, 2 (2003), pp. 151–167.

1 Varieties of Political Order in the Latin West

1. Fulcher of Chartres, *Chronicle*, in Edward Peters (ed.), *The First Crusade: The Chronicle of Fulcher of Chartres and Other Source Materials*, 2nd edn (Philadelphia, PA, 1998), p. 49.

2. Thomas N. Bisson, *The Crisis of the Twelfth Century: Power, Lordship, and the Origins of European Government* (Princeton, NJ, 2009), p. 6.

3. Robert Somerville, 'The Council of Clermont (1095), and Latin Christian Society', *Archivum Historiae Pontificiae*, 12 (1974), pp. 55–90.

4. Fulcher of Chartres, *Chronicle*, in *The First Crusade*, pp. 52–53.

5. For a new interpretation of Alexius' motivations, see Peter Frankopan, *The First Crusade: The Call from the East* (Cambridge, MA, 2012), esp. pp. 87–100.

6. Ibid., p. 53.

7. On the problem of defining 'Crusade', see C. J. Tyerman, 'Were There Any Crusades in the Twelfth Century?' *English Historical Review*, 110 (1995), pp. 553–577.

8. 'The Speech of Urban: The Version of Robert of Rheims', in *The First Crusade*, p. 27.

9. Mark Gregory Pegg, *A Most Holy War: The Albigensian Crusade and the Battle for Christendom* (Oxford, 2008), pp. 179–180.

10. Susan Reynolds, 'Government and Community', in Robert Fossier (ed.), *The New Cambridge Medieval History*, vol 4, part 1 (Cambridge, 2008), pp. 86–87.

11. Thomas N. Bisson, 'The Feudal Revolution', *Past and Present*, 142 (1994), pp. 208–225, with responses by Stephen D. White and Dominique Barthélemy as 'Debate: The Feudal Revolution', *Past and Present*, 152 (1996), pp. 196–205, 205–223, and Chris Wickham, 'Debate: The Feudal Revolution', *Past and Present*, 155 (1997), pp. 196–208.

12. Gerd Tellenbach, *Church, State and Christian Society at the Time of the Investiture Contest*, trans. R. F. Bennett (Oxford, 1940, reprinted Toronto, ON, 1991); J. A. Watt, 'Spiritual and Temporal Powers', in J. H. Burns (ed.), *The Cambridge History of Medieval Political Thought* (Cambridge, 1988), pp. 367–423.

13. Joseph R. Strayer, *On the Medieval Origins of the Modern State*, new ed. (Princeton, NJ, 2005).

14. R. I. Moore, *The First European Revolution, c. 970–1215* (Oxford, 2000), pp. 14–146; M. T. Clanchy, *From Memory to Written Record: England 1066–1307*, 2nd edn (Oxford, 1993).

15. Geoffrey Koziol, 'Political Culture', in Marcus Bull (ed.), *France in the Central Middle Ages* (Oxford, 2002), pp. 43–76.

16. Elizabeth A. R. Brown, 'The Tyranny of a Construct: Feudalism and Historians of Medieval Europe', *American Historical Review*, 79 (1974), pp. 1063–1088; Susan Reynolds, *Fiefs and Vassals: The Medieval Evidence Reinterpreted* (Oxford, 1996).

17. See Gerd Althoff, *Family, Friends and Followers: Political and Social Bonds in Early Medieval Europe*, trans. Christopher Carroll (Cambridge, 2004), pp. 136–159; Susan Reynolds, *Kingdoms and Communities in Western Europe, 900–1300* (Oxford, 1997).

18. Timothy Reuter, 'Assembly Politics in Western Europe', and 'The Medieval German *Sonderweg*? The Empire and Its Rulers in the High Middle Ages', in Janet L. Nelson (ed.), his *Medieval Politics and Modern Mentalities* (Cambridge, 2006), pp. 388–412.

19. Geoffrey Koziol, *Begging Pardon and Favor: Ritual and Political Order in Early Medieval France* (Ithaca, NY and London, 1992), pp. 229–235.

20. Philippe Buc, '*Principes gentium dominantur eorum*: Princely Power Between Legitimacy and Illegitimacy in Twelfth-Century Exegesis', in Thomas N. Bisson (ed.), *Cultures of Power: Lordship, Status, and Process in Twelfth-Century Europe* (Philadelphia, PA, 1995), pp. 310–328.

21. Benjamin Arnold, *Medieval Germany, 500–1300: A Political Interpretation* (Toronto, ON and Buffalo, NY, 1997), pp. 1–12, 68–74.

22. Arnold, *Medieval Germany*, pp. 103–104; Janet Nelson, 'Kingship and Empire', in J. H. Burns (ed.), *The Cambridge History of Medieval Political Thought* (Cambridge, 1988), p. 250.

23. Otto of Freising and Rahewin, *The Deeds of Frederick Barbarossa*, trans. Charles Christopher Mierow (reprint, Toronto, ON, 1999), p. 115.

24. Bernd Kannowski, 'The Impact of Lineage and Family Connections on Succession in Medieval Germany's Elective Kingdom', in Frédérique Lachaud and Michael Penman (eds.), *Making and Breaking the Rules: Succession in Medieval Europe, c. 1000–c.1600* (Turnhout, 2008), pp. 13–22.

25. See John Gillingham, 'Elective Kingship and the Unity of Medieval Germany', *German History*, 9 (1991), pp. 124–135.

26. The Norman Anonymous, printed as the 'Anonymous of York', in Brian Tierney (ed.), *The Crisis of Church and State 1050–1300* (Toronto, ON, 1988), p. 77.

27. Humbert of Silva Candida, 'Three Books Against the Simoniacs', in *The Crisis of Church and State*, p. 40.

28. Uta-Renate Blumenthal, *The Investiture Controversy: Church and Monarchy from the Ninth to the Twelfth Century* (Philadelphia, PA, 1988), pp. 106–134.

29. Cited in I. S. Robinson, *Henry IV of Germany, 1056–1106* (Cambridge, 1999), p. 318.

30. 'The Life of Henry IV', in Theodor E. Mommsen and Karl F. Morrison (eds.), *Imperial Lives and Letters of the Eleventh Century* (New York, 2000), p. 120

31. Thomas Head and Richard Landis (eds.), *The Peace of God: Social Violence and Religious Response in France Around the Year 1000* (Ithaca, NY, 1992).

32. Letter of Henry IV to Philip I of France, in *Imperial Lives and Letters*, 190.

33. The Concordat of Worms, in *The Crisis of Church and State*, p. 91.

34. Bisson, *The Crisis of the Twelfth Century*, p. 229.

35. See John W. Bernhardt, *Itinerant Kingship and Royal Monasteries in Early Medieval Germany, c. 936–1075* (Cambridge, 2002), p. 58; Horst Fuhrman, *Germany in the High Middle Ages, c. 1050–1200*, trans. Timothy Reuter (Cambridge, 1986), p. 32.

36. Quotation from Acerbus Morena, cited in C. Stephen Jaeger, *The Origins of Courtliness: Civilizing Trends and the Formation of Courtly Ideals 939–1210* (Philadelphia, PA, 1985), p. 172.

37. See David Abulafia, *Frederick II: A Medieval Emperor* (Oxford, 1988).

38. Joachim Bumke, *Courtly Culture: Literature and Society in the High Middle Ages*, trans. Thomas Dunlap (Berkeley, CA and Los Angeles, CA, 1991), pp. 447–448.

39. Timothy Reuter, 'Mandate, Privilege, Court Judgment: Techniques of Rulership in the Age of Frederick Barbarossa', in *Medieval Politics and Modern Mentalities*, pp. 413–431.

40. Benjamin Arnold, 'Instruments of Power: The Profile and Profession of *Ministeriales* Within German Aristocratic Society, 1050–1225', pp. 36–55.

41. Otto of Freising and his Continuator, Rahewin, *The Deeds of Frederick Barbarossa*, trans. Charles Christopher Mierow (New York, 1953, reprint Toronto, ON, 1994), p. 194.

42. Horst Fuhrmann, *German in the High Middle Ages, c. 1050–1200*, trans. Timothy Reuter (Cambridge, 1986), pp. 155–156.

43. Otto of Freising, *Deeds of Frederick Barbarossa*, p. 193.

44. Ibid., p. 239.

45. Karl Jordan, *Henry the Lion: A Biography*, trans. P. S. Falla (Oxford, 1986).

46. Joachim Bumke, *Courtly Culture: Literature and Society in the High Middle Ages*, trans. Thomas Dunlap (Woodstock and New York, 2000), p. 285.

47. Benjamin Arnold, *Princes and Territories in Medieval Germany* (Cambridge, 1991), pp. 37–38.

48. Robert L. Benson, 'Political *Renovatio*: Two Models from Roman Antiquity', in *Renaissance and Renewal in the Twelfth Century*, pp. 339–386.

49. Hubert Houben, *Roger II of Sicily: A Ruler Between East and West*, trans. Graham A. Loud and Diane Milburn (Cambridge, 2002), pp. 1–7, 176–181.

50. Alexander of Telese, *The History of the Most Serene Roger, First King of Sicily*, in *Roger II and the Creation of the Kingdom of Sicily*, ed. and trans. Graham A. Loud (Manchester and New York, 2012), p. 78.

51. Kenneth Pennington, 'The Normans in Palermo: King Roger II's Legislation', *Haskins Society Journal*, 18 (2006), pp. 140–167.

52. On George, see Hubert Houben, *Roger II*, pp. 33–34.

53. Hiroshi Takayama, 'Central Power and *Multi-Cultural Elements* at the Norman Court of Sicily', *Mediterranean Studies*, 12 (2003), pp. 1–15.

54. Houben, *Roger II*, p. 121.

55. Ibid., pp. 110–111.

56. Romuald of Salerno, *Chronicon*, in *The History of the Tyrants of Sicily by 'Hugo Falcandus' 1154–69*, trans. Graham A. Loud and Thomas Wiedemann (Manchester, 1998), p. 220.

57. 'Hugo Falcandus', in *The History of the Tyrants of Sicily*, p. 206.

58. *The Travels of Ibn Jubayr*, trans. R. J. C. Broadhurst (London, 1952), pp. 340–341.

59. Abulafia, *Frederick II*, pp. 140–142.

60. Ibid., 202–226.

61. Ibid., 251–267.

62. Translated as *The Art of Falconry By Frederick II of Hohenstaufen*, trans. Casey A. Wood and F. Marjorie Fyfe (Stanford, 1943).

63. 'Philip of Novara on Frederick II's Crusade', in *The Crusades: A Reader*, ed. S. J. Allen and Emilie Amt (Toronto, ON, 2003), p. 286.

64. 'Frederick II on His Taking of Jerusalem', in *The Crusades: A Reader*, p. 257.

65. 'Philip of Novara on Frederick II's Crusade', p. 286.

66. Thomas Glick, 'Convivencia: An Introductory Note', in Thomas Glick et al. *Convivencia: Jews, Muslims and Christians in Medieval Spain* (New York, 1992), pp. 1–9.

67. See 'Tanto amare, tanto amare', in *Lyrics of the Middle Ages: An Anthology*, ed. James J. Wilhelm (New York: 1990), p. 238.

68. *Historia Roderici,* in *The World of El Cid,* trans. Simon Barton and Richard Fletcher (Manchester, 2000), p. 105.
69. Jonathan Phillips, *The Second Crusade: Extending the Frontiers of Christendom* (New Haven, CT, 2007), pp. 253–257.
70. Ibid., pp. 145–159.
71. *De expugnatione Lisbonensi: The Conquest of Lisbon,* ed. and trans. Charles Wendell David, new edition (New York, 2001), pp. 130–133, 180–181.
72. Giles Constable, 'The Second Crusade as Seen by Contemporaries', *Traditio,* 9 (1953), pp. 213–279.
73. 'Statutes of León (1188)', in Olivia Remie Constable (ed.), *Medieval Iberia: Readings from Christian, Muslim, and Jewish Sources,* trans. Simon Doubleday (Philadelphia, PA, 1997), p. 165.
74. 'Statutes of Girona (1188)', trans. Thomas N. Bisson, in *Medieval Iberia,* pp. 167–172.
75. Thomas N. Bisson, 'A General Court of Aragon (Daroca, February 1228)', *English Historical Review,* 92 (1977), pp. 107–124.
76. Bisson, *Crisis of the Twelfth Century,* pp. 570–571.
77. Adam J. Kosto, 'The Limited Impact of the *Usatges de Barcelona* in Twelfth-Century Catalonia', *Traditio,* 56 (2001), pp. 53–88.
78. *The Usatges of Barcelona: The Fundamental Law of Catalonia,* trans. Donald J Kagay (Philadelphia, PA, 1994), pp. 67, 75.
79. Ibid., p. 73.
80. Ibid., p. 68.
81. Adam J. Kosto, *Making Agreements in Medieval Catalonia: Power, Order, and the Written Word, 1000–1200* (Cambridge, 2001), pp. 272–278.
82. C. Warren Hollister, 'The Strange Death of William Rufus', *Speculum,* 48 (1973). pp. 637–653; Judith Green, *Henry I: King of England and Duke of Normandy* (Cambridge, 2006), pp. 38–41.
83. 'The "Coronation Charter" of Henry I (5 August 1100)', in *English Historical Documents,* vol 2 (New York: 1953), p. 401.
84. Green, *Henry I,* p. 64.
85. David Crouch, 'Robert of Beaumont, Count of Meulan and Leicester: His Lands, His Acts, and His Self-Image', in *Henry I and the Anglo-Norman World: Studies in Memory of C. Warren Hollister,* ed. Donald F. Fleming and Janet M. Pope, *Haskins Society Journal,* 17 (special volume, 2006), pp. 91–116.
86. Suger, *The Deeds of Louis the Fat,* trans. Richard Cusimano and John Moorhead (Washington, DC, 1992), p. 114.
87. Orderic Vitalis, Marjorie Chibnall (ed.), *The Ecclesiastical History of Orderic Vitalis,* vol 6 (Oxford, 1978), pp. 22–28.
88. Suger, *The Deeds of Louis the Fat,* p. 115.
89. C. Warren Hollister, *Henry I,* ed. Amanda Clark Frost (New Haven, CT, 2001), pp. 117–125.
90. C. Warren Hollister and John W. Baldwin, 'The Rise of Administrative Kingship: Henry I and Philip Augustus', *American Historical Review,* 83

(1978), pp. 867–905; W. L. Warren, 'The Myth of Norman Administrative Efficiency: The Prothero Lecture', *Transactions of the Royal Historical Society*, 5th ser., 34 (1984), pp. 113–132.

91. M. T. Clanchy, *From Memory to Written Record: England 1066–1307*, 2nd edn (Oxford, 1993), p. 58.

92. John Hudson (ed.), *Historia Ecclesiae Abbendonensis: The History of the Church of Abingdon*, vol II (Oxford, 2002), pp. 132–133.

93. Stephanie Mooers Christelow, 'The Fiscal Management of England under Henry I', in *Henry I and the Anglo-Norman World*, pp. 158–182.

94. Henry of Huntingdon, *The History of the English*, in *English Historical Documents* II, p. 305.

95. Guibert of Nogent, *Monodies*, in *Guibert of Nogent: Monodies and On the Relics of Saints: The Autobiography and a Manifesto of a French Monk from the Time of the Crusades*, trans. Joseph McAlhany and Jay Rubenstein (London, 2011), pp. 143–145.

96. Bisson, *Crisis of the Twelfth Century*, p. 230.

97. Suger, *Deeds of Louis the Fat*, p. 35.

98. Blumenthal, *The Investiture Controversy*, pp. 159–167; I. S. Robinson, *The Papacy 1073–1198: Continuity and Innovation* (Cambridge, 1990), p. 424.

99. Marc Bloch, *The Royal Touch: Sacred Monarchy and Scrofula in England and France*, trans. J. E. Anderson (London, 1973); Frank Barlow, 'The King's Evil', *English Historical Review*, 95 (1980), pp. 3–27; Philippe Buc, 'David's Adultery with Bathsheba and the Healing Power of the Capetian Kings', *Viator*, 24 (1993), pp. 101–120.

100. John W. Baldwin, 'Crown and Government', in *The New Cambridge Medieval History*, vol 4.2, pp. 510–511.

101. Paul Brand, 'Henry II and the Creation of English Common Law', in Christopher Harper-Bill and Nicholas Vincent (eds.), *Henry II: New Interpretations* (Woodbridge, VA, 2007), pp. 215–241.

102. Robert Bartlett, *Trial by Fire and Water: The Medieval Judicial Ordeal* (Oxford, 1986); John W. Baldwin, 'The Intellectual Preparation for the Canon of 1215 against Ordeals', *Speculum*, 36 (1961), pp. 613–636.

103. Nick Barratt, 'Finance and the Economy in the Reign of Henry II', in *Henry II: New Perspectives*, p. 251.

104. Ralph V. Turner, '*Miles Litteratus*: How Rare a Phenomenon?', in his *Judges, Administrators and the Common Law in Angevin England* (London and Rio Grande, 1994), pp. 119–166.

105. 'The Constitutions of Clarendon', in *English Historical Documents*, vol II, pp. 718–722.

106. Michael Staunton, *Thomas Becket and His Biographers* (Woodbridge, VA, 2006), p. 103.

107. Martin Aurell, *The Plantagenet Empire 1154–1224*, trans. David Crouch (Harlow, 2007), pp. 251–262.

108. Cited in John D. Cotts, *The Clerical Dilemma: Peter of Blois and Literate Culture in the Twelfth Century* (Washington, DC, 2009), p. 222.

109. W. L. Warren, *Henry II* (Berkeley, CA and Los Angeles, CA, 1973), p. 626; G. Koziol, 'England, France, and the Problem of Sacrality in Twelfth-Century Ritual', in T. N. Bisson (ed.), *Cultures of power: Lordship, Status, and Process in Twelfth-Century Europe* (Philadelphia, 1995), p. 138.

110. John W. Baldwin, *The Government of Philip Augustus: Foundations of French Royal Power in the Middle Ages* (Berkeley, CA and Los Angeles, CA, 1986), pp. 6–7.

111. 'Rigord and His *Deeds of Philip Augustus*', trans. Paul R. Hyams, http://falcon.arts.cornell.edu/prh3/408/texts/Rigord1.html.

112. John W. Baldwin, *The Government of Philip Augustus*, pp. 160–161.

113. 'Rigord and His *Deeds of Philip Augustus*', http://falcon.arts.cornell.edu/prh3/408/texts/Rigord9.html.

114. Ralph V. Turner, 'The Problem of Survival for the Angevin "Empire" ': Henry II's and His Sons' Vision versus Late Twelfth-Century Realities', *American Historical Review*, 100 (1995), pp. 78–96.

115. Cited in Joseph R. Strayer, *The Albigensian Crusades*, new edn (Ann Arbor, MI, 1992), p. 142.

116. 'Rigord and His Deeds of Philip Augustus', http://falcon.arts.cornell.edu/prh3/408/texts/Rigord5.html.

117. Turner, 'The Problem of Survival for the Angevin "Empire" ', pp. 91–93.

118. John Gillingham, 'The Fall of the Angevin Empire', in his *Richard Coeur de Lion: Kingship, Chivalry and War in the Twelfth Century* (London and Rio Grande, 1994), pp. 193–200.

119. Gillingham, 'Magna Carta and Royal Government', in *Richard Coeur de Lion*, pp. 201–210.

120. Quotations from Magna Carta are cited from the British Library's translation, 'The Text of Magna Carta', http://www.fordham.edu/Halsall/source/magnacarta.asp.

121. Bisson, *Crisis of the Twelfth Century*, p. 427.

122. *Morkinskinna: The Earliest Icelandic Chronicle of the Norwegian Kings (1030–1157)*, trans. Theodore M. Andersson and Kari Ellen Gade (Ithaca, NY and London, 2000), pp. 313–322.

123. Bartlett, *Making of Europe*, pp. 9, 16; Brigit Sawyer and Peter Sawyer, *Medieval Scandinavia: From Conversion to Reformation, circa 800–1500* (Minneapolis, MN and London, 1993), pp. 60–61.

124. Knut Helle, 'Towards Nationally Organised Systems of Government: Introductory Survey', in *The Cambridge History of Scandinavia, Vol. 1: Prehistory to 1520*, ed. Halle (Cambridge, 2003), p. 347.

125. *Njal's Saga*, trans. Robert Cook (London, 2001), p. 181.

126. Jesse Byock, *Viking Age Iceland* (London, 2001), p. 309.

127. William Ian Miller, *Bloodtaking and Peacemaking: Feud, Law, and Society in Saga Iceland* (Chicago, IL and London, 1990).

128. Eric Christiansen, *The Northern Crusades*, new edn (London, 1997), p. 110.

129. Phillips, *The Second Crusade*, pp. 230–231.

130. Bernard of Clairvaux, *The Letters of St Bernard of Clairvaux*, trans. Bruno Scott James, new edn (Stroud, 1998), p. 467.
131. Christiansen, *The Northern Crusades*, p. 55.
132. Tadeusz Manteuffel, *The Formation of the Polish State: The Period of Ducal Rule 963–1194*, trans. Andrew Gorski (Detroit, 1982), pp. 105–118.
133. Lisa Wolverton, *Hastening Toward Prague: Power and Society in the Medieval Czech Lands* (Philadelphia, PA, 2001), p. 126.
134. Ibid., pp. 265–276.
135. Otto of Freising, *Deeds of Frederick Barbarossa*, p. 66.
136. Nora Berend, *At the Gate of Christendom: Jews, Muslims, and 'Pagans' in Medieval Hungary* (New York, 2001), pp. 163–171.
137. *Laws of the Medieval Kingdom of Hungary. Volume 1: 1000–1301*, eds. and trans. János M. Bak, György Bónis, and James Ross Sweeney (Idyllwild, CA, 1999), p. 35.
138. James Ross Sweeney, 'Hungary in the Crusades, 1169–1218', *The International History Review*, 3 (1981), pp. 467–481.

2 People, Economy, and Social Relations

1. Guibert of Nogent, *Monodies*, in *Guibert of Nogent: Monodies and On the Relics of Saints: The Autobiography and a Manifesto of a French Monk from the Time of the Crusades*, trans. Joseph McAlhany and Jay Rubenstein (London, 2011), p. 131.
2. Thomas N. Bisson, *Tormented Voices: Power, Crisis, and Humanity in Rural Catalonia 1140–1200* (Cambridge, MA, 1998).
3. John D. Cotts, *The Clerical Dilemma: Peter of Blois and Literate Culture in the Twelfth Century* (Washington, DC, 2009), p. 211.
4. Linda Paterson, *The World of the Troubadours: Medieval Occitan Society c. 1100–c.1300* (Cambridge, 1993), pp. 130–133.
5. Robert Fossier, 'The Rural Economy and Demographic Growth', in David Luscombe and Jonathan Riley-Smith (ed.), *The New Cambridge Medieval History*, vol 4.1 (Cambridge, 2004), pp. 11–46, and David Nicholas, 'Economy', in Daniel Power (ed.), *The Central Middle Ages*, Short Oxford History of Europe (Oxford, 2006), pp. 57–90.
6. Georges Duby, *The Early Growth of the European Economy: Warriors and Peasants from the Seventh to the Twelfth Century*, trans. Howard B. Clarke (Ithaca, NY, 1974), p. 182. For a comparison between high medieval growth rates and those of the modern world, with a special emphasis on England, see Robert Bartlett, *The Making of Europe: Conquest, Colonization and Cultural Change, 950–1300* (Princeton, NJ, 1993), p. 110.
7. J. C. Russell, 'Population in Europe, 500–1000', in Carlo M. Cipolla (ed.), *The Fontana Economic History of Europe, Volume I: The Middle Ages* (New York, 1976), pp. 36–41.
8. See Malcolm K. Hughes and Henry F. Diaz (eds.), *The Medieval Warm Period*, special issue of *Climatic Change* 26.2–3 (Dordrecht, 1994).

9. On the unpredictability of climate, and for a highly skeptical interpretation of weather-related data, see Robert Fossier, *The Axe and the Oath: Ordinary Life in the Middle Ages*, trans. L. G. Cochrane (Princeton, NJ, 2010), pp. 146–149.

10. Robert Fossier, *Peasant Life in the Middle Ages*, trans. Juliet Vale (Oxford, 1988), p. 10.

11. Georges Duby, 'The Culture of the Knightly Class', in *Renaissance and Renewal in the Twelfth Century* (Toronto, ON, 1999), pp. 243–268.

12. Bartlett, *Making of Europe*, pp. 115, 139–143.

13. Derek Keene, 'Towns and the Growth of Trade', in *New Cambridge Medieval History, Volume 4* (Cambridge, 2004), pp. 47–85, here at 52–54.

14. Ibid., p. 51.

15. Robert S. Lopez, *The Commercial Revolution of the Middle Ages, 950–1350* (Cambridge, 1976).

16. Bartlett, *Making of Europe*, pp. 134–138.

17. Werner Rösner, *Peasants in the Middle Ages*, trans. Alexander Stützer (Oxford, 1992), pp. 57–62.

18. Alain Boureau, *The Lord's First Night: The Myth of the Droit de Cuisage*, trans. Lydia G. Cochrane (Chicago, 1998).

19. Ruth Mazo Karras, *Sexuality in Medieval Europe: Doing Unto Others* (New York, 2005), pp. 59–86.

20. Rösner, *Peasants in the Middle Ages*, p. 187.

21. Ibid., pp. 70–76.

22. Fossier, 'Rural Economy', pp. 14–16; Röesner, *Peasants in the Middle Ages*, pp. 95–101.

23. Röesner, *Peasants in the Middle Ages*, pp. 85–88.

24. Fossier, *Peasant Life in the Middle Ages*, p. 134.

25. Bisson, *Tormented Voices*, pp. 7–27.

26. This debate is summarized in Nicholas, 'Economy', pp. 60–62.

27. Duby, 'The Culture of the Knightly Class', pp. 248–252.

28. Rösner, *Peasants in the Middle Ages*, pp. 40–42; Bartlett, *Making of Europe*, pp. 121–123.

29. Cited in Bartlett, *Making of Europe*, p. 136.

30. *The Usatges of Barcelona: The Fundamental Law of Catalonia*, trans. Donald Kagay (Philadelphia, PA, 1994), p. 67.

31. Scholars disagree considerably about how to use the terms 'nobility' and 'aristocracy'. I favor the latter term since it can consistently refer to a group of landholders that were referred to by a variety of terms in the Middle Ages. 'Nobility' here refers to a self-consciousness of qualities of those who rule through a combination of military skill and heredity, which ideally went together. For a historian who prefers 'aristocracy', see David Crouch, *The Image of the Aristocracy in Britain, 1000–1300* (London, 1992), esp. pp. 2–9. For a sensible introduction that focuses on nobility, see Constance Brittain Bouchard, *Strong of Body, Brave and Noble: Chivalry and Society in Medieval France* (Ithaca, 1998), and for an excellent study that uses the terms more or less interchangeably without apparent ill

effect, see Simon Barton, *The Aristocracy in Twelfth-Century León and Castile* (Cambridge, 1997).

32. Bouchard, *Strong of Body, Brave and Noble*, pp. 1–27.

33. Benjamin Arnold, 'Instruments of Power: The Profile and Profession of *Ministeriales* Within German Aristocratic Society, 1050–1225', in Thomas N. Bisson (ed.), *Cultures of Power: Lordship, Status and Process in Twelfth-Century Europe* (Philadelphia, 1995), pp. 36–55; John B. Freed, 'Nobles, Ministerials and Knights in the Archdiocese of Salzburg', *Speculum*, 62 (1987), pp. 575–611.

34. Geoffrey Koziol, 'England, France, and the Problem of Sacrality in Twelfth-Century Ritual', in *Cultures of Power*, p. 135.

35. Chrétien de Troyes, *Erec and Enide*, trans. Burton Raffel (New Haven, CT, 1997), p. 13.

36. Cotts, *The Clerical Dilemma*, p. 17.

37. Hollister, *Henry I* , pp. 365–366.

38. David Crouch, *William Marshal: Knighthood, War and Chivalry, 1147–1219*, 2nd edn (London, 2002).

39. Frank Barlow, *Thomas Becket* (Berkeley, CA and Los Angeles, CA, 1986), pp. 24–40.

40. Bouchard, *Strong of Body, Brave and Noble*, pp. 123–129.

41. John Hine Mundy, *Liberty and Political Power in Toulouse 1050–1230* (New York, 1954), p. 116.

42. Cited in Norman J. G. Pounds, *An Historical Geography of Europe 450 B.C.–A.D. 1330* (Cambridge, 1973), p. 268.

43. Jacques Rossiaud, 'The City-Dweller', in Jacques Le Goff (ed.), *The Medieval World*, trans. Lydia G. Cochrane (London, 1990), pp. 142–143.

44. Bartlett, pp. 170–172.

45. Ibid., 172–177.

46. Guibert of Nogent, *Monodies*, p. 135.

47. Ibid., p. 167.

48. 'William Clito, Count of Flanders: Charter for the Town of St Omer', Internet Medieval Sourcebook, http://www.fordham.edu/Halsall/source/1127stomer.asp.

49. 'Urban Privileges: Charter of Lorris, 1155', Internet Medieval Sourcebook, http://www.fordham.edu/Halsall/source/lorris.asp.

50. Karl Jordan, *Henry the Lion: A Biography*, trans. P. S. Falla (Oxford, 1986), pp. 70–71.

51. Keene, 'Towns and the Growth of Trade', p. 81.

52. Mundy, *Liberty and Political Power*, p. 99.

53. Steven A. Epstein, *Wage Labor and Guilds in Medieval Europe* (Chapel Hill, NC, 1991), pp. 51–52.

54. Ibid., p. 54; for the text of the charter, 'Adalbert, Bishop of Worms: Grant of a Craft Guild to Fishermen, 1106–1107', Internet Medieval Sourcebook, http://www.fordham.edu/Halsall/source/1105 fishermangild.asp.

55. W. J. Millor and C. N. L. Brooke (eds.), *The Letters of John of Salisbury, Volume II* (Oxford, 1986), pp. 6–7.

56. John F. Appleby (ed.), *The Chronicle of Richard of Devizes of the Time of King Richard the First* (London, 1963), pp. 65–66.

57. Leah Lydia Otis, *Prostitution in Medieval Society: The History of An Urban Institution in Languedoc* (Chicago, IL 1985), 17–19.

58. Jacques Rossiaud, 'The City-Dweller', in Jacques Le Goff (ed.), *The Medieval World*, trans. Lydia G. Cochrane (London, 1990), p. 151.

59. Keen, 'Towns and the Growth of Trade', p. 76.

60. David Nicholas, *Urban Europe, 1100–1700* (Basingstoke, 2003), p. 165.

61. Benjamin of Tudela, *The Itinerary of Benjamin of Tudela*, trans Marcus Adler, new edn (Malibu, CA, 1983), p. 62. See also Daniel Waley, *The Italian City-Republics* (New York, 1969), p. 175.

62. Lopez, *Commercial Revolution*, pp. 70–71; Robert S. Lopez and Irving W. Raymond (eds.), *Medieval Trade in the Mediterranean World: Illustrative Documents* (London, 1955), p. 145.

63. On the development of minting and coinage, see Peter Spufford, *Money and Its Use in Medieval Europe* (Cambridge, 1988), pp. 74–131, 240–266.

64. Spufford, p. 241.

65. 'Sir Penny', in *The Goliard Poets*, trans. George F. Wichler (New York, 1949), p. 147.

66. Lopez, *The Commercial Revolution*, pp. 85–102; Keene, 'Towns and the Growth of Trade', pp. 63–66.

67. Jonathan Philips, *The Second Crusade: Expanding the Frontiers of Christendom* (New Haven, CT and London, 2007), p. 254.

68. Eric Christiansen, *The Northern Crusades*, new edn (London, 1997), pp. 97–100.

69. David Abulafia, 'Trade and Crusade, 1050–1250', in Michael Goodich, Sophia Menache, and Sylvia Schein (eds.), *Cross Cultural Convergences in the Crusader Period: Essays Presented to Aryeh Grabois on His Sixty-Fifth Birthday* (New York, 1995), pp. 1–20.

70. Donald M. Nicol, *Byzantium and Venice: A Study in Diplomatic and Cultural Relations* (Cambridge, 1988), p. 193.

71. Edwin S. Hunt and James M. Murray, *A History of Business in Medieval Europe* (Cambridge, 1999), pp. 23–30.

72. Lopez and Raymond, p. 158.

73. Jacques Le Goff, *Your Money or Your Life: Economy and Religion in the Middle Ages* (New York, 1988), pp. 17–32.

74. Hunt and Murray, *A History of Business in Medieval Europe*, pp. 70–73.

75. Lester K. Little, *Religious Poverty and the Profit Economy in the Middle Ages* (Ithaca, NY, 1978), pp. 42–57; Lopez, *Commercial Revolution*, pp. 60–62.

76. Lopez and Raymond (eds.), p. 164.

77. Lopez, *Commercial Revolution*, pp. 73–79.

78. Bartlett, *Making of Europe*, p. 169.

3 Spirituality and Its Discontents

1. Thomas de Cantimpré, *The Life of Margaret of Ypres*, trans. Margot H. King (Toronto, ON, 1999), p. 19.
2. Anselm of Canterbury, 'Prayer to Christ', in *The Prayers and Meditations of Saint Anselm*, trans. Benedicta Ward (Harmondsworth, 1973), p. 97.
3. Catherine M. Mooney, 'Voice, Gender, and the Portrayal of Sanctity', in Catherine M. Mooney (ed.), *Gendered Voices: Medieval Saints and their Interpreters* (Philadelphia, PA, 1999), pp. 1–15.
4. For an overview of this scholarship see John Van Engen, 'The Christian Middle Ages as an Historiographical Problem', *American Historical Review*, 91 (1986), pp. 519–552. Among the classic evocations of the spiritual energy of the twelfth century are Morris, *Discovery of the Individual*, esp. pp. 139–157; Jean Leclercq, *The Love of Learning and the Desire for God*, trans. Catherine Misrahi (New York, 1961); see also the dated (first published in German in 1935) Herbert Grundmann, *Religious Movements in the Middle Ages*, trans. Steven Rowan (Notre Dame, 1995).
5. Malcolm Lambert, *Medieval Heresy: Popular Movements from the Gregorian Reform to the Reformation*, 3rd edn (Oxford, 2002), p. 415.
6. Jean Delumeau, *Catholicism Between Luther and Voltaire: A New View of the Counter-Reformation* (London and Philadelphia, PA, 1977).
7. For a good, recent summary see Bernard Hamilton, 'Religion and the Laity', in David Luscombe and Jonathan Riley-Smith (eds.), *The New Cambridge Medieval History* 4.2 (Cambridge, 2004), pp. 499–533.
8. The charms are translated in John Shinners (ed.), *Medieval Popular Religion, 1000–1500: A Reader* (Toronto, ON), pp. 282–285. See also Karen Louise Jolly, *Popular Religion in Late Anglo-Saxon England: Elf Charms in Context* (Chapel Hill, NC, 1996).
9. John D. Cotts, *The Clerical Dilemma: Peter of Blois and Literate Culture in the Twelfth Century* (Washington, DC, 2009), p. 235.
10. Leonard E. Boyle, 'Innocent III and Vernacular Versions of Scripture', in Katherine Walsh and Diana Wood (eds.), *The Bible in the Medieval World: Essays in Memory of Beryl Smalley*, Studies in Church History Subsidia 4 (Oxford, 1985), pp. 97–108.
11. Ruth Mazo Karras, *Sexuality in Medieval Europe: Doing Unto Others* (New York, 2005), pp. 43–45; Caroline Walker Bynum, 'Jesus as Mother and Abbot as Mother', in *Jesus as Mother: Studies in the Spirituality of the High Middle Ages* (Berkeley, CA and Los Angeles, CA, 1984), pp. 110–169.
12. Robert Bartlett, *Making of Europe: Conquest, Colonization and Cultural Change, 950–1300* (Princeton, 1993), pp. 5–23.
13. 'Meditation on Human Redemption', in *The Prayers and Meditations of St Anselm & The Proslogion* (London, 1979), p. 230.
14. Hildegard of Bingen, *Selected Writings*, p. 10.

15. Giles Constable, 'The Idea of the Imitation of Christ', in *Three Studies in Medieval Religious and Social Thought* (Cambridge, 1995), pp. 145–248.

16. Cited in Constable, 'Idea of the Imitation of Christ', p. 210.

17. Aelred of Rievaulx, *Spiritual Friendship*, trans. Mary Eugenia Laker (Kalamazoo, MI, 1977), p. 74.

18. 'Prayer to St Paul', in *The Prayers and Meditations of St Anselm*, p. 153.

19. Cited in Bynum, 'Jesus as Mother and Abbot as Mother: Some Themes in Twelfth-Century Cistercian Writing', in *Jesus as Mother*, p. 123.

20. Ibid., pp. 146–154.

21. Constable, 'The Idea of the Imitation of Christ', pp. 184–185.

22. Thomas of Celano, *The First Life of Francis of Assisi* in *Francis of Assisi: The First and Second Life of St Francis with Selections from the Treatise on the Miracles of Blessed Francis*, trans. Placid Hermann (Chicago, 1963), p. 85.

23. Constable, 'The Idea of the Imitation of Christ', pp. 216–217.

24. 'Prayer Before Receiving the Body and Blood of Christ', in *The Prayers and Meditations of St Anselm*, p. 101.

25. Norman P. Tanner, ed., *The Decrees of the Ecumenical Councils, Volume I: Nicea I to Lateran V* (London, 1990), p. 231.

26. Cotts, *The Clerical Dilemma*, p. 231.

27. 'Payer to St Mary Magdalene', in *The Prayers and Meditations of St Anselm*, p. 202.

28. See, for example, Gautier de Coincy's *Miracles of the Virgin Mary*, trans. Renate Blumenfeld-Kosinski, in Thomas Head (ed.), *Medieval Hagiography: An Anthology* (New York, 2000), pp. 631–644.

29. Guibert of Nogent, *On the Relics of the Saints*, in *Guibert of Nogent: Monodies and On the Relics of Saints*, p. 207.

30. Robinson, *The Papacy, 1073–79: Continuity and Innovation* (Cambridge, 1990), pp. 110–113; Moore, *First European Revolution*, pp. 174, 269.

31. Pauline Matarasso, introduction to '*The Vita Prima* by William of St Thierry, Arnald of Bonneval and Geoffrey of Auxerre', in Pauline Matarasso (ed. and trans.), *The Cistercian World: Monastic Writings of the Twelfth Century* (Harmondsworth, 1993), p. 19.

32. *The Saga of Bishop Jón of Hólar*, trans. Margaret Cormack, in *Medieval Hagiography: An Anthology*, pp. 595–626.

33. Jocelin of Brokeland, *The Chronicle of the Abbey of Bury St Edmunds*, trans. Diana Greenway and Jane Sayers (Oxford, 1989), p. 100.

34. Patrick J. Geary, *Furta Sacra: Thefts of Relics in the Central Middle Ages* (Princeton, NJ, 1991).

35. John Hudson (ed.), *Historia Ecclesiae Abbendonensis: The History of the Church of Abingdon*, vol II (Oxford, 2002), pp. 220–225.

36. Guibert of Nogent, *On the Relics of the Saints*, p. 210.

37. Jonathan Riley-Smith, *The Crusades: A History*, 2nd edn (New Haven, CT and London, 2005), pp. 12–16; J. M. Jensen, 'Peregrinatio sive Expeditio: Why the First Crusade was not a Pilgrimage', *Al-Masaq: Islam and the Medieval Mediterranean*, 15 (2003), 119–137.

38. See excerpts in S. J. Allen and Emilie Amt (eds.), *The Crusades: A Reader*, pp. 99–108.

39. *The Pilgrim's Guide to Santiago de Compostela*, trans. William Melczer (New York, 1993).

40. C. W. Wilson (ed.), *The Pilgrimage of the Russian Abbot Daniel to the Holy Land, 1106–07 A. D.* (London, 1895); Joyce Hill, 'From Rome to Jerusalem: an Icelandic Itinerary of the Mid-Twelfth Century', *Harvard Theological Review*, 76 (1983), pp. 175–203; Jesse Byock, *Viking Age Iceland* (London, 2001), pp. 369–372.

41. Bartlett, *Making of Europe*, pp. 294–295.

42. In Erwin Panofsky (ed. and trans.), *Abbot Suger on the Abbey Church of St-Denis and Its Art Treasures*, 2nd edn (Princeton, NJ, 1979), p. 89.

43. Diana Webb (ed. and trans.), *Pilgrims and Pilgrimage in the Medieval West* (London, 2001), pp. 246–248.

44. *Radulfus Niger—De re militari et triplici via peregrinationis ierosolim-mitane (1187/88)*, ed. Ludwig Schmugge Beiträge zur Geschichte und Quellenkunde des Mittelalters 6 (Berlin, 1977), p. 97. My translation.

45. 'The Foundation Charter of Cluny' in *Readings in Medieval History*, 3rd edn (Peterborough, ON, 2003), pp. 321–323.

46. *Prayers and Meditations of St Anselm*, p. 197.

47. Peter of Celle, *On the Discipline of the Closter* in Hugh Feiss (ed. and trans.), *Peter of Celle: Selected Works* (Kalamazoo, MI, 1987), pp. 81–82.

48. *The Letters of Hildegard of Bingen, Volume I*, trans. Joseph L. Baird and Radd K. Ehrman (New York and Oxford, 1994), pp. 128–130.

49. 'The Foundation Charter of Cluny', p. 323.

50. H. E. J. Cowdrey, *The Cluniacs and the Gregorian Reform* (Oxford, 1970).

51. Barbara H. Rosenwein, *To Be the Neighbor of St Peter: The Social Meaning of Cluny's Property, 909–1049* (Ithaca, NY, 1989).

52. Jocelin of Brokeland, p. 117.

53. Guibert of Nogent, *Monodies*, in *Guibert of Nogent: Monodies and On the Relics of Saints*, p. 27.

54. 'The Little Exord', in *The Cistercian World*, p. 5.

55. Ibid., p. 6.

56. William of St Thierry, '*The Vita Prima*', in *The Cistercian World*, p. 21.

57. 'The Little Exord', p. 7.

58. Bartlett, *Making of Europe*, p. 258.

59. Bernard of Clairvaux, *An Apologia to Abbot William*, trans. Michael Casey, in *The Works of Bernard of Clairvaux, Volume I: Treatises I* (Spencer, MA, 1970), p. 56.

60. 'The Little Exord', p. 7.

61. C. H. Lawrence, *Medieval Monasticism*, 2nd edn (London, 1989) pp. 178–179.

62. Bernard of Clairvaux, *Five Books on Consideration*, trans. John D. Anderson and Elizabeth T. Keenan (Kalanazoo, MI, 1976), p. 25.

63. Constance Berman, *The Cistercian Evolution: The Invention of a Religious Order in Twelfth-Century Europe* (Philadelphia, PA, 2000), p. 174.
64. Walter Map, *De Nugis Curialium: Courtiers' Trifles*, ed., trans., M. R. James, revised by C. N. L. Brooke and R. A. B. Mynors (Oxford, 1983), p. 111.
65. Lester K. Little, *Religious Poverty and the Profit Economy*, p. 93.
66. Bernard of Clairvaux, *On the Song of Songs I*, trans. Kilian Walsh, The Works of Bernard of Clairvaux 2 (Kalamazoo, MI, 1971), p. 10.
67. Leclercq, *The Love of Learning and the Desire for God*, p. 86.
68. 'Bernard of Clairvaux: In Praise of the New Knighthood', in *The Crusades: A Reader*, p. 197.
69. Ibid., p. 199.
70. Malcolm Barber, *The New Knighthood: A History of the Order of the Temple* (Cambridge, 1994).
71. Jonathan Phillips, *The Second Crusade: Extending the Frontiers of Christendom* (New Haven, CT, 2007), p. 202.
72. Jonathan Riley-Smith, *The Crusades*, pp. 76–79; see also Helen Nicholson, *The Knights Hospitaller* (Woodbridge, VA, 2001).
73. See the selection in *Sainted Women of the Dark Ages*, ed. and trans. Jo Ann McNamara, John E. Halborg, and Gordon Whatley (Durham, NC, 1992).
74. Bruce L. Venarde, *Women's Monasticism and Medieval Society: Nunneries in France and England, 890–1215* (Ithaca, NY, 1997), p. 102.
75. *Hildegard of Bingen: Selected Writings*, p. 9.
76. Giles Constable, *The Reformation of the Twelfth Century* (Cambridge, 1995), p. 65.
77. Grundmann, *Religious Movements*, pp. 91–92.
78. Anne E. Lester, 'A shared imitation: Cistercian Convents and Crusader Families in Thirteenth-Century Champagne', *Journal of Medieval History*, 35 (2009), pp. 353–370.
79. *The Letters of Abelard and Heloise*, trans. Betty Radice, rev. Michael Clanchy (London, 2003), p. 94.
80. Ibid., pp. 130–210.
81. Barbara Newman, 'Flaws in the Golden Bowl: Gender and Spiritual Formation in the Twelfth Century', *Traditio*, 45 (1989–1990), pp. 111–146.
82. 'Marbode of Rennes, Letter to Robert of Arbrissel', in *Robert of Arbrissel: A Medieval Religious Life*, trans. Bruce L. Venarde (Washington, DC, 2003), p. 93.
83. See *The Book of St Gilbert*, ed. Raymonde Foreville and Gillian Keir (Oxford, 1987).
84. Penelope D. Johnson, *Unequal in Monastic Profession: Religious Women in Medieval France* (Chicago, 1991), p. 148.
85. *The Life of Christina of Markyate: A Twelfth Century Recluse*, ed. and trans. C. H. Talbot (Oxford, 1959), p. 43.
86. Ibid., p. 99.
87. Ibid., p. 115.

88. Jacques de Vitry, *The Life of Marie d'Oignies*, trans. Margot H. King, in *Two Lives of Marie d'Oignies* (Toronto, ON, 1998), p. 54.

89. Constable, *Reformation of the Twelfth Century*, p. 66.

90. Caroline Walker Bynum, 'Women Mystics in the Thirteenth Century: The Case of the Nuns of Helfta', In *Jesus as Mother*, pp. 170–262.

91. Thomas of Cantimpré, *The Life of Lutgard of Aywières*, trans. Margot L. King (Toronto, 1991), p. 38.

92. Thomas of Cantimpré, *The Life of Christina the Astonishing*, trans. Margot L. King, 2nd edn (Toronto, 1999), p. 29.

93. Lambert, *Medieval Heresy*, pp. 14–21.

94. In R. I. Moore (ed.), *The Birth of Popular Heresy* (London, 1975), pp. 111–112.

95. Ibid., p. 35.

96. On the Waldensians and Humiliati, see Malcolm Lambert, *Medieval Heresy*, pp. 70–80; Little, *Religious Poverty*, pp. 113–128; Frances Andrews, *The Early Humiliati* (Cambridge, 1999).

97. Malcolm Lambert, *The Cathars* (London, 1998).

98. Moore, *Birth of Popular Heresy*, p. 124.

99. Mark Gregory Pegg, *A Most Holy War: The Albigensian Crusade and the Battle for Christendom* (Oxford, 2008); cf. Hamilton, 'Religion and the Laity', esp. pp. 516–532.

100. Thomas of Celano, *The Second Life of St Francis*, in *Francis of Assisi*, p. 144.

101. 'The Canticle of Brother Sun', in *Francis and Clare: The Complete Works*, trans. Regis J. Armstrong and Ignatius C. Brady (New York, 1982), pp. 37–39.

102. This account of Dominic follows that of Jordan of Saxony, *On the Beginnings of the Order of Preachers*, trans. Simon Tugwell (Dublin, 1982), here at p. 6.

103. R. I. Moore, *The Formation of a Persecuting Society: Authority and Deviance in Western Europe, 950–1250*, 2nd edn (Oxford, 2007).

104. Jo Ann Hoeppner Moran Cruz, 'Popular Attitudes Toward Islam in Medieval Europe', in *Western Views of Islam in Medieval and Early Modern Europe: Perception of Other*, ed. David R. Blanks and Michael Frassetto (New York, 1999), pp. 55–88.

105. John V. Tolan, *Saracens: Islam in the Medieval European Imagination* (New York, 2002), p. 110.

106. John V. Tolan, 'Muslims ad Pagan Idolaters in Chronicles of the First Crusade', in *Western Views of Islam in Medieval and Early Modern Europe*, pp. 97–118.

107. Cited in Tolan, *Saracens*, p. 135.

108. Cited in James Kritzeck, *Peter the Venerable and Islam* (Princeton, NJ, 1964), p. 124; see also the more recent Thomas E. Burman, *Reading the Qur'an in Latin Christendom, 1140–1560* (Philadelphia, PA, 2007), pp. 60–87.

109. Alex Metcalfe, *The Muslims of Medieval Italy* (Edinburgh, 2009), p. 142.

110. Tolan, *Saracens,* pp. 182–186.
111. *The Itinerary of Benjamin of Tudela,* p. 63.
112. Robert Chazan, 'The Jews in Europe and the Mediterranean Basin', in *The New Cambridge Medieval History* 4.1, pp. 623–657.
113. Anna Sapir Abulafia, *Christians and Jews in the Twelfth-Century Renaissance* (London, 1995).
114. *The First Crusade,* p. 126.
115. Cited in Jonathan Phillips, *The Second Crusade,* p. 85.
116. Giles Constable (ed.), *The Letters of Peter the Venerable,* vol 1 (Cambridge, MA, 1967), p. 328. My translation.
117. Thomas of Monmouth, *The Life and Passion of St William of Norwich,* in *Medieval Hagiography: An Anthology,* p. 523.
118. *Gentile Tales: The Narrative Assault on Late Medieval Jews* (New Haven, CT, 1999), pp. 7–39.
119. 'The Jewish Martyrs of Blois', in *Medieval Hagiography,* p. 551.
120. Little, *Religious Poverty and the Profit Economy in Medieval Europe,* pp. 42–57.
121. Robert Stacey, 'Jews and Christians in 12th Century England: Some Dynamics of a Changing Relationship', in *Jews and Christians in Twelfth-Century Europe,* ed. Michael A. Signer and John Van Engen (Notre Dame, IN, 2001), pp. 340–354.
122. Rigord, *Deeds of Philip Augustus,* http://falcon.arts.cornell.edu/prh3/408/texts/Rigord1.html.
123. Jane Sayers, *Innocent III: Leader of Europe, 1198–1216* (Cambridge, 1994).
124. Norman P. Tanner (ed.), *The Decrees of the Ecumenical Councils, Volume I: Nicea I to Lateran V* (London, 1990), p. 230.
125. Ibid., p. 243.
126. Ibid., p. 253.
127. Ibid., p. 240.
128. Ibid., p. 245.
129. Ibid., p. 253.
130. Ibid., p. 244.
131. Ibid., p. 265.
132. Ibid., p. 266.

4 Intellectual Syntheses

1. *The Vinland Sagas: The Icelandic Sagas about the First Documented Voyages Across the North Atlantic,* trans. Keneva Kunz (London, 2008), p. 47.
2. Jesse Byock, *Viking Age Iceland* (London, 2001), pp. 369–372.
3. John D. Cotts, *The Clerical Dilemma: Peter of Blois and Literate Culture in the Twelfth Century* (Washington, DC, 2009), pp. 113–115; R. N. Swanson, *The Twelfth-Century Renaissance* (Manchester, 1999), pp. 43–50.

4. R. W. Southern, *Saint Anselm: A Portrait in a Landscape* (Cambridge, 1990), p. 128.

5. *Proslogion*, in *The Prayers and Meditations of St Anselm & The Proslogion* (London, 1979), pp. 244–245.

6. For a good summary of the argument, see Southern, *St Anselm: A Portrait in a Landscape*, pp. 132–134.

7. *Proslogion*, p. 255.

8. William Tronzo, 'The Medieval Object-Enigma, and the Problem of the Capella Palatina in Palermo', in Eva R. Hoffman (ed.), *Late Antique and Medieval Art of the Mediterranean World* (Oxford, 2007), pp. 317–349.

9. *Adelard of Bath: Conversations With His Nephew*, trans. Charles Burnett (Cambridge, 1988), p. 91.

10. John Tolan, *Petrus Alfonsi and His Medieval Readers* (Gainesville, FL, 1993), pp. 59–61.

11. Edward Grant (ed.), *A Source Book in Medieval Science* (Cambridge, MA, 1974), p. 35.

12. C. Stephen Jaeger, *The Envy of Angels: Cathedral Schools and Social Ideals in Medieval Europe, 950–1200* (Philadelphia, PA, 1994); Édouard Jeauneau, *Rethinking the School of Chartres*, trans. Claude Paul Desmaris (Toronto, ON, 2009).

13. John of Salisbury, *Metalogicon*, trans. Daniel D. McGarry (Berkeley, CA, 1955), p. 36.

14. Beryl Smalley, *The Study of the Bible in the Middle Ages* (Notre Dame, 1964), pp. 46–66.

15. *Historia Calamitatum*, in *The Letters of Abelard and Heloise*, trans. Betty Radice, rev. M. T. Clanchy (London, 2003), pp. 3–43.

16. A. J. Minnis and A. B. Scott (eds.), *Medieval Literary Theory and Criticism: The Commentary Tradition*, revised ed. (Oxford, 1991).

17. *Historia Calamitatum*, p. 24.

18. M. T. Clanchy, *Abelard: A Medieval Life* (Oxford, 1997), pp. 307–314.

19. R. W. Southern, *Scholastic Humanism and the Unification of Europe. Volume I: Foundations* (Oxford, 1995), p. 223.

20. Marcia L. Colish, *Peter Lombard* (Leiden, 1994), 2 vols; Philipp W. Rosemann, *The Story of a Great Medieval Book: Peter Lombard's Sentences* (Toronto, ON, 2007).

21. 'Rules of the University of Paris, 1215', in Lynn Thorndkie (ed.), *University Records and Life in the Middle Ages* (New York, 1971), pp. 27–31.

22. See M. T. Clanchy, 'The *Moderni* in Education', *Speculum*, 50 (1975), pp. 671–688.

23. John D. Cotts 'Monks and Clerks in Search of the *Beata Schola*: Peter of Celle's Warning to John of Salisbury Reconsidered', in Sally N. Vaughn and Jay Rubenstein (eds.), *Teaching and Learning in Northern Europe, 1000–1200* (Turnhout, 2006), p. 263.

24. 'Frederick II: Lictere Generales, Establishing the University of Naples, 1224', Internet Medieval Sourcebook, http://www.fordham.edu/halsall/source/1224fred2-lictgen.asp.

25. J. W. Baldwin, '*Studium et Regnum*'; The Penetration of University Personnel into French and English Administration at the Turn of the Eleventh and Twelfth Centuries', in *Medieval Education in the West* (Paris, 1977), pp. 119–215.

26. David Spear, 'Power, Patronage, and Personality in the Norman Cathedral Chapters, 911–1204', *Anglo-Norman Studies*, 20 (1998), pp. 205–221.

27. Cotts, *The Clerical Dilemma*, pp. 63–73.

28. 'The Confession of Golias', in *The Goliard Poets*, pp. 106–119.

29. Cotts, *The Clerical Dilemma*, pp. 165–175.

30. Gerald of Wales, *De invectionibus*, in *Opera*, ed. J. S. Brewer, Rolls Series 21.1 (London, 1861), p. 151. My translation.

31. John F. Benton, 'The Court of Champagne as a Literary Center', *Speculum*, 36 (1961), pp. 551–591.

32. Abulafia, *Frederick II*, pp. 254–264.

33. See Nancy Partner, *Serious Entertainments: The Writing of History in Twelfth-Century England* (Chicago and London, 1977).

34. Henry, Archdeacon of Huntington, *Historia Anglorum (History of the English People)*, ed. and trans. Diana Greenaway (Oxford, 1996), pp. 3, 7.

35. Cosmas of Prague, *The Chronicle of the Czechs*, trans. Lisa Wolverton (Washington, DC, 2009), p. 31.

36. Otto of Freising, *The Two Cities: A Chronicle of Universal History to the Year 1146 A.D., by Otto, Bishop of Freising*, trans. Charles Christopher Mierow, new edn (Toronto, ON, 2002), p. 91.

37. Nicholas L. Paul, 'Crusade, Memory and Regional Politics in Twelfth-Century Amboise', *Journal of Medieval History*, 31(2005), 127–141.

38. John Gillingham, 'A Historian of the Twelfth-Century Renaissance and the Transformation of English Society, 1066–ca. 1200', in Thomas F. X. Noble and John Van Engen (eds.), *European Transformations: The Long Twelfth Century* (Notre Dame, 2012), pp. 45–74.

39. On general issues of women and literacy, see Elisebeth van Houts, *Gender and Memory in Medieval Europe, 900–1200* (Toronto, ON, 1999).

40. *Historia Calamitatum*, p. 10.

41. Clanchy, *Abelard: A Medieval Life*, pp. 173–174.

42. *Historia Calamitatum*, p. 17.

43. 'Letter 2, Heloise to Abelard', in *The Letters of Abelard and Heloise*, p. 54.

44. 'Letter 4, Heloise to Abelard', in *The Letters of Abelard and Heloise*, p. 68.

45. Clanchy, *Abelard: A Medieval Life*, pp. 169–172, 277–282.

46. 'Peter the Venerable: Letter (115) to Heloise', in *The Letters of Abelard and Heloise*, p. 217.

47. *Hildegard of Bingen: Selected Writings*, trans. Mark Atherton (London, 2001), p. 31.

48. *Hildegard of Bingen: Selected Writings*, p. 24.

49. Ibid., p. 96.

50. Barbara Newman, *Sister of Wisdom: Hildegard of Bingen's Theology of the Feminine*, 2nd edn (Berkeley, CA and Los Angeles, CA, 1998).

51. *Hildegard of Bingen: Selected Writings*, pp. 31, 118.
52. Fiona Griffiths, 'Herrad of Hohenbourg: A Synthesis of Learning in *The Garden of Delights*', in Constant J. Mews (ed.), *Listen, Daughter: The Speculum Virginum and the Formation of Religious Women in the Middle Ages* (Basingstoke, 2001), pp. 221–243.
53. John of Salisbury, *Metalogicon: A Twelfth-Century Defense of the Verbal and Logical Arts of the Trivium*, trans. Daniel D. McGarry (Berkeley, CA and Los Angeles, CA, 1955), p. 167.
54. Cotts, 'Monks and Clerks in Search of the Beata Schola', pp. 272–273.
55. Franklin T. Harkins, *Reading and the Work of Restoration: History and Scripture in the Theology of Hugh of Saint Victor* (Toronto, ON, 2009).
56. Hugh of St Victor, *The Didascalicon of Hugh of Saint Victor: A Medieval Guide to the Arts*, trans. Jerome Taylor (New York, 1961), p. 46.
57. Ibid., p. 77.
58. Boyd Taylor Coolman, *The Theology of Hugh of St Victor: An Interpretation* (Cambridge, 2010).
59. John W. Baldwin, *Masters, Princes, and Merchants: The Social Views of Peter the Chanter and His Circle* (Princeton, NJ, 1970), 2 vols.
60. Monique Boutry (ed.), *Petri Cantoris Parisiensis Verbum Adbreviatum Textus Conflatus* (Turnhout, 2004), p. 7. My translation.
61. Ibid., pp. 328–337.
62. Alan of Lille, *Anticlaudianus, or the Good and Perfect Man*, trans. James J. Sheridan (Toronto, ON, 1973), p. 150.
63. Ibid., p. 162.
64. Anders Winroth, *The Making of Gratian's* Decretum (Cambridge, 2000).
65. Steven Epstein, *Guilds and Wage Labor*, pp. 80–81.
66. John of Salisbury, *Policraticus: Of the Frivolities of Courtiers and the Footprints of Philosophers*, trans. Cary J. Nederman (Cambridge, 1990), p. 126.
67. Ibid., p. 25.
68. Chrétien de Troyes, *Erec and Enide*, p. 76.
69. Chrétien de Troyes, *Lancelot: The Knight of the Cart*, trans. Burton Raffel (New Haven, CT and London, 1997), p. 13.
70. Wolfram von Eschenbach, *Parzival and Titurel*, trans. Cyril Edwards (Oxford, 2006), pp. 123, 141.
71. Gottfried von Strassburg, *Tristan and Isolde*, trans. A. T. Hatto, rev. Francis G Gentry (New York, 1988), p. 171.
72. Ibid., p. 250.
73. Andreas Capellanus, *The Art of Courtly Love*, trans. John Jay Perry and ed. Frederick W. Locke (New York, 1957).
74. Gerald of Wales, *The Journey through Wales and the Description of Wales*, trans. Lewis Thorpe (London, 1978), p. 141.
75. See Matthew Gabriele, *An Empire of Memory: The Legend of Charlemagne, the Franks, and Jerusalem before the First Crusade* (Oxford, 2011).
76. *The Song of Roland*, trans. Glyn Burgess (Harmondsworth, 1990), p. 65.

77. Burton Raffel, trans., *The Song of the Cid: A Dual Language Edition with Parallel Text* (London, 2009), p. 5. I have modified Raffel's translation to reflect the language or lord and vassal in the Spanish.
78. Ibid., p. 59.
79. Mariane Ailes (trans.), with notes by Malcolm Barber, *The History of the Holy War: Ambroise's Estoire de la Guerre Sante. Volume II: Translation* (Rochester, NY, 2003), p. 53.
80. Villehardouin, *The Conquest of Constantinople*, in Caroline Smith (trans.), *Chronicles of the Crusades* (London, 2008), p. 53.
81. In James J. Wilhelm (ed.), *Lyrics of the Middle Ages: An Anthology* (New York, 1990), p. 171.
82. Ibid., p. 28.
83. R. Howard Bloch, *The Scandal of the Fabliaux* (Chicago, 1986).
84. In John DuVal (trans.), *Fabliaux Fair and Foul* (Binghamton, NY, 1992), p. 38.
85. *Audigier*, in Paul Brians (ed.), *Bawdy Tales from the Courts of Medieval France* (New York, 1973), p. 58.

5 The Crusades and the Idea of Christendom

1. Joyce Hill, 'From Rome to Jerusalem: An Icelandic Itinerary of the Mid-Twelfth Century', *Harvard Theological Review*, 76 (1983), p. 180.
2. David Woodward, 'Medieval Mappaemundi', in J. B. Harley and David Woodward (ed.), *The History of Cartography, 1: Cartography in Prehistoric, Ancient and Medieval Europe and the Mediterranean* (Chicago, 1987), pp. 286–370.
3. Gerald of Wales, *The History and Topography of Ireland*, trans. John O'Meara (London, 1982), p. 31.
4. See Elizabeth Pastan, 'Charlemagne as Saint? Relics and the Choice of Window Subjects at Chartres Cathedral', in Matthew Gabriele and Jace Stuckey (eds.), *The Legend of Charlemagne in the Middle Ages: Power, Faith, and Crusade* (New York, 2008), pp. 97–136.
5. Norman Housley, *Contesting the Crusades* (Malden, MA and Oxford, 2006), pp. 1–23; C. J. Tyerman, 'Were There Any Crusades in the Twelfth Century', *English Historical Review*, 110 (1995).
6. Robert Bartlett, *Making of Europe: Conquest, Colonization and Cultural Change, 950–1300* (Princeton, NJ, 1993), pp. 262–263, 279; Jonathan Riley-Smith, *The Crusades: A History*, 2nd edn (New Haven, CT and London, 2005), p. 161.
7. Jonathan Riley-Smith, 'The Motives of the Earliest Crusaders and the Settlement of Latin Palestine, 1095–1100', *English Historical Review*, 98 (1983), pp. 721–736.
8. Jay, Rubenstein, *Armies of Heaven: The First Crusade and the Quest for Apocalypse* (New York, 2011), p. 25.

9. Ibn al-Athir, 'The Franks Seize Antioch', in *Arab Historians of the Crusades*, trans. Francesco Gabrieli and E. J. Costello (Berkeley, CA and Los Angeles, CA, 1969), p. 3.

10. Jonathan Riley-Smith, *The First Crusaders, 1095–1131* (Cambridge, 1997), p. 33.

11. 'The Speech of Urban: The Version of Robert of Rheims', in *The First Crusade*, p. 27.

12. Penny J. Cole, 'O God, the Heathen Hath Come into Your Inheritance' (Ps. 78.1). The Theme of Religious Pollution in Crusade Documents', in Maya Shatzmiller (ed.), *Crusaders and Muslims in Twelfth-Century Syria* (Leiden, 1993), pp. 84–111.

13. 'The Speech of Urban—The Version of Baldric of Dol', in *The First Crusade*, p. 31.

14. 'The Speech of Urban—The Version of Guibert of Nogent', in *The First Crusade*, pp. 34–35.

15. Rubenstein, *Armies of Heaven*, pp. 29–30.

16. Ibid., p. 49.

17. 'The Slaughter of the Jews: The Version of Albert of Aachen', in *The First Crusade*, p. 111.

18. See, for example, Marcus Bull, *Knightly Piety and the Lay Response to the First Crusade: The Limousin and Gascony, c. 970-c. 1130* (Oxford, 1993).

19. Rubenstein, *Armies of Heaven*, pp. 205–228.

20. 'The Frankish Triumph: The Version of Raymond d'Aguilers', in *The First Crusade*, pp. 259–260.

21. See Rubenstein, *Armies of Heaven*, pp. 286–292.

22. Peter Frankopan, *The First Crusade: The Call from the East* (Cambridge, MA, 2012), p. 171.

23. Cited in Joshua Prawer, 'The Roots of Medieval Colonialism', in *The Meeting of Two Worlds: Cultural Exchange between East and West during the Period of the Crusades* (Kalamazoo, MI, 1986) p. 25.

24. Christopher MacEvitt, *The Crusades and the Christian World of the East: Rough Tolerance* (Philadelphia, PA, 2008), esp. pp. 136–156; cf. Prawer, 'The Roots of Medieval Colonialism', pp. 33–36.

25. See, for example, 'Laws of the Kingdom of Jerusalem', in *The Crusades: A Reader*, pp. 93–99.

26. 'Analyses of the Second Crusade', in *The Crusades: A Reader*, pp. 145–147.

27. Loud, 'Some Reflections on the Failure of the Second Crusade'; Jonathan Phillips, *The Second Crusade: Extending the Frontiers of Christendom* (New Haven, CT, 2007), pp. 269–279.

28. John Gillingham, *Richard I* (New Haven, 1999), pp. 108–110.

29. Robert Chazan, 'Emperor Frederick I, the Third Crusade, and the Jews', *Viator*, 8 (1977), pp. 83–93.

30. Michael Markowski, 'Richard Lionheart: Bad King, Bad Crusader?' *Journal of Medieval History*, 23 (1997), pp. 351–365.

31. Michael Angold, 'The Anglo-Saxon Historiography of the Fourth Crusade: A Crime Against Humanity or Just an Accident', in Gherardo Ortalli, Giorgio Ravegnani, and Peter Schreiner (eds.), *Quarta Crociata: Venezia-Bisanzio-Imperio Latin*, vol 1 (Venice, 2006), pp. 301–316.

32. Villehardouin, *The Conquest of Constantinople*, p. 53.

33. Stephan Kuttner and Antonio Garcia y Garcia, 'A New Eyewitness Account of the Fourth Lateran Council', *Traditio*, 20 (1964), pp. 115–178, here at 128–129, 165–166.

34. Phillips, *The Second Crusade*, pp. 87–87.

35. Riley-Smith, *The Crusades: A History*, 2nd edn (New Haven, CT and London, 2005), p. 137.

36. 'Papal Bull of Gregory VIII, 1187', in *The Crusades: A Reader*, p. 165.

37. 'Accounts of the Children's Crusade' in *The Crusades: A Reader*, pp. 249–251.

38. Gary Dickson, *The Children's Crusade: Medieval History, Modern Mythhistory* (Basingstoke and New York, 2008).

39. Norman P. Tanner, *The Decrees of the Ecumenical Councils*, vol 1 (Washington, DC, 1990), p. 267.

40. Ibid., p. 269.

41. Ibid., p. 270.

42. Ibn al-Athir, 'The Franks Conquer Jerusalem', in *Arab Historians of the Crusade*, p. 11.

43. 'Imad ad-Din, in *Arab Historians of the Crusades*, pp. 151–152.

44. Tolan, *Saracens*, 225n.41.

45. 'The End of the "Crusade of the People": The Version of Anna Comnena', in *The First Crusade*, pp. 143–144.

46. Odo of Deuil, *De Profectione Ludovici in Orientem: The Journey of Louis VII to the East*, ed. and trans. Virginia Gingerick Berry (New York, 1948), p. 69.

47. 'Letters of Innocent III', in *The Crusades: A Reader*, pp. 238–240.

48. 'Guyuk Khan's Letter to Pope Innocent IV', in Christopher Dawson (ed.), *Mission to Asia*, reprint (Toronto, ON, 1980), pp. 85–86.

49. William of Rubruck, *The Journey of William of Rubruck*, in *Mission to Asia*, p. 157.

50. Erwin Panofsky, *Gothic Architecture and Scholasticism* (London and New York, 1951).

51. See R. W. Southern, *Scholastic Humanism and the Unification of Europe*, vol 1, pp. 3–13.

52. R. W. Southern, *Western Society and the Church in the Middle Ages* (London, 1970), p. 302.

53. David Burr, *The Spiritual Franciscans: From Protest to Persecution in the Century After Saint Francis* (University Park, PA, 2001).

Suggestions for Further Reading

Approaches to the twelfth century and its 'renaissance'

Barber, Malcolm, *The Two Cities: Medieval Europe 1050–1320* (London and New York, 1992).

Bartlett, Robert, *The Making of Europe: Conquest, Colonization and Cultural Change, 950–1300* (Princeton, NJ, 1993).

Benson, Robert L., Giles Constable, and Carol D. Lanham (eds.), *Renaissance and Renewal in the Twelfth Century*, reprint (Toronto, ON, 1999).

Bisson, Thomas N., *The Crisis of the Twelfth Century: Power, Lordship, and the Origins of European Government* (Princeton, NJ, 2009).

Constable, Giles, *The Reformation of the Twelfth Century* (Cambridge, 1995).

Haskins, Charles Homer, *The Renaissance of the Twelfth Century* (Cambridge, MA, 1927).

Luscombe, David and Jonathan Riley-Smith (eds.), *The New Cambridge Medieval History, Volume 4* (Cambridge, 2004), 2 parts.

Moore, R. I., *The First European Revolution, c. 970–1215* (Oxford, 2000).

Power, Daniel (ed.), *The Central Middle Ages*, Short Oxford History of Europe (Oxford, 2006).

Swanson, R. N., *The Twelfth-Century Renaissance* (Manchester, 1999).

Political life and national histories

Political culture

Althoff, Gerd, *Family, Friends and Followers: Political and Social Bonds in Early Medieval Europe*, trans. Christopher Carroll (Cambridge, 2004).

Bisson, Thomas N. (ed.), *Cultures of Power: Lordship, Status, and Process in Twelfth-Century Europe*, ed. Thomas N. Bisson (Philadelphia, PA, 1995).

Kaeuper, Richard, *Chivalry and Violence in Medieval Europe* (Oxford, 1999).

Koziol, Geoffrey, *Begging Pardon and Favor: Ritual and Political Order in Early Medieval France* (Ithaca, NY and London, 1992).

Reuter, Timothy, *Medieval Polities and Modern Mentalities*, ed. Janet L. Nelson (Cambridge, 2006).

Reynolds, Susan, *Kingdoms and Communities in Western Europe, 900–1300* (Oxford, 1997).

———, *Fiefs and Vassals: The Medieval Evidence Reinterpreted* (Oxford, 1996).

Stephen Jaeger, C., *The Origins of Courtliness: Civilizing Trends and the Formation of Courtly Ideals, 939–1210* (Philadelphia, PA, 1985).

Strayer, Joseph R., *On the Medieval Origins of the Modern State*, new ed. (Princeton, NJ, 2005).

The Papacy, the Holy Roman Empire, and Italy

Abulafia, David, *Frederick II: A Medieval Emperor* (Oxford, 1988).

Arnold, Benjamin, *Medieval Germany, 500–1300: A Political Interpretation* (Toronto, ON and Buffalo, NY, 1997).

———, *Princes and Territories in Medieval Germany* (Cambridge, 1999).

Blumenthal, Uta-Renate, *The Investiture Controversy: Church and Monarchy from the Ninth to the Twelfth Century* (Philadelphia, PA, 1988).

Fuhrman, Horst, *Germany in the High Middle Ages, c. 1050–1200*, trans. Timothy Reuter (Cambridge, 1986).

Haverkamp, Alfred, *Medieval Germany, 1056–1200*, trans. Helga Braun and Richard Mortimer, 2nd edn (Oxford, 1992).

Jordan, Karl, *Henry the Lion: A Biography*, trans. P. S. Falla (Oxford, 1986).

Raccagni, Gianluca, *The Lombard League, 1167–1225* (Oxford, 2010).

Robinson, I. S., *Henry IV of Germany* (Cambridge, 1999).

———, *The Papacy, 1073–1198: Continuity and Innovation* (Cambridge, 1990).

Sayers, Jane, *Innocent III* (Cambridge, 1994).

Tellenbach, Gerd, *Church, State and Christian Society at the Time of the Investiture Contest*, trans. R. F. Bennett, reprint (Toronto, ON, 1991).

———, *The Church in Western Europe from the Tenth to the Early Twelfth Centuries* (Cambridge, 1993).

Waley, Daniel, *The Italian City-Republics* (New York and Toronto, ON, 1969).

Iberia and Sicily

Bisson, Thomas N., *The Medieval Crown of Aragon: A Short History* (Oxford, 1991).

Houben, Hubert, *Roger II of Sicily: A Ruler Between East and West*, trans. Graham A. Loud and Diane Milburn (Cambridge, 2002).

Kosto, Adam J., *Making Agreements in Medieval Catalonia: Power, Order, and the Written Word, 1000–1200* (Cambridge, 2001).

Matthew, Donald, *The Norman Kingdom of Sicily* (Cambridge, 1992).

Riley, Bernard F., *The Medieval Spains* (Cambridge, 1993).

Shadis, Miriam, *Berenguela of Castile (1180–1246) and Political Women in the High Middle Ages* (New York, 2009).

England and France

Aurell, Martin, *The Plantagent Empire, 1154–1224*, trans. David Crouch (Harlow, 2007).

Baldwin, John W., *The Government of Philip Augustus: Foundations of French Royal Power in the Middle Ages* (Berkeley, CA and Los Angeles, CA, 1986).

Barlow, Frank, *Thomas Becket* (Berkeley, CA and Los Angeles, CA, 1986).

Bartlett, Robert, *England under the Norman and Angevin Kings, 1075–1225* (Oxford, 2000).

Bradbury, Jim, *Philip Augustus, King of France 1180–1223* (London and New York, 1998).

Chibnall, Marjorie, *The Empress Matilda: Queen Consort, Queen Mother and Lady of the English* (Oxford, 1991).

Clanchy, M. T., *From Memory to Written Record: England 1066–1307*, 2nd edn (Oxford, 1993).

Gillingham, John, *Richard I* (New Haven, CT and London, 1999).

Green, Judith, *Henry I: King of England and Duke of Normandy* (Cambridge, 2006).

Hallam, Elizabeth M., *Capetian France, 987–1328* (London and New York, 1980).

Harper-Bill, Christopher and Nicholas Vincent (eds.), *Henry II: New Interpretations* (Woodbridge, VA, 2007).

Hollister, C. Warren, *Henry I*, ed. Amanda Clark Frost (New Haven, CT and London, 2001).

Turner, Ralph, *King John* (London and New York, 1994).

———, *Eleanor of Aquitaine: Queen of France, Queen of England* (New Haven, CT and London, 2009).

Warren, W. L., *Henry II* (Berkeley, CA and Los Angeles, CA, 1973).

Northern and Eastern Europe

Bagge, Sverre, *From Viking Stronghold to Christian Kingdom: State Formation in Norway, c. 900–1350* (Copenhagen, 2009).

Berend, Nora, *Christianization and the Rise of Christian Monarchy: Scandinavia, Central Europe and Rus' c. 900–1200* (Cambridge, 2007).

———, *At the Gate of Christendom: Jews, Muslims, and 'Pagans' in Medieval Hungary* (New York, 2001).

Byock, Jesse, *Viking Age Iceland* (London, 2001).

Christiansen, Eric, *The Northern Crusades*, new edn (London, 1997).

Helle, Knut (ed.), *The Cambridge History of Scandinavia, Vol. 1: Prehistory to 1520* (Cambridge, 2003).

Manteuffel, Tadeusz, *The Formation of the Polish State: The Period of Ducal Rule 963–1194*, trans. Andrew Gorski (Detroit, 1982).

Miller, William Ian, *Bloodtaking and Peacemaking: Feud, Law, and Society in Saga Iceland* (Chicago and London, 1990).

Sawyer, Brigit and Peter Sawyer, *Medieval Scandinavia: From Conversion to Reformation, circa 800–1500* (Minneapolis, MN and London, 1993).

Wolverton, Lisa, *Hastening Toward Prague: Power and Society in the Medieval Czech Lands* (Philadelphia, PA, 2001).

Demography, economy, and society

Bisson, Thomas N., *Tormented Voices: Power, Crisis, and Humanity in Rural Catalonia 1140–1200* (Cambridge, MA, 1998).

Bouchard, Constance Brittain, *Strong of Body, Brave and Noble: Chivalry and Society in Medieval France* (Ithaca, NY, 1998).

Crouch, David, *The Image of the Aristocracy in Britain, 1000–1300* (London, 1992).

———, *William Marshal: Knighthood, War and Chivalry, 1147–1219*, 2nd edn (London, 2002).

Duby, Georges, *The Early Growth of the European Economy: Warriors and Peasants from the Seventh to the Twelfth Century*, trans. Howard B. Clarke (Ithaca, NY, 1974).

Epstein, Steven A., *Wage Labor and Guilds in Medieval Europe* (Chapel Hill, 1991).

Fossier, Robert, *The Axe and the Oath: Ordinary Life in the Middle Ages*, trans. L. G. Cochrane (Princeton, NJ, 2010).

———, *Peasant Life in the Middle Ages*, trans. Juliet Vale (Oxford, 1988).

Hunt, Edwin S. and James M. Murray, *A History of Business in Medieval Europe* (Cambridge, 1999).

Karras, Ruth Mazo, *Sexuality in Medieval Europe: Doing Unto Others* (New York, 2005).

Le Goff, Jacques, *Your Money or Your Life: Economy and Religion in the Middle Ages* (New York, 1988).

Little, Lester K., *Religious Poverty and the Profit Economy in the Middle Ages* (Ithaca, NY and London, 1978).

Lopez, Robert S., *The Commercial Revolution of the Middle Ages, 950–1350* (Cambridge, 1976).

Nicholas, David, *Urban Europe, 1100–1700* (Basingstoke, 2003).

Otis, Leah Lydia, *Prostitution in Medieval Society: The History of and Urban Institution in Languedoc* (Chicago, 1985).

Paterson, Linda, *The World of the Troubadours: Medieval Occitan Society c. 1100–c.1300* (Cambridge, 1993).

Pounds, Norman J. G., *An Historical Geography of Europe 450 B.C.–A.D. 1330* (Cambridge, 1973).

Rösner, Werner, *Peasants in the Middle Ages*, trans. Alexander Stützer (Oxford, 1992).

Spufford, Peter, *Money and its Use in Medieval Europe* (Cambridge, 1988).

Religious life

Barber, Malcolm, *The New Knighthood: A History of the Order of the Temple* (Cambridge, 1994).

Berman, Constance, *The Cistercian Evolution: The Invention of a Religious Order in Twelfth-Century Europe* (Philadelphia, PA, 2000).

Bynum, Caroline Walker, *Jesus as Mother: Studies in the Spirituality of the High Middle Ages* (Berkeley, CA and Los Angeles, CA, 1984).

Constable, Giles, *Three Studies in Medieval Religious and Social Thought* (Cambridge, 1995).

Fulton, Rachel, *From Judgment to Passion: Devotion to Christ and the Virgin Mary, 800–1200* (New York, 2002).

Grundmann, Herbert, *Religious Movements in the Middle Ages*, trans. Steven Rowan (Notre Dame, 1995).

Johnson, Penelope D., *Unequal in Monastic Profession: Religious Women in Medieval France* (Chicago, 1991).

Lambert, Malcolm, *Medieval Heresy: Popular Movements from the Gregorian Reform to the Reformation*, 3rd edn (Oxford, 2002).

———, *The Cathars* (London, 1998).

Lawrence, C. H., *Medieval Monasticism*, 2nd edn (London, 1989).

Leclercq, Jean, *The Love of Learning and the Desire for God*, trans. Catherine Misrahi (New York, 1961).

Metcalfe, Alex, *The Muslims of Medieval Italy* (Edinburgh, 2009).

Mooney, Catherine M. (ed.), *Gendered Voices: Medieval Saints and their Interpreters* (Philadelphia, PA, 1999).

Moore, R. I., *The Formation of a Persecuting Society: Authority and Deviance in Western Europe, 950–1250*, 2nd edn (Oxford, 2007).

Morris, Colin, *The Discovery of the Individual, 1050–1300*, reprint (Toronto, ON, 1987).

Nicholson, Helen, *The Knights Hospitaller* (Woodbridge, 2001).

Rosenwein, Barbara H., *To Be the Neighbor of St. Peter: The Social Meaning of Cluny's Property, 909–1049* (Ithaca, NY and London, 1989).

Tolan, John V. *Saracens: Islam in the Medieval European Imagination* (New York, 2002).

Venarde, Bruce L. *Women's Monasticism and Medieval Society: Nunneries in France and England, 890–1215* (Ithaca, NY, 1997).

Webb, Diana, *Medieval European Pilgrimage* (Basingstoke, 2002).

Intellectual life

Baldwin, John W., *The Language of Sex: Five Voices from Northern France around 1200* (Chicago and London, 1994).

———, *Masters, Princes, and Merchants: The Social Views of Peter the Chanter and His Circle*, 2 vols (Princeton, NJ, 1970).

Bouchard, Constance Brittain, *Every Valley Shall Be Exalted: The Discourse of Opposites in Twelfth-Century Thought* (Ithaca, NY and London, 2003).

Clanchy, M. T., *Abelard: A Medieval Life* (Oxford, 1997).

Colish, Marcia L. *Peter Lombard*, 2 vols (Leiden, 1994).

Coolman, Boyd Taylor, *The Theology of Hugh of St. Victor: An Interpretation* (Cambridge, 2010).

Cotts, John D., *The Clerical Dilemma: Peter of Blois and Literate Culture in the Twelfth Century* (Washington, DC, 2009).

Flanagan, Sabina, *Doubt in an Age of Faith: Uncertainty in the Long Twelfth Century* (Turnhout, 2009).

Jaeger, C. Stephen, *The Envy of Angels: Cathedral Schools and Social Ideals in Medieval Europe, 950–1200* (Philadelphia, PA, 1994).

Jeauneau, Édouard, *Rethinking the School of Chartres*, trans. Claude Paul Desmaris (Toronto, ON, 2009).

Newman, Barbara, *Sister of Wisdom: Hildegard of Bingen's Theology of the Feminine*, 2nd edn (Berkeley, CA and Los Angeles, CA, 1998).

Partner, Nancy, *Serious Entertainments: The Writing of History in Twelfth-Century England* (Chicago and London, 1977).

Rosemann, Philipp, W., *The Story of a Great Medieval Book: Peter Lombard's Sentences* (Toronto, ON, 2007).

Rubenstein, Jay, *Guibert of Nogent: Portrait of a Medieval Mind* (New York, 2002).

Smalley, Beryl, *The Study of the Bible in the Middle Ages* (Notre Dame, 1964).

Southern, R. W., *Scholastic Humanism and the Unification of Europe*, 2 vols (Oxford, 1995–2001).

———, *Saint Anselm: A Portrait in a Landscape* (Cambridge, 1990).

The Crusades

Asbridge, Thomas, *The First Crusade: A New History* (Oxford, 2004).

Dickson, Gary, *The Children's Crusade: Medieval History, Modern Mythhistory* (Basingstoke and New York, 2008).

Edgington, Susan B. and Sarah Lambert (eds.), *Gendering the Crusades* (Cardiff, 2001).

Frankopan, Peter, *The First Crusade: The Call from the East* (Cambridge, MA, 2012).

Hillenbrand, Carole, *The Crusades: Islamic Perspectives* (Chicago and London, 1999).

Harris, Jonathan, *Byzantium and the Crusades* (London, 2003).

Housley, Norman, *Contesting the Crusades* (Malden, MA and Oxford, 2006).

Jotischky, Andrew, *Crusading and the Crusader States* (Harlow and New York, 2004).

MacEvitt, Christopher, *The Crusades and the Christian World of the East: Rough Tolerance* (Philadelphia, PA, 2008).

Madden, Thomas F, *The New Concise History of the Crusades* (New York, 2005).

Pegg, Mark Gregory, *A Most Holy War: The Albigensian Crusade and the Battle for Christendom* (Oxford, 2008).

Phillips, Jonathan, *The Second Crusade: Expanding the Frontiers of Christendom* (New Haven, CT and London, 2007).

————, *The Fourth Crusade and the Sack of Constantinople* (New York, 2004).

Riley-Smith, Jonathan, *The Crusades: A History*, 2nd edn (New Haven, CT and London, 2005).

Rubenstein, Jay, *Armies of Heaven: The First Crusade and the Quest for Apocalypse* (New York, 2011).

Index

234